Charles Bukowski

Titles in the series Critical Lives present the work of leading cultural figures of the modern period. Each book explores the life of the artist, writer, philosopher or architect in question and relates it to their major works.

In the same series

Georges Bataille Stuart Kendall	Fyodor Dostoevsky Robert Bird	Karl Marx Paul Thomas
Charles Baudelaire Rosemary Lloyd	Marcel Duchamp Caroline Cros	Edweard Muybridge Marta Braun
Simone de Beauvoir Ursula Tidd	Sergei Eisenstein Mike O'Mahony	Vladimir Nabokov Barbara Wyllie
Samuel Beckett Andrew Gibson	Michel Foucault David Macey	Pablo Neruda Dominic Moran
Walter Benjamin Esther Leslie	Mahatma Gandhi Douglas Allen	Octavio Paz Nick Caistor
Jorge Luis Borges Jason Wilson	Jean Genet Stephen Barber	Pablo Picasso Mary Ann Caws
Constantin Brancusi Sanda Miller	Allen Ginsberg Steve Finbow	Edgar Allan Poe Kevin J. Hayes
William S. Burroughs Phil Baker	Derek Jarman Michael Charlesworth	Ezra Pound Alec Marsh
Coco Chanel Linda Simon	Alfred Jarry Jill Fell	Jean-Paul Sartre Andrew Leak
Noam Chomsky Wolfgang B. Sperlich	James Joyce Andrew Gibson	Erik Satie Mary E. Davis
Jean Cocteau James S. Williams	Franz Kafka Sander L. Gilman	Gertrude Stein Lucy Daniel
Salvador Dalí Mary Ann Caws	Lenin Lars T. Lih	Simone Weil Palle Yourgrau
Guy Debord Andy Merrifield	Stéphane Mallarmé Roger Pearson	Ludwig Wittgenstein Edward Kanterian
Claude Debussy David J. Code	Gabriel García Márquez Stephen M. Hart	Frank Lloyd Wright Robert McCarter

Charles Bukowski

David Stephen Calonne

REAKTION BOOKS

For my father Pierre Calonne
and to the memory of
my mother Mariam Galoostian

Published by Reaktion Books Ltd
33 Great Sutton Street
London EC1V 0DX, UK

www.reaktionbooks.co.uk

First published 2012

Printed and bound in Great Britain
by Bell & Bain, Glasgow

British Library Cataloguing in Publication Data
Calonne, David Stephen, 1953–
     Charles Bukowski. – (Critical lives)
     1. Bukowski, Charles.
     2. Authors, American –20th century – Biography.
     I. Title II. Series
     818.5'409-dc23

ISBN 978 1 78023 023 8

Contents

Charles Bukowski in 1978.

Deutschland, Vaterland, The Name of the Father: 1920–1943

'Hello, it's good to be back.' So spoke Charles Bukowski in Hamburg, Germany, during his standing room only reading at the Markthalle on 18 May 1978. These words were delivered dramatically, for the writer had returned to his *Heimat*, the land of *Dichter und Denker*, the birthplace of many geniuses he admired: George Frideric Handel, Richard Wagner, Friedrich Nietzsche, Johannes Brahms, Ludwig van Beethoven, J. S. Bach, Arthur Schopenhauer. Although Charles Bukowski (Heinrich Karl Bukowski, Jr) had been born on 16 August 1920 in a tall corner house on Aktienstrasse 12 and baptized in the Mariendom in Andernach, a town on a lovely stretch of the Rhine 40 kilometres south of Bonn, this was the first time he had set foot in Germany since his departure at the age of two. His father Henry Charles Bukowski, though born in Pasadena, California in 1895, was of German extraction and during the First World War had been stationed in Andernach with the American Army of Occupation as a GI, where he met and courted Katharina Fett, a seamstress. Although Bukowski sometimes claimed he had been born out of wedlock, the marriage records in Andernach confirm that his parents were in fact married on 15 July 1920.[1]

Andernach, in the district of Mayen-Koblenz in the Rhineland-Palatinate, is one of the most ancient towns in Germany. The Roman general Nero Claudius Drusus constructed a fortified citadel in 12 BC on the site of a Celtic settlement; the Romans named the place Antunnacum and the foundations of the town walls they constructed

Bukowski's birthplace in Andernach, Aktienstrasse 12.

are visible today.[2] Bukowski's cultural connection to Andernach on the Rhine already surfaces in his first published story 'Aftermath of A Lengthy Rejection Slip' (1944) in which he described the 'fuzzy blackness, impractical meditations, and repressed desires of an Eastern European' in contradistinction to the 'Browns and Smiths' of America: 'The Browns and Smiths are good writers but there are too many of them and they all write alike.' The narrator sees himself, on the contrary, in the tradition of Dostoevsky and Gorky; although this self-description is meant to be taken partially tongue-in-cheek, it is in fact how Bukowski conceived his literary ancestry.[3]

As the German economy continued to implode following the First World War, Bukowski's parents decided to come to America. They left Bremerhaven on 18 April 1923 for Baltimore, Maryland,

ss *President Fillmore* passenger list documenting the Bukowski family's
embarkation from Bremerhaven, 18 April 1923.

and then moved on to California. They settled first at Trinity Street,
near downtown Los Angeles, and ultimately returned to Bukowski
Sr's father Leonard's (*b*. 1861) birthplace in Pasadena.[4] Leonard had
left Germany in the 1880s and met his wife Emily Krause (*b*. 1865) –
also a German immigrant – in Cleveland. They moved to Pasadena
and were married in September 1887. Leonard drank heavily and
Emily left him around 1920.[5] The three-year-old Bukowski bonded
with his grandfather Leonard, who gave him a German cross and
his gold pocket watch – the grandson thought his grandfather 'was
the most beautiful man I had ever seen and I wasn't afraid'.[6]

In the novel devoted to his childhood and adolescence, *Ham on
Rye* (1982), there is an eerie scene depicting the infant Bukowski
sitting beneath a table: the furniture and sunlight are more real
than the human beings surrounding him. After describing both
of his parents, Bukowski turns to his grandmother:

Sometimes there was a third, a fat one who wore dresses with lace at the throat. She wore a large brooch, and had many warts on her face with little hairs growing out of them. 'Emily,' they called her. These people didn't seem happy together. Emily was the grandmother, my father's mother.[7]

Emily also comes in for cool treatment in the poem 'Emily Bukowski':

at 87
she died one evening
while feeding her
canary.
she liked to
drop the seed
into the cage
while making these
little
bird sounds.
she wasn't very
interesting
but few people
are.[8]

The dominant note in Bukowski's recollections of his childhood is that of existential *thrownness* – Heidegger's *Geworfenheit*, Jim Morrison's 'into this world we're thrown'. Bukowski describes the empty 'white air' all around him, and the overpowering sensation of being a stranger in an alien world marks his vision from the beginning.

The Bukowski family then moved to 2122 South Longwood Avenue in Los Angeles, the residence Bukowski would later remember as 'the house of horrors'. His mother spoke primarily

Bukowski with his parents in Pasadena, 1924.

German, her English remained tentative and Bukowski himself spoke German. The boy also had dyslexia: Bukowski's later manuscripts reveal a tendency to reverse letter order as well as some difficulty with correct spelling. In 1925 he began his education at San Marino School, south of Pasadena, and then attended Virginia Road grammar school.[9] As was the German custom, his parents attired him in velvet pants and shirts with elaborate collars.[10] The boy was also dissuaded from making friends – the adult Bukowski recalled his father intentionally dressing him in Native American costumes, which incited the wrath of the other boys, who played cowboys. Bukowski reports with his typical gallows humour that his parents also tried to prevent him from being left-handed during infancy: 'I was born left-handed and my parents bent my slop spoon so if I put it to my jaw with my left hand all I got was this frustration thing and a slap across the mouth for failing. Besides, riches ain't everything – especially after you've gotten away from parents like that.'[11]

2122 South Longwood Avenue, 1978.

As Bukowski remembered in a late poem, 'being the German kid in the 20's in Los Angeles / was difficult': other children called him 'Heinie', the derogatory term for Germans during the post-First World War period.[12] He wrote in a letter to John William Corrington on 14 January 1963: 'Between the imbecile savagery of my father, the disinterestedness of my mother, and the sweet hatred of my playmates: 'Heinie! Heinie! Heinie!' things were pretty hot all around.'[13] The lovelessness and rejection he experienced from his family as well as the outsider status he sensed as a German-American would be the initial elements which shaped Bukowski's personality: he would be forced to develop a tough, pugnacious independence to retaliate against the world's bullies.

Bukowski's young life was further scarred by his abusive father who beat him regularly. In his essay 'Ah, Liberation, Liberty, Lilies on the Moon!' he recalled:

> I well remember my childhood. I was held in total slavery. Saturday was lawnmowing and watering day. Sunday was

church. The other days were school, homework, and tasks. I was beaten 3 or 4 times a week by a bully of a father, a hateful man. He used a razor strop. My mother's only comment was: 'Respect him. After all, he is your father.'

I was a slave. I'd think, god, I'm only 3 feet tall. I can't get a job. I must stay here and take these beatings in order to have a place to sleep and something to eat. This sounds a bit humorous to me now but it wasn't then.[14]

The bedrock institutions of American life – family, school, church – are here revealed as oppressive systems: the enslavement of the individual by what the Marxist philosopher Louis Althusser named the ideological state apparatus. Bukowski spent his life attempting to undo the damage these modes of indoctrination had wreaked upon him: 'We are here to unlearn the teachings of the church, state, and our educational system. We are here to drink beer. We are here to kill war. We are here to laugh at the odds and live our lives so well that Death will tremble to take us.'[15] In this regard he resembles a writer with whom he felt himself to have nothing in common – William S. Burroughs – who also portrayed a modern world dominated by various systems of 'control'. Bukowski sought through the alchemy of art and his total dedication to the written word to liberate himself from what William Blake called in 'London' the 'mind-forged manacles' of the contemporary world.[16]

The German virtues of *Ordnung, Pünktlichkeit und Sauberkeit* – order, punctuality and cleanliness – and the fear of the Prussian father are seen in Franz Kafka, as well as in the American poet Theodore Roethke, who was born of German parents in Saginaw, Michigan. In his cycle of poems 'The Lost Son', Roethke described his fear as his father approached: 'Ordnung, Ordnung, papa is coming!'[17] As Bukowski tells us in *Ham on Rye*, his father 'was the dark covering the sun, the violence of him made everything else utterly disappear'.[18] Bukowski would frequently claim that it was his father 'who made me a writer'. He was well prepared for an intractable world, for an existence that Thomas Hobbes famously described as 'solitary, poor, nasty, brutish and short', for 'pain without reason'. His literary style was forged in the crucible of his youthful anguish: he would learn to handle words as if they were his fists, pounding back at the injustices he had endured. Writing became one means of fighting his way out, of steeling himself to avoid self-destruction. His skin had been removed: the emotional directness of his art had its source in naked, extreme vulnerability.

This early and repeated abuse ultimately led Bukowski to develop a kind of psychological dissociation: he was alienated not only from his self and body but also both separated from and a remote observer of the external world. A recurring pattern of imagery in his writings illustrates this estrangement. In the poem 'the recess bells of school', which begins 'my father's feet stank and his smile was like a / pile of dog shit', he describes how his suffering began to transform his perception of reality: 'to be the very blood of that hated blood / made the windows intolerable, / and the music and the flowers and the trees / ugly . . . brutal were the calla lilies / brutal the nectar and the kiss / brutal the recess bells of school. / brutal the softball games / brutal soccer and volleyball / the skies were white and high, / and I'd look at the faces of the game- / players / and they were strangely masked'.[19] This disorientation recurs in *Ham on Rye*: 'The first children of my age that I knew were in kindergarten. They seemed very strange, they laughed and talked and seemed happy. I didn't like them. I always felt as if I was going to be sick, to vomit, and the air seemed strangely still and white.'[20] This is a typical response to trauma – the other children taking part in games have faces which are 'strangely masked' – the alienation of the soul from itself, the 'othering' of the world, the self as stunned and neutral observer. And in both passages we note that the air is 'white' and 'high' – it is a remote aether in which he is emotionally anaesthetized rather than a blue, welcoming, accepting sky.

The historical background of these childhood traumata was equally difficult: the Depression arrived in 1929 and Bukowski often returned to his memories of this convulsive period in the United States.[21] The Depression revealed class and ethnic divisions which would alter the shape of American literature. In later life, Bukowski saw himself as a writer who identified with the literary generation of the Thirties, although at the time he was still an adolescent. Indeed, Bukowski in many ways saw himself as a writer of the same generation to which two of his favourite writers – the Armenian-American William Saroyan (*b*. 1908) and the Italian-American John Fante (*b*. 1909) belonged, although he himself had been born more than a decade later. He would repeatedly invoke them, as well as figures such as H. L. Mencken and Whit Burnett. The poverty, hopelessness and violence of the period as well as its literary innovations shaped his sensibility: it was also between the two world wars that he believed the greatest writers had flourished and Bukowski felt that since then there had been a precipitous decline in the quality of literature.

The first sign of Bukowski's future literary vocation manifested itself during the beginning years of the Depression while he was in the fifth grade. His teacher suggested the students write an account of President Herbert Hoover's visit to Los Angeles in 1932 to celebrate the opening of the Olympic Games.[22] His essay garnered accolades from the teacher as an especially well-written piece of prose: the irony was that he had never actually attended the event and the story was entirely invented. This was the moment that Bukowski first became aware that he had talent as a writer. He then began attending Mount Vernon Junior High School and in 1933 broke out with an extreme case of *acne vulgaris*. In a letter to Sheri Martinelli, he described the illness as well as the treatment he received at Los Angeles County General Hospital: 'I became covered with boils the size of baseballs. Not pimples, baseballs. And they sat me under the electric needle and drilled drillllled drilled deep into the flesh I could feel the little needle getting hot . . . like a wood drill punching into wood . . . and I could smell the oil.'[23] He now composed his first short story: 'The first thing I ever remembered writing was about a German aviator with a steel hand who shot hundreds of Americans out of the sky during World War I. It was in long hand in pen and it covered every page of a huge memo ringed notebook. I was about 13 at the time and I was in bed covered with the worst case of boils the medics ever remembered seeing.'[24] Already Bukowski's secret literary compositions began to function as a counterbalance to the terrors of his actual life. Freud's notion that creative writing, daydreaming, fantasy and the resolution of neurotic conflict are connected is borne out by Bukowski's youthful literary compulsions.

In January 1936 he graduated from Junior High School but his dermatological problems worsened and he stayed home from school from February to September 1936.[25] The explosion of acne over his shoulders, back, face and even his eyelids signalled the somatizing of his father's constant beatings, the body's primal screams: he had now registered his violation both emotionally and physically. One recalls Franz Kafka's story 'In Der Strafkolonie' ('In the Penal Colony', 1914) about a man whose punishment for a non-existent crime is to have his body engraved with the name of his infraction with sharp knives.[26] The centrality of the suffering body would become a central trope in Bukowski's work. 'All the Assholes in the World and Mine', for example, written in his mid-forties, documents humorously his painful haemorrhoid operation and, as we shall see, his letters of the 1960s overflow with a litany of physical complaints. The link between spiritual struggle and physical extremity was pondered by the Greek writer Nikos Kazantzakis when he experienced a mysterious skin disease during the composition of his great work, *The Saviors of God*.

Kazantzakis wrote: 'I understand those hermits now who were attacked suddenly with leprosy when in their retreat they reached out toward God. Skin diseases were the most usual manifestations.'[27] Bukowski would join the ROTC (Reserve Officers' Training Corps) – not due to any sense of military obligation or patriotic feeling – but because he wanted to avoid the embarrassment of having to disrobe in front of the other young men during physical education class and thus reveal his disfigured body.

In the wake of these multiple onslaughts, it is understandable that when Bukowski first drank alcohol as an adolescent he greeted it as his salvation. In chapter Twenty-two of *Ham on Rye* he describes going into the cellar of his friend Baldy's house where there were wine barrels. He samples the wine from the spigot, becomes nauseous, and spits it out. He then tries again and notices that he 'was beginning to feel good'.[28] He continues going 'from barrel to barrel. It was magic. Why hadn't someone told me? With this, life was great, a man was perfect, nothing could touch him . . . now I have found something, I have found something that is going to help me, for a long long time to come.'[29] Thus began his lifelong love affair with alcohol, a passion shared by scores of American writers including Edgar Allan Poe, Jack London, Sinclair Lewis, William Faulkner, Ernest Hemingway, John Berryman, F. Scott Fitzgerald, Hart Crane, John Steinbeck and Eugene O'Neill.[30] He began to leave his house through his bedroom window at night when his parents were asleep and frequent the bars in downtown Los Angeles. He named his torment 'The Frozen Man Stance' – a psychological state of total, anaesthetized unfeeling remoteness: 'I began drinking about 17 with older boys who roamed the streets and robbed gas stations and liquor stores. They thought my disgust with everything was a lack of fear, that my non-complaining was a soulful bravado. I was popular and I didn't care whether I was popular or not. I was Frozen.'[31]

As the Depression intensified, life at home became increasingly fraught. In the late poem 'we ain't got no money, honey, but we got rain', Bukowski describes a torrential rainstorm during which helpless unemployed husbands quarrel with their wives as their houses are foreclosed by the banks.[32] Bukowski depicts his attempt to intervene as his father beats his mother. In 1936 Bukowski's father lost his job as a milkman, but continued to drive to work so the neighbours would believe that he was still employed. In the poem 'waiting', Bukowski writes:

> hot summers in the mid-30's in Los Angeles,
> nothing to do, nowhere to go, listening to
> the terrified talk of our parents
> at night:
> 'what will we do? What will we
> do?'
>
> 'god, I don't know . . .'
> starving dogs in the alleys, skin taut
> across ribs, hair falling out, tongues
> out, such sad eyes, sadder than any sadness
> on earth[33]

Bukowski began Susan Miller Dorsey High School in September 1936 and transferred the following year to Los Angeles High School, graduating in 1939. The poem 'my old man' reveals that when he was sixteen, his father found the manuscripts of his stories and was so infuriated by what he read that he threw Bukowski's clothing and belongings out of the house onto the front lawn.[34] In 1937 their conflict reached a culminating point. Bukowski had returned from a drunken evening and vomited on the living room floor. His father pushed his face down into the vomit on the rug, telling his son that this is how one deals with a dog. In his poem 'The Rat', Bukowski memorialized the scene: 'with one punch, at the age of 16 and $^1/_2$, / I knocked out my father, / a cruel shiny bastard with bad breath,

/ and I didn't go home for some time, only now and then to try to get a dollar from / dear momma. / It was 1937 in Los Angeles and it was a hell of a / Vienna.'[35]

Bukowski now discovered a 'small library near La Cienega and West Adams boulevards' where he found D. H. Lawrence, Turgenev, Upton Sinclair, Sinclair Lewis, Gorky, Dostoevsky.[36] It was also during his late adolescence that he discovered John Fante. In a late short story, 'I Meet the Master' (1984) in which he names Fante 'Bante', he recalled: 'I was not a hero-worshipper. Bante was my first. It was the words, the simply clarity of them. They made me want to weep yet they made me feel like walking through walls.'[37] Bukowski describes his visit to Angel's Flight in Bunker Hill to find the hotel in which Fante set the love story of Arturo Bandini and Carmen in his novel *Ask the Dust*. He had gone by the room 'for months on my way to the Grand Central Market or my favorite green bar, or just to go downtown to walk around'.[38] He finally decided to go up to see the room but encountered an old lady who angrily sent him away.[39] This intense admiration of writers signalled that the discovery of the 'magic' of literature was to be as grand as – or grander than – the discovery of the 'magic' of alcohol. As he revealed in *Ham on Rye*: 'To me, these men who had come into my life from nowhere were my only chance. They were the only voices that spoke to me.'[40]

He also devoured Turgenev and Gorky: 'Turgenev was a very serious fellow but he could make me laugh because a truth first encountered can be very funny. When someone else's truth is the same as your truth, and he seems to be saying it just for you, that's great.'[41] And in *Notes of a Dirty Old Man* he wrote: 'First of all, read Céline. The greatest writer of 2,000 years. Of course, *The Stranger* by Camus must fit in. *Crime and Punishment*. *The Brothers*. All of Kafka. All the works of the unknown writer John Fante. The short stories of Turgenev.'[42] Turgenev's limpid, descriptive style in which each sentence packs abundant visual detail surely appealed to Bukowski;

as Sherwood Anderson remarked, in the Russian writers, 'one feels life everywhere, in every page'.[43] Gorky is as frequently invoked: 'Oh, I like Céline, early Hemingway, Dostoevski, early Gorki short stories. I like Jeffers, that's about it.' Bukowski loved Gorky (not however what he wrote after the Revolution) and he must have identified with Gorky's brutal treatment by his grandfather, drinking, suicide attempt at age nineteen, many lowly jobs as well as his youthful enraptured discovery of literature.[44]

In the summer of 1939 he graduated from high school: he went to the senior prom with his face covered in bandages from his *acne vulgaris* treatment and peered through the window at the dancing students. He spent time in the bars on 6th street and at Pershing Square where he listened to the debates on God's existence.[45] From 1939 to 1941 Bukowski took his first job, at Sears & Roebuck on Pico Boulevard and in September 1939 matriculated at Los Angeles City College to study journalism and English. Bukowski wrote of his time at college: 'Tuition fee was two dollars but the old man said he couldn't afford to send me anymore. I went to work in the railroad yards, scrubbing the sides of trains with Oakite. I drank and gambled at night. Had a small room above a bar on Temple Street in the Filipino district, and I gambled at night with the aircraft workers and pimps and etc.'[46] Rooming houses and small apartments would take on an infernal symbolic meaning in his life and work: the frayed couches, torn lampshades and shrieking landladies; the shared bathroom down the hall; the mice, roaches and rats that kept him company through the long, solitary, drunken nights as he typed and listened to his radio playing Brahms, Stravinsky, Mahler, Shostakovich and his favourite – Sibelius.

Bukowski disliked his time in college, and he described these years as a waste of time. His first publication was a humorous letter to the editor under the title 'Why Crab?', published in the 24 May 1940 issue of the *Los Angeles Collegian*, the Los Angeles City College newspaper:

Dear Cubby Hole: In answer to R.D.'s complaints about our street car service, I would like to step forth as a valiant defender of that vehicle.

I find that: the violent rocking not only awakens me for class but also allows me to kick heck out of the guy next to me, if I don't like his looks. I never have to give my seat to a lady – I never get one. I have developed a marvelous muscular coordination by the continued process of holding a strap with one hand, my books with another, while treading heavily (and of course accidentally) upon some person's feet in an effort to blitzkrieg my way to a seat.

All this for 7 cents! Why crab?

Henry Bukowski[47]

The letter shows that already at the age of twenty – although he was still 'Henry Bukowski' and not yet 'Charles'– he had begun to evolve his characteristic sarcasm, tough guy persona and his combination of courtly style with rough-house antics. His way of coping with reality was by rebelling, revolting against everything, with a bit of charming humour thrown into the mix.

The perhaps intentionally incendiary use here of the word 'blitzkrieg' may subtly allude to the fact that Germany had invaded Poland on 1 September 1939: the onset of the Second World War began to stir Bukowski's latent pro-German sympathies. His parents had been members of the Deutsche Haus, a German-American group, and his mother had voiced positive feelings about Hitler: Bukowski himself may have briefly attended meetings of the German American Bund.[48] This has been one of the most controversial episodes in Bukowski's life and has been variously interpreted by his biographers. His behaviour seems to have been motivated by his penchant for taking the opposite position of the pro-American 'masses', to answer the prejudice he had experienced as a German-American child as well as his desire to play the role of *provocateur*. Yet there was primarily an element of cultural pride in his identification with Germany. As an American of German descent, Bukowski was declaring solidarity with what he perceived as his own history rather than declaring any sympathy for Fascism, Nazism or anti-Semitism. It is perhaps noteworthy that when he became financially successful in the late 1970s he acquired a succession of BMW and Audi automobiles and also purchased higher quality wine than he had been accustomed to: German Bernkasteler Riesling.

Bukowski left Los Angeles City College in June 1941 without taking a degree. He would spend his entire life – apart from a few journeys to other American cities – in Los Angeles: as he put it, 'I have it in my bones.' Unlike other major American cities, Los Angeles is spread out across hundreds of miles into various sections and he knew intimately all of its different areas: Santa Monica and Venice Beach, the seedy streets of East Hollywood, the racetracks at Santa Anita, Hollywood Park, Los Alamitos and Del Mar, his grandparents' house in Pasadena, the Olympic Auditorium on Grand Avenue where he would watch the fights, and later the harbour town of San Pedro. Following the Second World War, the defence and aerospace industry would become a major engine of the economy and Bukowski would witness the change from a prelapsarian Los Angeles with palm trees, uncongested roads, clear air and water and a congenial number of inhabitants to the megalopolis which began to emerge in the 1950s and 1960s: omnipresent freeways, a polluted Pacific Ocean, the triumph of billboard advertising, gas stations, neon, strip malls, smog and endless telephone poles and wires crisscrossing an occluded sky. Charles Phoenix's *Southern California in the Fifties* contains photographs from the period which illustrate a Los Angeles in rapid, surreal transformation: Disneyland, 'space age' modernist architecture, the birth of fast-food behemoth McDonald's, Hollywood, Knott's Berry Farm, Pacific Ocean Park.[49] One of the most significant developments was the expansion of the transportation system in Los Angeles and the retiring of the railcars of Bukowski's childhood. Soon the city would be dominated by several major freeways, which are frequently depicted in his works: Harbor, Ventura, San Diego and Hollywood. Los Angeles is a city in which everyone owns one car (at least) as a birthright and car-pooling is frowned upon. A good portion of every Angeleno's life is spent in an automobile: driving somewhere over long distances, or trapped for hours in stop-and-go, snarling traffic stretching for miles on end.

Yet culturally backward Los Angeles had also become, paradoxic-ally, a place of high intellectual cachet because many European artists and intellectuals as well as American expatriates had been 'exiled in Paradise' during the 1930s and 1940s, between the mountains and the sea, beneath the dome of the then smog-free blue sky. Some visited and settled in southern California by necessity due to the rise of Fascism in Europe and others came for personal reasons: Bertolt Brecht, Thomas Mann, Theodor Adorno, Arnold Schoenberg, Aldous Huxley, Igor Stravinsky, Henry Miller.[50] Huxley, whose novel *Point Counter Point* Bukowski admired, lived nearby. When asked during his first 1963 interview about Huxley – 'Does it bother you that Aldous Huxley is in a position to spit on you? From the window, if you stick your head out far enough, and look hard enough, you can see the lights in Aldous Huxley's house up the hill, where the successful live' – Bukowski responded: 'I haven't even thought about it, but no, it doesn't bother me.'[51]

Bukowski would inhabit inexpensive 'courts' – areas containing several bungalows in typically Los Angeles Spanish-style architec-ture: red tile roofs, white stucco, arched windows and entryways. The lush tropical foliage of the city surrounded him: azaleas, invoked in the poem 'the passing of a dark gray moment' –

'standing here, / doing what? / as exposed as an azalea / to a bee'
– bougainvillea, bottle brush, poinsettia, tournefortia, guava, the
omnipresent palm.[52] The coastal beach communities of Venice
and Santa Monica looked out upon the Pacific Ocean, which sat
inscrutable, symbol of that variously silent, indifferent or hostile
Nature which Bukowski frequently invoked as in his famous poem,
'I Met a Genius':

> I met a genius on the train
> today
> about 6 years old,
> he sat beside me
> and as the train
> ran down along the coast
> we came to the ocean
> and then he looked at me
> and said,
> it's not pretty.
>
> it was the first time I'd
> realized
> that.[53]

Los Angeles becomes his cosmos, a place the Spanish stole from the
Native Americans, despoiled with their destructive 'Christianity'
and which the subsequent white settlers carved up, exploited and
turned into a dream factory selling the illusions of Disneyland and
Hollywood to the masses.

Bukowski would leave Los Angeles: he needed to free himself
from his familial psychodrama and in 1942 he began his *wander-
jahre* throughout the United States. He did not go 'on the road'
in the romantic manner of Jack Kerouac in search of spiritual
illumination; he had nowhere to go, so he went everywhere

and gathered material for his writing – many of his experiences would find their way into his stories, poems, novels and essays. It is difficult to determine Bukowski's whereabouts with any certainty during the 1940s: the primary evidence is his own memory, which was not always reliable. When he left Los Angeles, he headed for New Orleans. He thought the French Quarter phony and 'stayed west of Canal Street, sleeping with the rats'.[54] He found work with a newspaper, as he reveals in the autobiographical note he appended to *Longshot Pomes for Broke Players* (1962): 'the closest I ever got to being a reporter was as an errand boy in the composing room of the *New Orleans Item*. Used to have nickel beers in a place out back and the nights passed quickly.'[55]

He was also writing obsessively during this period – he began to write six to ten stories a week which he would hand print in ink and submit to the *New Yorker*, *Atlantic Monthly* and *Harper's* – but they were rejected.[56] Later in life, when he was investigated by the FBI, the dossier the agency compiled included an 'OPF' (Official Personnel File) dated 26 December 1957, which Bukowski completed for the Post Office. This contains a 'Standard Form 85: Security Investigation Data for Nonsensitive Position' that names the places he claims he lived from January 1937 to December 1957. He lists only Los Angeles – from January 1937 to December 1941 and from September 1945 to December 1957, with one period from January 1942 to August 1945 in Philadelphia.[57] In a letter to John William Corrington he says that in New Orleans he 'went to work in a comic book house, and soon moved on. Miami Beach. Atlanta. New York. St. Louis. Philly. Frisco. L.A. again. New Orleans again. Then Philly again. Then Frisco again. L.A. again. Around and around. A couple of nights in East Kansas City. Chicago. I stopped writing. I concentrated on drinking. My longest stays were in Philly.'[58]

He spent time in Atlanta where he lived in the infamous 'tar paper shack'. This episode attained an iconic importance in

Bukowski's self-mythologizing. It was here that he ran out of paper on which to write and in desperation began to scrawl on the edges of newspapers (which served as the floor for the shack) with a stubby pencil while he starved, froze in the cold and made an attempt at suicide.[59] In a poem published in 1962, 'love song to a woman I saw Wednesday at the racetrack', he mentions also living in Savannah, Georgia: 'remembering Savannah 20 years ago / a four poster bed / and streets full of helmets and hunters / things I did then / left welts . . .'.[60] If this chronology is correct, that would place him in Savannah in the early 1940s, around the time he was in Atlanta. This incredible dedication to writing becomes symbolic of his last connection to life – the hanging thread which tenuously keeps him alive, the sustenance without which he will spiritually die. He also apparently read Knut Hamsun's *Hunger* during this period: he would later recall that he had read Hamsun during his 'starving writer days'.

He did not resort to trying to eat his own flesh, as did the hero of *Hunger*. However, as he remembers in the poem 'a note upon starvation': 'I'm not sure where I starved the worst: / Savannah, Atlanta, New Orleans, Philadelphia / or Los Angeles. / starving is not as terrible as it might / seem. / the first two or three days without / food / are the worst / about the fourth day / you begin to feel almost intoxicated.'[61] Hamsun's novel about a poor writer – like Saroyan's 'Daring Young Man on the Flying Trapeze' alone in a small room fighting to keep alive for his art and dying while reading Proust, or John Fante's Arturo Bandini in *Ask the Dust* – supplied Bukowski with another archetypal model of the artist ready to perish to realize his calling. In 'Another Portfolio' Bukowski writes that a year or so after he submitted his story '20 Tanks from Kasseldown' to Caresse Crosby's *Portfolio*, 'I am in a tar paper shack for $1.25 a week in Atlanta, no water, no heat, no light.' He describes writing to Crosby for financial help but receives none. He claims he 'got out of Atlanta by signing on with a railroad track gang going west . . .'.[62]

His novel *Factotum* (1975) describes his various jobs in Philadelphia, Atlanta, New York, Houston, St Louis, San Francisco,
New Orleans, El Paso, Savannah. These cities appear throughout
his work and the consistency of these references suggests he spent
at least some time in each of them. In 1942 he was in San Francisco
and drove a truck for the Red Cross.[63] In one of his best tales from
his 'Notes of a Dirty Old Man' series he wrote: 'I sat in a hard wooden
chair and peered at the San Francisco Bay Bridge.' A friendly landlady named 'Mama Fazzio' gives him ice for his beer and wine: he
drinks ecstatically, listens to classical music and has an affair with
the wife of an Italian Communist.[64] San Francisco is also the setting
for his early story 'Hard Without Music' (1946): 'I was a young
man in San Francisco spending whatever money I could get feeding
symphonies to the hungry insides of my landlady's wooden, man-
high victrola. I think those were the best days of them all, being
very young and seeing the Golden Gate Bridge from my window.
Almost every day I discovered a new symphony.'[65] And in the
poem 'we, the artists –' he wrote: 'in San Francisco the landlady,
80, helped me drag the green / Victrola up the stairway and I
played Beethoven's 5th / until they beat on the walls / there was
a large bucket in the center of the room / filled with beer and
winebottles'.[66] The poem ends as the Second World War arrives
and the narrator lands in New Orleans.[67]

He confirms his stay in San Francisco and his refusal to join
the military in the poem 'ww2': 'I was in frisco a dandy place with
lakes or something / i could see the gold bridge and it wasn't teeth
from my window / enough to drink almost always enough to drink
/ I wrote the old man down in l.a. you might as well get a story /
ready for your god damned neighbors because i am not going
to yr / war.'[68] His father remonstrates with him, saying that his
country is at war and his son would not exist if had he not met his
mother during the First World War. The poem then shifts: 'I don't
know how much later but some time later i am sitting in another /

cheap room philly i am drinking a bottle of port have a record /
player and i am listening to the 2nd movement of brahms' 2nd
symphony.'[69] It was in Philadelphia where he would spend the
most time away from Los Angeles and in the documents Bukowski
filed with the Post Office he states he lived on 603 North 17th
Street.[70] Here he sat daily at the bar immortalized in *Barfly* (1984),
located on the corner of 17th and Fairmont Street. Bukowski lists
his employment at Fairmount Motor Works at 16th Street and
Fairmont. Thus the twin poles of his life – bar and work – were
conveniently in close proximity. Bukowski had arrived in the city
of brotherly love in the footsteps of another American literary man
of genius with a daimonic imagination who a century previously
for six years (1838–44) had also haunted drunk its dark streets:
Edgar Allan Poe.

2

Solitude and Music in Small Rooms: First Stories and Poems, 1944–1959

Although Bukowski spent considerable time changing residences and employment while criss-crossing America from 1942 to 1947, this did not impede his creativity. He continued to compose obsessively and in 1944 at the age of 24 made his precocious debut with the publication of 'Aftermath of a Lengthy Rejection Slip' in *Story*, one of America's premier literary magazines. Founded by husband and wife Whit Burnett (1899–1973) and Martha Foley (1897–1977) in 1931, many distinguished writers – including William Faulkner, J. D. Salinger, Carson McCullers, Norman Mailer, William Saroyan and Sherwood Anderson – had appeared in its pages.[1] 'Aftermath' is a clever, whimsical, metafictional tale – the writing of fiction about the writing of fiction. He shapes his plot around an actual event – the rejection by Burnett of his submission to *Story* – and even includes as a prelude the (presumably) actual rejection letter. Bukowski was *au courant* with the major literary currents of his time such as Imagism and Surrealism: here he anticipates metafiction, one of the dominant self-conscious narrative modes of the 1960s. The plot demonstrates his early mastery of farce, colloquialisms, rapid dialogue and deft irony.

'Aftermath' also introduces Bukowski's favourite thematic holy trinity *Wein, Weib und Gesang* – Wine, Woman and Song – which would typify his later work. As the narrator observes his acquaintances Carson and Shipkey – described sarcastically as 'painters who couldn't make up their minds whether to paint like Salvador Dali

From the German edition (2007) of 'Aftermath', Bukowski's first published short story (1944).

or Rockwell Kent, and they worked at the shipyards while trying to decide' – drink and play cards, his girlfriend Millie, a lady of questionable virtue, appears and flirts with him and then enters into a mock seduction of the presumed literary man Burnett (for whom he plays a recording of Tchaikovsky's Sixth Symphony) – who, unknown to the narrator, is in reality an insurance man.[2] We are reminded of James Thurber, a writer (and artist) Bukowski greatly admired, and his 'The Secret Life of Walter Mitty' – about a man who escapes into fantasy, the artist as gentle dreamer. As Sigmund Freud argued in 'Creative Writers and Day-Dreaming', 'the creative writer does the same as the child at play. He creates a world of phantasy which he takes very seriously.'[3] The story also demonstrates Bukowski's early ability to shape and time his plot for maximum comic effectiveness as well as the surprise reversal of expected reality typical of successful jokes: at one point the narrator hilariously attempts to teach a cat tricks which dogs are normally expected to perform. Indeed, this humorous vitality is what Bukowski found lacking in the work of Ernest Hemingway.

Following the publication of his first story, Bukowski left Philadelphia and made a brief trip to New York City where he stayed three months. In his essay 'Dirty Old Man Confesses', he recalled:

> Then it seemed I was in the Village in New York – the old Village, a chickenshit place full of phonies as I might guess the new Village is now. The artist must always move on, one step ahead of the jellymen.
>
> While I was in the Village I passed a drugstore, and in the magazine rack was the then-famous *Story* mag edited by Whit Burnett and Martha Foley . . . I reached for the mag to look through it, then saw *my* name on the cover! They'd published me. At twenty-four. I'd been moving so fast the mail hadn't caught up or had been lost.[4]

Bukowski describes seeing Burnett on the streets of New York and being disappointed when he saw 'this look of pain in his eyes, but I caught it as rather spoiled and sheltered pain, even though his eyes were beautiful. But I knew then that we were *very* different.'[5] Bukowski was proud of his publication in *Story*, although he was disappointed that 'Aftermath' appeared in the 'end pages' of the magazine rather than in a more prominent location. He would correspond with Burnett over the next ten years, submitting to him many stories for consideration.[6]

One of Bukowski's major innovations was the way he narrowed the gap between poetry and prose: he sometimes wrote poems which appear to be short stories broken up into lines of verse. Bukowski's earliest poems appeared from 1946 to 1951 in *Matrix*, a little magazine based in New York and Philadelphia edited by

Joseph Moskovitz and Frank Brookhouser. His first two appeared in the Summer 1946 issue. One is entitled 'Hello', while the other, 'Soft and Fat Like Summer Roses' is a mini-short story: 'Rex was a two-fisted man / Who drank like a fish / And looked like a purple gargoyle.' At once we have the bizarre simile coupled with colloquial American English ('two-fisted', 'drank like a fish') and the poem continues as an uninterrupted narrative. After Rex is injured at work, his wife leaves him and we encounter the first example of the 'obscenity' for which Bukowski was to become notorious as the husband exclaims: '"Bitch. Cheap—bitch," he said. / She climbed on the bed, fully dressed . . .'.[7] The plot resembles James M. Cain's *The Postman Always Rings Twice* (1934): we have an injured man, a waitress, and the 'other man' is a Greek who comes to the restaurant and tries to take her away from him. In Cain's novel, the owner of the restaurant is Greek, while the man comes to steal his waitress wife. If the poem was indeed a subliminal remembering of Cain's novel, it would be early evidence of Bukowski's interest in hardboiled crime fiction which resurfaces in works such as his final novel *Pulp*.[8]

In this same issue of *Matrix* 'The Reason behind Reason' was published, the first of a quartet of short stories which would appear in the magazine. It was followed over the next two years by 'Love, Love, Love', 'Cacoethes Scribendi' and 'Hard without Music' (1948). They are remarkable not only for their style but because they introduce for the first time the major themes of Bukowski's subsequent career: his familial psychodrama, manic literary compulsion, alcohol, romantic yearnings, madness and love of classical music. 'The Reason behind Reason' features a baseball player named 'Chelaski' (the first fictional version of the name of Bukowski's alter ego Henry Chinaski) who has been seized by an existential crisis in the middle of the game. From the outset he is estranged from reality and Nature: 'There are days when you feel a little different. Things don't set right. Like now, even the sun looked a little sick, the green of the fences too green, the sky much too high . . .'.[9] These are images of remoteness, emptiness, space – as if the integral core of the self is absent. He refuses to continue playing and the story ends with 'reporters . . . making their way down to Chelaski to ask him what was wrong'.[10]

The most accomplished of the sequence, 'Hard without Music', depicts Larry, a young man who is selling his record collection to two nuns. Sister Celia (Saint Cecilia is the patron saint of music) tells him: 'You have such good taste. Almost all of Beethoven, and Brahms, and Bach and . . .'.[11] This mirrors Bukowski's own preferences in classical music, for he eschewed vocal music.[12] Larry's ecstatic speech celebrating the 'inwardness' of listening – 'there are moments, I have found, when a piece, after previous listenings that were sterile and dry . . . I have found that a moment comes when the piece at last unfolds itself fully to the mind . . . like the buzzing of countless little steel bees whirling in ever-heightened beauty and knowing' – echoes German philosophical thought concerning the power of symphonic music.[13] As Peter Watson observes in *The German Genius*: 'The symphony, for example, was associated with Kant's notion of the sublime, a form of art defined by reference to its vastness of scope and its "oceanic" capacity to overwhelm the senses. Many philosophers and artists argued that contemplation of the infinite through the sublime offered insights that the merely beautiful could not provide. "The massed forces" of the symphony supported this idea.'[14] So too, Bukowski's characters are often beaten by life and lured by the sublime, beset by *Sehnsucht* – the yearning for something beyond the quotidian which tormented the German Romantics.[15]

As we have seen, Bukowski claims he spent only three months in New York and then returned to Philadelphia: 'Aftermath' had appeared in the March/April 1944 issue of *Story*. He recalls this period in a work of 1960, 'Portions from a Wine-Stained Notebook':

When I was 24 or 5 I ran errands for sandwiches and cleaned venetian blinds and answered questions on the classics in a bar in Philly straight East of the Eastern pen. Most days were memory-less but not meaningless: I was feeling toward the classic of self, almost found it one day when I failed my errand and fell in an alley like a great wounded bird, white belly up to sun, and children came up and poked at me, and I heard a woman's voice: 'Now you leave that man alone!' and I laughed quietly inside myself, on such a fine Spring day to be a castrat-edly inept, a young man printed on both sides of the Atlantic, and somebody's fine sandwich in the dirt.[16]

Here is the famous bar immortalized in *Barfly* where he played the role of court jester: he would entertain and go on errands for patrons and be rewarded with drinks. His self-portrayal is at once comic and terrible: he laughs to himself as the children taunt his drunken body in an alleyway, realizing that he as at once 'castratedly inept' and yet 'printed on both sides of the Atlantic'. He is the poet as mystic fool, both answering 'questions on the classics' for the bar's clientele and 'feeling toward the classic of self' – coming into his own interiority, discovering himself as a poet as he revels in ecstatic drunkenness. The 'holy fool' – the wise man with spiritual depth and power who pretends to be 'dumb' – would become a dominant trope in Bukowski's later work.[17]

The reference to the 'Eastern pen' alludes to another sub-plot in Bukowski's life, for as the Second World War drew to its final year, he became involved in a private war of his own. On 22 July 1944 he was arrested in Philadelphia for draft dodging by the FBI.[18] Just as he had been 'moving so fast' that he had not received his first published story in the mail from the publisher, he apparently had neglected to notify the draft board of his whereabouts. He spent seventeen days in the Philadelphian 'Eastern pen', Moyamensing Prison ('pen' is American slang for 'penitentiary'). The poem 'ww2' and short story 'Doing Time with Public Enemy No. 1' also describe his arrest and his meeting in prison with the infamous criminal Courtney Taylor.[19] Bukowski took a medical and psychological test on 7 August 1944 and was exempted from service.

Bukowski's second publishing coup, '20 Tanks from Kasseldown'[20] (1946), appeared in the colourful socialite Caresse Crosby's (1892–1970) *Portfolio* along with Henry Miller, Jean-Paul Sartre, Federico García Lorca and Jean Genet. It depicts a man jailed following a trial on political charges and its brooding tone is in marked contrast to 'Aftermath of a Lengthy Rejection Slip' and may allude to Bukowski's time in Moyamensing. The solitary 'dark night of the soul' is a spiritual struggle waged by Bukowski's anti-heroes: they must work out their inner destiny alone. The story recalls German Expressionism with its dreamlike atmosphere and emphasis on extreme states of emotion. Bukowski had read more French writers – Artaud, Camus, Céline, Genet and – later in life, Sartre – than German ones, although he is directly in the line of German literature stretching from E.T.A. Hoffman and Hölderlin to Brecht. Brecht is mentioned briefly in a letter to Carl Weissner in a list of writers he admires: 'Brecht in portions.'[21] His appearance in *Portfolio* was significant because the magazine was considered to be avant-garde in its time. He wrote in his 1967 essay for *A Tribute to Jim Lowell*: 'the "little magazines" are not little in circulation because the writers write badly, but because there are not enough readers to understand, enjoy, digest advanced writing.'[22] Indeed, he would be published later in Wallace Berman's *Semina*, Andy Warhol's *Intransit* and many other publications devoted to 'advanced writing' and art.

Bukowski returned to Los Angeles in 1945 for a brief period. In his 1974 *Berkeley Barb* interview, he described the starvation he endured during his travels: he had been 200 lb (91 kg), but by the time he reached LA he had gone down to 131 lb (59 kg).[23] In his story 'Love, Love, Love' he describes being charged for room and board by his parents. He then returned to Philadelphia – we know he was in Philadelphia since when he wrote to Caresse Crosby in

1946–7 he included his return address as '2020 Mt. Vernon St. Phila 30 Pa'. He came back to Los Angeles in April 1947 where he would remain. A photograph taken three months later in July depicts him in a double-breasted suit standing in his parents' yard.[24] A bizarre sub-plot in Bukowski's already weird family inferno developed when his father – in his effort to improve his employment prospects – informed his supervisor at the Los Angeles County Museum of Art that he himself was the author of the story '20 Tanks from Kasseldown' (father and son shared the same name) and thus received a promotion. Bukowski was flabbergasted by this – he wrote to the bibliographer Jim Roman in 1965 that his father had also stolen both of his copies of *Portfolio*. He again fled, finding a room downtown, this time near Alvarado Street.[25] Bukowski continued composing between 1946 and 1951, despite his later claim that he went on a 'ten-year drunk' after 1946 during which he wrote nothing. Apparently during periods when he had no typewriter (which he periodically pawned or sold for financial reasons) he hand-printed his stories and decorated them with his clever cartoons. An example is the story 'A Kind, Understanding Face' (1948) which spins a bizarre plot around a weird young man named Ralph who leaves a suicide note covered on the reverse with odd quotations from Rabelais and Santayana.

By far the most cataclysmic event of 1947 was Bukowski's encounter with the woman who would become his muse for the next decade and haunt him for the rest of his life: he meets Jane Cooney Baker at a bar on Alvarado Street.[26] He frequently recounted how he walked into the Glenview one night. He was warned that the lady he observed sitting by herself was 'crazy' and that he should be careful, but naturally he approached and sat beside her. This dramatic moment would be told and retold in story, essay, novel as well as the film *Barfly*. Jane was born in 1910 in Carlsbad, California, then lived in Glencoe and Roswell, New Mexico and was thus ten years older than Bukowski. She was a deeply troubled woman

Jane Cooney Baker in the Roswell High School Yearbook, 1927.

who felt guilt over the death of her alcoholic ex-husband in a car accident.[27] Jane was another wounded misanthrope trapped in a brutal world, their relationship a *folie à deux*. In his poem 'my first affair with that older woman', he remembered: 'she was ten years older / and mortally hurt by the past / and the present; / she treated me badly: desertion, other / men; / she brought me immense / pain, / continually'; and in 'the tragedy of the leaves', Bukowski described his landlady screaming mercilessly at him for the rent and he concluded that the reason for her irrational anger was 'because the world had failed us both'.[28] The same might be said of Jane and himself: the world had failed them both. In one of his first 'Notes from a Dirty Old Man' columns from *Open City* in 1967, he recalled their early days together: 'There was a hotel at Beverly and Vermont. We were on the wine. My ladyfriend and I. Jane was a natural. And she had delicious legs and a tight little gash and a face of powdered pain. And she knew me. She taught me more than the philosophy books of the ages.'[29]

Bukowski worked at the Sunbeam Lighting Company from 1949 to March 1951 when he lived at 521 and 503 Union Drive. From 11 to 27 December 1950 he got a job at the Post Office as a Temporary Substitute Carrier. Following his last appearance in *Matrix* in 1948, Bukowski's next publication was the poem 'The Look' in *Matrix* in March 1951, after which he would not appear again in print until 1956. He took a variety of jobs and lived in various locations around Los Angeles. In April 1951 he moved to 268 4/6 S Coronado St. He then worked for three years as an 'Indefinite Mail Carrier' from 5 March 1952 until 1955, living at 323 $\frac{1}{2}$ N Westmoreland Avenue as well as 2325 Ocean View Avenue and at 1237 W 11th Street. His relationship with Jane continued to be volatile. Although Bukowski claimed that he and Jane never married, in the FBI report a document is included (redacted in the text but visible upon close inspection) stating: 'On March 4, 1952, BUKOWSKI married to JANE S. COONYE [sic] who [was born] in 1918, at Roswell, New Mexico.'[30] This contradicts what is stated by Bukowski's biographers – that they never married, and also that Jane was ten years older than he – this would make her just two years his elder. However, it is probable that given the strictures against cohabitation during this time in America, Bukowski claimed they had been married on his employment forms to avoid obloquy.

The couple was repeatedly evicted from their domiciles due to their constant drinking and fighting. Despite his violent and unsettled life with Jane, Bukowski continued to submit to poetry journals, as we see in a letter he wrote to Judson Crews dated 4 November 1953:

Except for the new ones on top, these poems have been rejected by *Poetry* magazine and a new outfit *Embryo*. Favorable remarks, ect., [sic] but they do not think my stuff is poetry. I know what they mean. The idea is there but I can't break thro the skin.

I can't work the dials. I'm not interested in poetry. I don't know what interests me. Non-dullness, I suppose. Proper poetry is dead poetry even if it looks good.[31]

Here we have one of the earliest statements of what will become Bukowski's prevailing attitude towards poetry: that 'proper poetry is dead poetry even if it looks good'. He wants to break away from the strictures that have defined verse as an elitist activity for the few, and to re-energize it – to 'make it new', as Ezra Pound advised.

Bukowski had been drinking alcohol for close to twenty years when the stress on his body finally reached a climax in 1954: he entered the Los Angeles County Hospital to be treated for an internal haemorrhage from which he nearly died. In a letter to Doug Blazek he remembered: 'I ended up in the charity ward of the hospital spewing blood out of my mouth and ass, completely fallen apart, done. They let me lay there 2 days before somebody came along and decided I needed a transfusion . . . I came out 900 years older'; he recounts this event with his typical mix of comedy and horror in his story 'Life and Death in the Charity Ward'.[32] Due to his poverty he was almost denied blood and the priest was brought in for the last rites, but Bukowski refused to see him. Fortunately, however, his father had some 'blood credits' so he received the requisite transfusion. Miraculously he survived and Jane now introduced him to horse racing as a presumed replacement for alcohol (he would continue however, contra doctor's orders, to drink). The track would occupy in Bukowski's imagination the same place as bullfighting for Hemingway: the arena in which a life and death struggle took place governed by the laws of determinism and contingency. It is also likely that he was aware of the large role gambling played in the lives of two of his literary heroes, Dostoevsky and Saroyan.

Following his near-death experience, Bukowski was driven to write poetry as if possessed: suddenly he was covering page after page with lines which seemed to appear magically, unbidden. It was as if his second chance at life stimulated his creativity to move in powerful new directions. Following his hospital stay, his behaviour became less manic and his speech had also slowed: he speculated that he had likely suffered some brain damage during his ordeal.[33] This recalls the experience of Jorge Luis Borges, whose serious head injury in 1938 signalled his breakthrough into the haunting, labyrinthine, cerebral stories of *Ficciones* for which he became famous, as well as C. G. Jung's struggle with madness – his *Red Book* (1914–30) charting his overwhelming yet ultimately fecundating confrontation with his volcanic unconscious.[34] Edmund Wilson, in his essay 'The Wound and the Bow', recounts the story of Sophocles' Philoctetes, the Greek archer wounded by a snake bite, whose seeming liability becomes the spur to excellence.[35]

It is difficult not to see Bukowski as a classic case of the links between genius and madness, to see the connections between the extreme states of consciousness with which he had been familiar since childhood and the initial breaking of the dam which led to the astonishing outpouring of poetry, stories, essays, novels, book reviews and journalism over the next forty years. Surviving his health crisis also added to the myth of his seemingly superhuman resilience and ability to prevail: as Nietzsche wrote, '*Aus der Kriegs-schule des Lebens: was mich nicht umbringt, macht mich starker*': 'Out of life's school of war: What does not destroy me makes me stronger.'[36] Bukowski himself acknowledged this in a letter to Carl Weissner: 'it's funny, if and when one does break out of the suicide knot, one feels stronger, better, a hell of a lot tougher, can take almost *anything*. The suicide thing may even be a process of growth – you fall back almost to zero, then lift back. It's a kind of rebirth process.'[37] Modern students of creativity such as Andrew Robinson have speculated that persons of genius take ten years to incubate their as yet inchoate conceptions and achieve the breakthrough into new discoveries.[38] Bukowski's original style –

Bukowski with
Barbara, December
1956.

a mixture of sensitivity, violence, humour, desperation, sometimes
grotesque imagery and lyric, open vulnerability – had indeed evolved
slowly over a ten-year period from approximately 1946 to 1956.

Thus began his *anni mirabiles*, and Bukowski's prolific output
would soon find an outlet when he began to correspond with a
literary lady in Texas named Barbara Frye, who edited the magazine
Harlequin. In their frequent exchange of letters, Frye made it clear
that she was seeking a husband. He described their early relationship in the poem 'A Literary Romance': 'I met her somehow through
correspondence or poetry or magazines / and she began sending me
very sexy poems about rape and lust, / and this being mixed in with
a minor intellectualism / confused me somewhat . . .'.[39] As we see
in this poem from 1962, Bukowski began quite early to stake out
his territory as a forthright poet writing openly and frequently
humorously about personal and sexual matters in an ironic, witty
and hip way: the 'Dirty Old Man' began to create his image/mask
rather earlier than many readers may have suspected. Bukowski's

relationship with Jane had become increasingly fraught, and he was probably seeking an escape route: in a drunken moment, he agreed to marry Barbara and she came to Los Angeles. They were married on 29 October 1955 in Las Vegas. Frye had a congenital birth defect: she was afflicted with virtually no neck and hence was unable to move her head. They lived together in a court apartment at 2254½ Branden St during 1955–6. The following year he began to edit *Harlequin* with her and he also made a trip to her home in Wheeler, Texas (later humorously recalled in an episode from his novel *Post Office*).

Bukowski now discovered James Boyer May's *Trace* magazine. This was significant because May included a directory of publications to which Bukowski could submit his work. Bukowski ultimately sent his writings to literally hundreds of the 'little magazines', which would supply him with a vast backlog of material which was then assembled into his early chapbooks. His volumes over the years would include many poems which had originally been published decades earlier, thus often making it difficult for readers to place them in the correct chronological sequence of composition. Bukowski also would establish a personal connection with his editors – beginning as we have seen with Whit Burnett and Caresse Crosby – which he nourished by continual epistolary exchanges. These letters were often fascinating and his editors frequently chose to feature them in their magazines: May in *Trace*, John Bryan in *Renaissance*, Jon Webb in *The Outsider*, Tom Mc-Namara in *Down There*, Margaret Randall in *El Corno Emplumado*, Allen De Loach in *Intrepid*, Carl Weissner in *Klactoveedsedsteen*, Will Inman in *Kauri*, William Packard in *The New York Quarterly*.

Bukowski's mother Katharina died on 23 December 1956. In the poem 'cancer', collected in *Septuagenarian Stew*, he describes his nausea when he visits her in the hospital, and she finally acknowledges: 'you know, you were right, your father / is a terrible man'.[40] His feelings for his mother had always been remote since he blamed her for not intervening to protect him from his father during the abuse he had suffered as a child. She herself had taken to alcohol due to her unhappy marriage and Bukowski often described her emotional coldness, again recalling that other famous German-American writer Henry Miller's relationship to his forbidding, Nordic, harsh mother: Miller experienced a similarly dramatic deathbed scene with the mother who had rejected him his entire life.

By 1956 the landscape of American culture had radically changed. Allen Ginsberg read 'Howl' in San Francisco and in 1957 Norman Mailer published his essay 'The White Negro', which described the rise of the 'hipster'. The shifts away from Eisenhower Corporate America began with 'subversive' books such as J. D. Salinger's *Catcher in the Rye* (1951) and continued with Jack Kerouac's *On the Road* (1957) and William S. Burroughs's *Naked Lunch* (1959). Bukowski's own work reflected this new focus on the sensitive, suffering person chained and buffeted by an increasingly cold and technocratic America. Indeed, it is a miswriting of literary history, for example, that the 'Confessional Poets' – Robert Lowell, John Berryman, Sylvia Plath, Theodore Roethke, Anne Sexton – are given sole credit for the invention of a new mode of self-revelation which dealt with the most intimate, hidden and painful aspects of the psyche, when actually Bukowski was doing this from the outset. Bukowski's directness also had a kind of Zen exactitude, humour and 'naturalness' about it, which may be one reason the poet Gary Snyder was fond of his work: he never shies away from the fact that human beings possess bodies.[41] During this period, while living at 580 North Kingsley Drive, Bukowski's wife Barbara also encouraged him to develop his artistic talents and he returned to Los Angeles City College briefly to study art from October 1956 to February 1957.[42] Over the next decades Bukowski would create not only his characteristic drawings and cartoons, but also hundreds of pastels, oils, acrylics and watercolours, many of which would be included in deluxe editions of his books.[43]

The issue of *Harlequin* Bukowski co-edited with Barbara Frye in 1957 contained a sequence of eight of his poems as well as three short stories. In 'Death Wants More Death', a horrified child encounters a spider killing a fly.[44] This poem begins a recurring pattern of insect and animal imagery in which Nature is depicted as 'red in tooth in claw', as Tennyson famously described. Ants, spiders, flies and roaches pullulate, infiltrating the seemingly safe human world and threatening the conventional bourgeois view of fairness, justice and (a favourite American bromide) 'a level playing field' governing social reality. The killing takes place in his 'father's garage', is 'almost like love' and may be interpreted as a symbolic drama replaying Bukowski's own victimization by his father. The universe is a vast eating machine in which the larger, more powerful creature consumes the weaker one. As Charles Darwin observed in his *Notebooks* on 12 March 1839: 'It is difficult to believe in the dreadful but quiet war of organic beings, going on in the peaceful woods & smiling fields.' This 'natural fact' also conditioned Bukowski's view of 'relationships' in which he sometimes envisions himself as a sacrificial victim controlled and then devoured by the all-consuming female: the sexual dance is a *Totentanz* – a dance which may lead to more vivid, intense life but which may also end in death. Bukowski once emphatically declared: 'Nature is not normal. Nature is not kind. Nature doesn't give a fuck, and I give a fuck.'[45]

Bukowski's philosophy finds one of its sources in his admiration for the California poet Robinson Jeffers (1887–1962), whom he read as early as the late 1930s. Jeffers was a fierce solitary character who built the Tor tower in Big Sur where he lived in isolation and his misanthropic 'anti-humanism' appealed immensely to Bukowski, as well as his anti-interventionist stance on American involvement in the Second World War. He was particularly fond of Jeffers's long narrative poems such as 'Roan Stallion' in which we find the lines: 'Humanity is the / start of the race; / I say / Humanity is the mould to break away from, the crust to break through, the / coal to break into fire, / The atom to be split.'[46] We recall Bukowski's 'Humanity, you never had it / from the beginning' from his poem 'those sons of bitches'.[47] Jeffers also represented – like Saroyan, Fante and Henry Miller – the new Californian literary tradition in which Bukowski began to conceptualize his own work. The West Coast was the place of new beginnings and experimentation in the arts, where writers defined themselves in opposition to the ossified traditions of the East Coast, New England, literary past.[48]

'The Rapist's Story' and '80 Airplanes Don't Put You in the Clear' are the most intriguing of the three short stories in *Harlequin*. Bukowski again balances his more eerie imaginings with playful, even lighthearted offerings for these two stories are worlds apart. 'The Rapist's Story', although technically awkward in terms of narrative skill, contains several startling and revealing passages. Bukowski's unnamed narrator tells us how he has been – he thinks, but seems unsure – unjustly accused of raping a mother and her young daughter. As he tells his tale, he describes descending into the cellar of the house where the crime is said to have taken place.

> I went down there and found an electric light. Click, it went on and it stank the cellar-stink down there. It made you think of wet gunnysacks and spiders or say a human arm buried somewhere in the mud with some of the sleeve around it, and if you lifted it out of the mud, a bunch of water bugs would run up and down its side, scurrying past each other in direct line paths, with now and then a bug or two shooting out of the constellation.[49]

The shift into the unconscious is symbolized by the descent into the cellar where he finds the rejected detritus of life and the spooky images reflect a perceptive and deeply troubled psyche. The story is noteworthy because it signals Bukowski's initial exploration of the criminal mind which he will pursue more deeply in his later work. '80 Airplanes', on the other hand, is a whimsical tale built around the biography of D. H. Lawrence and returns us to the comic, absurd world of 'Aftermath'.[50] It demonstrates Bukowski's knowledge of the life and work of Lawrence – his attempt to establish the colony of *Rananim* as well as his wife Frieda von Richthofen's kinship to Manfred von Richthofen, the 'Red Baron' of the First World War. Over his long career, Bukowski would compose hundreds of short stories, experimenting with an amazing variety of forms and approaches. During this period he also published the slight, ironic love poem 'Mine' in Wallace Berman's *Semina* in 1957.[51] This issue also included work by Michael McClure, Alexander Trocchi and Jean Cocteau, and signals Bukowski's at first peripheral and then more central connection to the counterculture. Berman was an experimental artist and writer who was influential in the promulgation of the avant-garde art scene in Southern California.[52]

Throughout his life, Bukowski listened to and was deeply moved by classical music: his favourite composers included Bach, Beethoven, Brahms, Bruckner, Handel, Haydn, Mahler, Mozart, Shostakovich, Sibelius and Stravinsky. Two poems from the late 1950s illustrate Bukowski's continuing absorption in the lives and works of the great composers. 'The Life of Borodin', from *Quicksilver* (1958), is an accomplished poem about the Russian master who was a professional chemist and engaged in his musical pursuits on the side, hounded by a difficult wife and enduring a variety of physical ailments.[53] 'When Hugo Wolf Went Mad', from *Odyssey* (1959), depicts the famous Austrian song composer's tribulations with his landlady (a frequent situation for Bukowski himself – 'the landlady execrating and final' in 'Old Man, Dead in a Room') who does not care that a gifted artist suffered and created in her room, but is more concerned about collecting her rent. He refers to Wolf's admiration of Richard Wagner obliquely yet effectively in the poem's opening: 'Hugo Wolf went mad while eating an onion / and writing his 253rd song; it was rainy / April and the worms came out of the ground / humming *Tännhauser* . . .'.[54] Over his long career, Bukowski would frequently depict the artist as a martyr who devotes his life (and it is indeed virtually always a man, except in the case of Carson McCullers, the one woman writer Bukowski admired) to the often-lost cause of creating beautiful things in a world which at once ignores and tries to destroy him. The artist symbolizes the outsider: his difference from the 'normal' and 'average' and 'healthy' simultaneously ostracizes and sanctifies him.

The poems of this phase also begin to explore territory which Bukowski would make very much his own – a kind of psychological dissociation in which the integrity of the speaker's mental life begins to fracture. For example in 'The Hunted', a poem which appeared in *Quicksilver* in 1958, we return to insect imagery, but now with an even more heightened sense of threat as the language breaks and divides into bizarre collocations of images:

> the ants are coming across the arms of chairs at me;
> a man climbs in the shell of the radio . . .
> I am frightened, away from my sea,
> and I am frightened up here, alone
> like some godless monk stuck in a cell; I lift a glass and
> drink the dog's pure nighthowl,
> and the last of two eyes
> like sun-banged webs thin into the structure before me
> and a face looks out and drinks and smiles
> behind the mouth of a howl
> behind the dull thick snout with nostrils like plagues
> behind a man tossed like a bone into a cat-scratched tomb.[55]

As did Allen Ginsberg for his title 'Howl', Bukowski turns here to canine imagery. The violent, spooky mood is emphasized by the guttural, dental, sibilant and plosive sounds in the monosyllabic hammering and repetition of 'g', 't / d', 's', 'p' and 'b' in 'glass', 'lift', 'drink', 'dog's', 'pure', 'banged', 'webs'.

We recall Edvard Munch's most famous painting *The Scream* in the lovely, tortured vision: 'the last of two eyes / like sun-banged webs thin out into the structure before me'. Bukowski's protagonists are indeed isolated misfits, screaming or howling alone, and resemble the 'godless monk' here depicted, for they pursue in solitude the same spiritual enlightenment – through poetry, music, love, alcohol – which drives some men to spend their lives in monasteries. His anti-heroes are 'godless' because they seek a kind of gnostic self-knowledge as well as redemption from a fallen, inscrutable world. The religious person and the artist are both engaged in an interior quest for meaning and authenticity in a world dedicated to material and superficial values. The poem ends in a frightened question: 'what do they want with me? / what the hell do they want / with me?' Bukowski's characters are sometimes imprisoned in their own consciousness, yet there is pleasure in his creative ability to transform these sensations of difficult emotions into the aesthetic form of a poem. The self is not fluid or stable in Bukowski – rather there is what Walter Pater in *The Renaissance* called a 'perpetual weaving and unweaving of ourselves', a constant movement of consciousness as it observes self and world.[56]

Bukowski returned to work at the Post Office on 2 January 1958, but now as a 'Temporary Substitute Distribution Clerk' – or mail sorter – at the Terminal Annex Building, Postal Employee Number 106160, where he would remain for the next twelve years. In March of 1959 he would work in the same position full-time.[57] Like Franz Kafka, caught in the monstrous, inhuman labyrinth of the Prague Workers' Insurance Bureau, Bukowski often bemoaned his Sisyphean labours at the Post Office. His experiences there surely prepared him to fully appreciate the Czech writer, as we see from a letter he wrote to Ann Bauman in late November 1962:

Kafka, unlike your Henry James, was not ordinarily intelligent and discerning. Kafka was a god damned petty clerk who lived a good damned [sic] petty life and wrote about it, the dream of it, the madness of it. There is one novel where a man enters this house, this establishment, and it appears that from the viewpoint of others that he is guilty of something but he does not know what. He is shuffled from room to room, endlessly, to the rattle of papers and bureaucracy, a silent simmering horrible living dream of ordinary mad and pressing, senseless everyday life. Most of his books are on this order: the shadow, the dream, the stupidity. Then there are other things – where a man turns into a bridge and lets people walk across him. Then there is another where a man gradually turns into a giant cockroach ('The Metamorphosis') and his sister feeds him as he hides under the bed. Others, others. Kafka is everything. Forget Henry James. James is a light mist of silk. Kafka is what we all know.[58]

This is a typical example of the concentrated force and energy of Bukowski's letters. Like Henry Miller in *The Books in My Life*, he exhibits an unflagging enthusiasm for writers he admires and his interpretations are chock full of sharp insights. Literature is always related directly to his own experience of living, to his own deepest needs. One derives more in a seemingly offhand pair of succinct sentences of Bukowski on Kafka than from a book-length study by a presumably learned academic: 'James is a light mist of silk. Kafka is what we all know.'

While Bukowski continued to make steady progress with his writing, his personal life continued to be war all the time. Barbara became pregnant, but lost the child in a miscarriage. Their essential incompatibility is recorded in a comic story depicting a quarrelling literary couple, 'Confession of a Coward', written during this period. Their marriage ended in divorce on

18 March 1958.[59] He memorialized the event in the poem 'The Day I Kicked a Bankroll Out the Window' in which he satirizes his ex-wife's rich relatives and their opulent Texas lifestyle, as well as in his novel *Post Office* (1971) in which Barbara is named 'Joyce'.[60] His relationships with women would continue to be volatile in the following years although the positive side of this acrimony is that it furnished him with a great deal of often hilarious material for his poems, stories and novels. Following his divorce he moved to 1623 Mariposa Avenue, #303, where he would live until 1 May 1964.[61]

In 1958 Bukowski again appeared in august literary company when two of his poems – 'I Cannot Stand Tears' and '10 Lions and the End of the World' (the latter collected in *Flower, Fist and Bestial Wail*) appeared in the first issue of the *San Francisco Review* along with e.e. cummings, William Saroyan, William Carlos Williams and Bertrand Russell.[62] The death of his father on 4 December 1958 occasioned one of his best-known poems, 'The Twins': 'he hinted at times that I was a bastard and I told him to listen / to Brahms, and I told him to learn to paint and drink and not be / dominated by women and dollars . . .'.[63] Bukowski inherited $15,000 from the sale of his father's house on Doreen Avenue in Temple City. He recounts how he had the neighbours come and take whatever they wanted from his father's belongings in the stories 'The Death of the Father I' and 'The Death of the Father II' in *Hot Water Music*.[64] Another work perhaps inspired by his parents' deaths is the elegiac poem 'I Taste the Ashes of Your Death' from *Nomad*, 1959, which possesses haiku-like simplicity and visual precision: 'the blossoms shake / sudden water / down my sleeve, / sudden water / cool and clean / as snow / as the stem-sharp / swords / go in / against your breast / and the sweet wild / rocks / leap over / and / lock us in'.[65] Bukowski reveals himself in such a short lyric as a fine craftsman, achieving the flash of intense poetry in a short space.

By the late 1950s Bukowski had begun to be a significant figure in the underground literary world and Jory Sherman, the West Coast editor of the magazine *The Outsider*, would bring him to the attention of Jon Webb. Sherman had first read Bukowski in *Epos* 1959, edited by Evelyn Thorne and her husband Will Tullos.[66] Evelyn told Sherman to write to Bukowski and she also showed him 'some of his strange, almost violent letters' when he visited her.[67] As 1960 and his 40th birthday approached, Bukowski had come a long way. He had found his genius and marked out his literary territory: the terror of existence was his subject matter.

3

Christ and Dionysus:
Flower, Fist and Bestial Wail to *Crucifix in a Deathhand*, 1960–1965

During the 1960s America was driven by Faustian ambitions and convulsed by political upheaval. The Cuban Missile Crisis precipitated a Red Alert on 15 October 1962; the arrival of the Beatles on *The Ed Sullivan Show* on 9 February 1964 catapulted teenage girls into Dionysian frenzies; on 22 November 1963 John F. Kennedy was assassinated; the war in Vietnam escalated; race riots erupted in Los Angeles and Detroit; the sexual revolution blossomed; by the conclusion of the decade, on 21 July 1969, America had landed a man on the moon – all powered both ecstatic visions and profound despair.[1] Although Bukowski frequently compared himself to the crucified Christ and his country appeared headed for apocalypse, he remained dedicated to his craft and sullen art, sustaining his galloping pace of composition. This hypergraphic compulsion was both a blessing and a curse: he was highly productive, yet he was possessed by what Juvenal in *Satire VII* called 'the furious itch to write' – *cacoethes scribendi*, as Bukowski titled his early 1946 story.[2] Psychologists have speculated on the link between creativity and self-therapy, and Bukowski himself declared that he wrote 'to keep myself from total madness'. His astonishing poetic creativity coincided with the proliferation of the little magazine movement in America – the use of mimeograph machines, the production of small chapbooks, broadsides and the underground newspapers. He would come to be known as 'The King of the Littles' since he began to acquire a reputation for the quality and quantity of his submissions.[3]

Yet Bukowski's opinion of most poetry was clear: he disliked it. In 1987 he told Sean Penn: 'I always remember the schoolyards in grammar school, when the word 'poet' or 'poetry' came up, all the little guys would laugh and mock it. I can see why, because it's a fake product. It's been fake and snobbish and inbred for centuries. It's over-delicate. It's over-precious . . . It's a con, a fake.'[4] And the academic poets were 'still standing still, playing secret and staid games, snob and inbred games which are finally anti-life and anti-truth'.[5] Poetry had become humourless, dull and sacralized: there should be no law against being entertained. He agreed with Lawrence Ferlinghetti, who lamented in his 'Populist Manifesto' (humorously alluding to the opening of Ginsberg's 'Howl'): 'We have seen the best minds of our generation / destroyed by boredom at poetry readings. / Poetry isn't a secret society, / It isn't a temple either.'[6] Bukowski wanted to take poetry down from Mount Parnassus and bring it to Hollywood Boulevard and Western Ave: as he declared in 'Notes of a Dirty Old Man', 'I'd rather hear about a live American bum than a dead Greek god.'[7] And the poet himself is simply a worker, a *maker* – ancient Greek *poietes* – who deserves no special status and whose gift is contingent. He wrote to A. D. Winans: 'A good poet never knows what he is, he's a dime from the edge, but there's nothing holy about it. It's a job. Like mopping a bar floor.'[8]

In his desire to revivify poetry, Bukowski was continuing a long American tradition beginning with Walt Whitman. The free verse of *Leaves of Grass* broke with staid European practice: its long, direct, vital, clear lines were rhythmically varied, unfettered by regular metre and rhyme. Bukowski had also read Ezra Pound as well as William Carlos Williams, one of whose strictures was 'no ideas but in things'.[9] The Imagists wanted to remove the vague, tired Romantic slush of the nineteenth-century pre-Raphaelites, just as Ernest Hemingway sought to make his prose lean, to trim the fat from the long, flowery, adjective-ridden sentences typical of

Victorian novelists and go straight to the syntactical bone. Pound also wanted the clear image, the 'hard, clean line' as Bukowski put it.[10] What Bukowski learned from Pound and the Imagists – as well as the great Chinese poet Li Po – to place a clear picture before the reader in every line – is a technique he also utilized in his prose style. In his dedication to artful 'simplicity', he was 'postmodern': based on actual (sometimes 'colloquial', 'vulgar' or 'obscene') American speech, his new 'talk poetry' was defined by clear narratives depicting the lives of 'ordinary', 'everyday' people. As Fredric Jameson observed in his essay 'Postmodernism and Consumer Society': 'The much simpler talk poetry . . . came out of the reaction against complex, ironic, academic modernist poetry of the 1960s.'[11]

Bukowski had other – sometimes unexpected – literary influences. In 1973, when Jack Matthews 'asked him what other poets he liked, he surprised me by mentioning the names of Robinson Jeffers and Conrad Aiken. The latter, especially, who in his mandarin excellence is far removed from the primal-energy-barbarian-image that Bukowski often projects.'[12] He also mentions Aiken in an interview as 'one of the few poets who turns me on with classical lines. I admire Conrad Aiken very much. But most of the – what shall I call them, purists? – don't pick me up.' [13] Aiken had also undergone a primal trauma in his own childhood – as witnessing the death of his parents – and it is probable that the muted pain and lush, complex imagery which infuse some of Bukowski's early poems had one source in Aiken's luxurious style.

Between 1960 and 1965, Bukowski published seven volumes of poetry: *Flower, Fist and Bestial Wail* (1960), *Run with the Hunted* (1962), *Poems and Drawings* (1962), *Longshot Pomes for Broke Players* (1962), *It Catches My Heart in Its Hands* (1963), *Cold Dogs in the Courtyard* (1965) and *Crucifix in a Deathhand* (1965). *Flower, Fist and Bestial Wail* is the first of several chapbooks (small pamphlets usually about 25–30 pages in length) and contains sixteen poems, fourteen of which appeared in magazines between 1957 and 1959.[14] Bringing the book to print caused Bukowski considerable anxiety, and he harried his publisher, E. V. Griffith, editor of *Hearse*, to complete the project. Griffith published 201 copies of a broadside of one of the poems – 'His Wife, The Painter' on 16 June 1960.[15] Griffith chose the poems to be included in the book and Bukowski wrote to him on 9 July 1958: 'I'm quite pleased with your selections.'[16] This is a practice which Bukowski would follow later in his career, when he typically turned over to his editors the responsibility of deciding what to print from his prolific output. When *Flower* finally appeared, he was overjoyed: upon receiving his author's copies, he wrote Griffith a deeply felt letter of gratitude.[17] Like Henry Miller, whose *Tropic of Cancer* (1934) appeared when the author was 43, Bukowski also had achieved his first book in middle age, and his frenetic pace of composition may well have had one motivation in his desire to play catch-up.

The title alludes to D. H. Lawrence's *Birds, Beasts and Flowers* and Bukowski's poetry is sometimes suffused with natural and sexual imagery. Like Lawrence, Bukowski sought instinctive, animal, 'blood knowledge', as Lawrence wrote in his famous letter to Ernest Collings: life should be lived 'with the blood' and 'the intellect is only a bit and a bridle'.[18] The juxtaposition of 'flower' and 'fist' also illustrates the doubleness of Bukowski's vision of a cosmos where the sensitive individual is always at risk of being crushed. In '10 Lions and the End of the World', Bukowski describes a photograph in a national magazine depicting lions crossing a village road and 'blocking traffic / while the roses bloomed'. In stopping the customary flow of automobiles, the lions have performed the salutary function of temporarily halting the insane, frenetic pace of modern 'civilization'. He imagines an apocalyptic future: the world has been destroyed and 'they turn out the lights / and the whole thing's over, / I'll be sitting here / in the chalky smoke / thinking of those 10 damned / (yes, I counted them) / lions . . . .'.

He hopes that all humans learn from these lions, 'while there's /
time' – and he spells the world 'time' vertically down the page.
The lions are heroic rebels who say 'no' to a stultifying status
quo. This desire for a return to the 'natural' is a recurring theme
of Bukowski's work, recalling Walt Whitman's 'I think I could turn
and live with the animals . . .'. Stylistically, the bare one-to-six word
lines of verse as well as the use of parenthentical comments and
final one-letter-per-line vertical spelling reveal the influence of
e.e. cummings's typographical play.[19]

During the 1960s Bukowski began to define his poetic practice in
a series of literary 'manifestos'. His first volley in his polemic against
the literary Establishment was his essay 'Manifesto: A Call for Our
Own Critics' (1960) in which Bukowski announces: 'It is difficult for
a single poet to stand against the university coterie. Perhaps we too
must invent our own history and choose our own gods if our portion
of American literature is to receive a hearing on some tomorrow.'[20]
This will become a recurring theme as the decade progressed: the
desire to mark out a territory for the dissident voices of the American
Underground.[21] As we have seen, Bukowski's major entry into the
underground literary scene occurred through his connection with
the New Orleans editor Jon Webb and it was through Jory Sherman
that he made the initial contact with Webb. Sherman – a writer
living in California and working as a 'West Coast talent scout'
for Webb, had written to him about Bukowski on 8 August 1960,
saying 'a chapbook for Buk sounds good.'[22] Bukowski wrote back
to Sherman on 17 August 1960 saying 'thanks for word on *Outsider*.
Finally got card from them through *Coastlines*. Asking me for
contributions. Ah, well.'[23] Thus began his long and productive
relationship with Webb and his wife, Gypsy Lou, and their Loujon
Press. In the Fall 1961 issue of *The Outsider*, 'A Charles Bukowski
Album' appeared, which included eleven of his poems.

Bukowski's contacts with the wider literary world also expanded
when in 1960 he began a correspondence with Sheri Martinelli, the

Bukowski and Gypsy Lou, 1967.

Bukowski and Jon Webb, 1965.

mistress of Ezra Pound during his incarceration for treason at St Elizabeth's Hospital in Washington, DC. Four of his poems appeared in her publication *Anagogic & Paideumic Review*, in January 1961, while one poem and a humorous sequence of texts and drawings depicting Pound, Aldous Huxley and G. B. Shaw appeared in issue 6 that September.[24] The fact that Martinelli had been involved with Pound impressed Bukowski, and in their exchange of letters he shared his literary enthusiasms with her, urging in a letter dated 21 December 1960 that she read Jeffers: 'Do especially read *Roan Stallion*. Robinson Jeffers. If you haven't. Please do this for me. It's the only thing I have ever asked of you! Isn't it?'[25]

The relationship to Martinelli also illustrates Bukowski's connection to the world of 'high culture', an aspect of his life and work usually ignored by commentators. For example, in a 12 April 1961 letter to J. W. Corrington, he suddenly remarks: 'Steiner . . . says in this quarterly the *Kenyon Review* that we are drifting toward mathematics and away from the word, and to this I must agree.'[26] Bukowski goes on to assert that in the *Kenyon Review* 'the articles are, in most cases, sound', while 'the poetry . . . remains almost unbelievably flat and lifeless'.[27] Although a manual labourer all his life, Bukowski was in the tradition of American 'proletarian' artists who might work as longshoremen or carpenters during the day and at night immerse themselves with pleasure in the *Kenyon Review*, Thucydides or Isaiah Berlin. Although relegated to the role of quasi-literate, drunken womanizer by academia, Bukowski was both widely read and intellectually curious, devouring a wide range of cultural sustenance throughout his career as a 'blue-collar' worker.

Run with the Hunted (1962), published by Midwest Poetry in Chicago and edited by R. R. Cuscaden, contains twenty poems, including 'I Am Visited by an Editor and a Poet', which first appeared in *Hearse* in 1961. The poem is noteworthy because it features 'Charles Bukowski' as a character in the narrative: he has just won $115 gambling, is lying naked on his bed 'listening to an opera by one of the Italians / and had just gotten rid of a very loose lady' when he is visited by someone claiming to be his publisher. He says he does not have a publisher 'and he screamed back, / you're Charles Bukowski, aren't you? and I got up and / peeked through the iron grill to make sure it wasn't a cop, / and I placed a robe upon my nakedness, / kicked a beercan out of the way and bade them enter, / an editor and a poet.'[28] Thus as early as 1961 he is beginning to perfect his image as the dishevelled yet courtly ('I placed a robe upon my nakedness'; 'bade them enter') poet 'Charles Bukowski', drinking beer, wary of the police, listening to classical music, firing sardonic salvos against the literary world of poets, publishers and editors, frolicking with 'loose women' as he plays out a comic variation on the theme of the *poète maudit* (the poem alludes to *Les Fleurs du mal*, Rimbaud and Villon). Unlike the great doomed French poets, however, Bukowski proves himself to be witty, laughing and wily. Bukowski draws self-portraits repeatedly from various angles: sometimes in comic caricature, sometimes as a mystical *voyant*.

Although Bukowski was extremely productive during the early 1960s, he was drinking heavily and incarcerated for drunkenness in June 1961. He struggled with depression and made an abortive suicide attempt which he recalled in a letter to Carl Weissner: 'I tried gas once. Turned on all the burners and laid down on the bed. It almost knocked me out, I was on the way, but something about breathing in all that gas, a kind of a grey-yellow feeling, and it gave me a headache, a terrible headache and the headache woke me up.'[29] His troubles mounted: on 22 January 1962, Jane Cooney Baker died. Bukowski confessed on that day to John William Corrington: 'I am unable to write. The woman I have known for so long has been critically ill since Saturday and died 2 hours ago. This is going to be the longest night of them all.'[30] Her funeral was held two days later, on 24 January.[31] The death of Jane occasioned some of Bukowski's most deeply felt poems. Several appeared in *The Days Run Away Like Wild Horses Over the Hills* (1969) which was dedicated to her, including 'for Jane': 'in this room / the hours of love / still make shadows. / when you left / you took almost / everything / I kneel in the nights / before tigers / that will not let me be'.[32]

In June 1962, Neeli Cherkovski – a young Los Angeles poet Bukowski had met the year previously who would become his friend and biographer – included a Bukowski poem in his magazine *The Black Cat Review*. Bukowski would establish connections with a number of aspiring Los Angeles poets including Gerald

Locklin, Ron Koertge and John Thomas.[33] On 5 August 1962, Bukowski also gave his first public reading on the KPFK radio station where he read a number of poems, including 'To the Whore Who Took My Poems', 'The Tragedy of the Leaves' and 'The Ants'.[34] He read in a slow, drawling voice (people sometimes commented that he sounded like W. C. Fields), apparently inebriated since he made offhand comments about his intoxicated state during his performance.

Bukowski now also garnered his first serious critical attention with R. R. Cuscaden's essay 'Charles Bukowski: Poet in a Ruined Landscape'. Cuscaden noted Bukowski's portrayal of the emptiness of modern life and his debt to Jeffers but observed: 'Bukowski rarely gives in completely to utter, hopeless despair, and this, not the variance in style and technique, marks the essential difference between him and Jeffers. The despair of Bukowski exists just because he continually hopes; Jeffers' despair is the result of no hope at all.'[35] He began to correspond with John William Corrington, a Southern writer teaching at Louisiana State University who would become a champion of Bukowski's work and to whom he dedicated *Run with the Hunted*. Corrington's 'Charles Bukowski and the Savage Surfaces' appeared the following year in *Northwest Review*.[36] When the two men finally met, Bukowski was appalled by Corrington's immersion in academic politics and literary gamesmanship.

Bukowski was given further encouragement when Jon Webb selected him for the 'Outsider of the Year' award. He admired Webb as an editor and wrote to him on 30 November 1962: 'Hang on, you're getting an *award* too, somewhere, somehow; this is lit. history like *Poetry* when Ez was European editor and full of beans, or even like Mencken's *Mercury*; or Dial; but you are essentially the new center and the part of this age, only people never realize the blood sweat weariness disgust breakdown & trial of soul that goes into it; and the puking little criticisms of milk-white jackasses.'[37] H. L. Mencken symbolized to Bukowski the glories of the 1920s and '30s American literary world when Modernism was born, and it is interesting that Bukowski drew a parallel between the revolution of Pound and the impact he felt Webb was making on the new literature of the 1960s.

In 1962 Bukowski began to submit his work to John Bryan, who would become a central figure in his turn towards journalism five years later. Bryan was an indefatigable editor in the vanguard of the Californian counterculture and an advocate of LSD.[38] He published three poems in his magazine *Renaissance* (no. 3, 1962) and in the next issue printed a letter Bukowski had written to him about war under the title 'Peace, Baby, Is Hard Sell'.[39] This is a significant statement of Bukowski's pacifist stance and would be important for setting the stage for his connection with the Californian counterculture of the 1960s. As we have seen, several of his poems of the late 1950s and early 1960s reflected the dark realities of the post-atomic age: Americans were now experiencing what W. H. Auden called 'The Age of Anxiety' and some Californians built 'bomb shelters' in their backyards to store provisions in case of a nuclear attack.

His work also appeared in the second issue of *The Outsider* in summer 1962 and he attracted the attention of an American writer who had gone to live in Paris at the famous 'Beat Hotel' (where Ginsberg, Burroughs, Corso and Bukowski's later friend Harold Norse hung out) named Kay Johnson, or 'Kaja'. She wrote to the Webbs about his poem 'sick leave': 'How do you pull the guts out of Bukowski, I mean, how do you do it? You are really an editor. How did you get it out of him so whole? So perfect? Cesarean [sic] operation? Did it come in a poem or in a letter? . . . anyhow you can sure pull the poems outa him. And this "sick leave" is right from the guts.'[40] And Diane Wakoski, after seeing the Bukowski tribute issue, wrote to Jon Webb: 'I was also surprised and pleased to see such a spread on Bukowski. He is making it this year – and well deserves to . . . Sometimes his work is inexpressibly vulgar and

I do not like it then. But despite this, when he writes about his experiences (especially with love) a kind of pure, almost ballad-like tone is set and he achieves beautiful moments. There is something fresh about his poems.'[41] Wakoski rightly remarks on the 'ballad-like tone' of the poems since this is a form Bukowski frequently employs: with its roots in folk tradition, the ballad typically is a narrative with regular refrains which perfectly suited his story-telling talents.

In addition to Bryan, Johnson and Wakoski, Bukowski would forge another link to the counterculture in 1962 in the person of Gerard Malanga, a student at Wagner College in New York and a member of Andy Warhol's entourage; in 1966 he and Warhol published Bukowski in *Intransit* and Malanga later included Bukowski in *Screen Tests*, a book of his photographs.[42] Bukowski also corresponded with the American poet Harold Norse as well as Marvin Malone, the publisher of the *Wormwood Review*, who would emerge as a central editor in his career. His first appearance in the magazine was the poem 'Thank God for Alleys' in vol. 2, no. 3, issue 7 in October 1962. Malone would publish several all-Bukowski issues of the magazine, including *Grip the Walls* (1964), *Beauti-ful* (1988) and *People Poems* (1991).

It Catches My Heart in Its Hands: New and Selected Poems, 1955–1963, published in 1963 by Loujon Press, was Bukowski's breakthrough book. It takes its title from a poem of Jeffers entitled 'Hellenistics': 'Whatever it is catches my heart in its hands, what-ever it is makes me shudder with love / And painful joy . . .'.[43] The book's colophon states that '777 copies of this book were printed by the editors of *Loujon Press*, one page at a time, handfed with as 12-point *Garamond Old Style* for the poems, 18-point *Pabst O.S.* for the titles – to an ancient 8 by 12 Chandler & Price letter-press; on *Linweave Spectra* paper throughout . . .'.[44] John William Corrington in his 'Introduction' wrote that Bukowski's poetry was 'the spoken voice nailed to paper'.[45] Reviewed in the *New York Times*

Book Review in July 1964 by Kenneth Rexroth, *It Catches* signalled
Bukowski's initial entry into the national literary world.[46] Rexroth
was the leading light of the San Francisco Renaissance and the
master of ceremonies during Ginsberg's reading of 'Howl' at
the Six Gallery in San Francisco on 7 October 1955. This was
by far Bukowski's most substantial work to date, containing 66
poems, several of which have become canonical in his oeuvre. 'Old
Man, Dead in a Room' opens: 'this thing upon me is not death /
but it's as real' and continues 'this thing upon me / crawling like
a snake, / terrifying my love of commonness, / Some call Art,
/ some call Poetry; / it's not death / but dying will solve its
power.'[47] The incantatory variations on the theme of poetry,
death, poverty, solitude, ecstasy and the immortality of art is
brought to a subtle close:

> and as my grey hands
> drop a last desperate pen
> in some cheap room
> they will find me there
> and never know
> my name
> my meaning
> nor the treasure
> of my escape.[48]

These mystical, hymning lines recall Walt Whitman, who in the
final section (52) of 'Song of Myself' wrote the beautiful envoy:

> I bequeath myself to the dirt to grow from the grass I love,
> If you want me again look for me under your boot-soles.
> You will hardly know who I am or what I mean,
> But I shall be in good health to you nevertheless,
> And filter and fibre your blood.

Failing to fetch me at first keep encouraged,
Missing me one place search another,
I stop somewhere waiting for you.

Bukowski ends in a less affirmative way than Whitman, yet 'they will find me', 'never know my name', and 'my meaning' echo Whitman's 'If you want me again look', 'you will hardly know who I am or what I mean'. Whitman was a significant figure for both Henry Miller and William Saroyan, and through Saroyan his long electric lines found their way into the music of Jack Kerouac's 'Bop Prosody' and into the ecstatic dithyrambs of Allen Ginsberg's 'Howl'.[49]

'The tragedy of the leaves', which had appeared in 1960 in *Targets* as well as *Longshot Pomes* (1962), also explores the solitude of the poet: 'I awakened to dryness and the ferns were dead.' The scene is a bleak hangover with 'empty bottles like bled corpses' scattered about the room.[50] The images of death and decay require some comic relief, 'a jester / with jokes upon absurd pain; / pain is absurd / because it exists, nothing more.' The poet himself who 'had been young and / said to have genius' enters 'a dark hall' where he encounters his landlady 'execrating and final, / sending me to hell, / waving her fat, sweaty arms / and screaming / screaming for rent / because the world had failed us / both'.[51] The poet and landlady are fellow inhabitants of Hell. The figure of the landlady becomes a regular fixture in Bukowski's infernal psychological landscapes, as in 'Conversation in a Cheap Room' from *Galley Sail Review*, 1960. One of the inhabitants, 'old Mr. Sturgeon died and / they carried him down the stair and / I was in / my underwear; as the rats ran after / him leaping with beautiful tails like the / as tails of young whores half-drunk on / wine'. Yet the death of as this man is of no significance for the landlady: 'Mrs. McDonald will / want her rent / that's all they / said.'[52] Bukowski has begun to chart his territory as a poet, and a complex of related images will recur throughout his later work: roominghouse, landlady, alcohol, walls, waiting, poetry, death, insects, animals, artist, solitude, music.

Bukowski described the submerged operations of his imagination in one of his letters to Corrington, 18 October 1963. In response to being asked: 'What do you do? How do write, create?', he responded: 'You don't, I told them. You don't try. That's very important: not to try, either for Cadillacs, creation or immortality. You wait, and if nothing happens, you wait some more. It's like a bug high on the wall. You wait for it to come to you. When it gets close enough you reach out, slap out and kill it. Or if you like its looks you make a pet out of it.'[53] In another letter to Corrington the following month (27 November), he expands this idea: 'I don't look into myself to see why certain wheels turn; I feel this is dangerous.'[54] Bukowski's notion that the activity of the unconscious should not be meddled with is quite similar to Rainer Maria Rilke's as well as to Igor Stravinsky's response when asked how he composed *The Rite of Spring*: 'I can wait as an insect waits . . . I did not compose *Le Sacre du Printemps* – I was the vessel through which it passed.' Bukowski interestingly also employs insect imagery to suggest a kind of passive receptiveness as a prelude to the act of composition and as a necessity for creative genius to flourish.

In 1963 Bukowski would become involved with the second literary lady of his life when he met Frances Elizabeth Dean. Like Barbara Frye, Frances wrote poetry and had attended the prestigious Smith College: she was known later as FrancEyE. She had informed Bukowski that she was a fan of his so he invited her to visit one evening and they commiserated over their emotional troubles. Bukowski was still ravaged by the death of Jane, while Frances's marriage had ended in divorce and she was separated from her children. They soon moved in together, first to 5126^1/$_4$ and then to 5124 De Longpre where Bukowski would live for eight years, until 1972. This was a furnished Spanish Colonial Revival Style bungalow, with a living room, bedroom, kitchen and bath.[55] According to

Bukowski's residence at 5124 De Longpre Avenue, 1982.

John Thomas, it 'looked like a place for transients. Obviously second hand furniture. Living room floor covered with cheap linoleum, one sheet of ugly linoleum that was rolled out like carpet, but all curled up around the edges.'[56] There was a bedroom with only a bed and dresser as well as a kitchen: 'small, grimy, nothing in the refrigerator except cans of Miller High Life and three eggs. On the dirty stove, a frying pan containing two partially eaten fried eggs and a tin fork. He obviously ate the fried eggs out of the frying pan, right over the stove.'[57]

Of the women in his life thus far, Frances was the most decidedly intellectual. He describes her in a letter of 17 February 1964 to Jon and Lou Webb 'reading "The Poverty of Historicism" by Karl Popper'.[58] She was committed to liberal causes and attended poetry workshops which Bukowski sometimes mocked. In one of his 'Dirty Old Man' essays in *Open City* about the black writer LeRoi Jones (later Imiri Baraka), he pillories her 'bleeding heart' stance and argues in his work at the Post Office – where many of his co-workers were black – that his own relationships to black Americans were more authentic and lived than hers.[59] Although Frances soon became unexpectedly pregnant – Bukowski had mistakenly thought she was beyond her child-bearing years – the couple decided against marriage.

In 1963 the Webbs published *The Outsider* with a photograph of Bukowski on the cover and reprinted Cuscaden's essay as well as several tributes from a number of little magazine editors and aficionados of his work. In his response to these homages, Bukowski defined his own poetics: 'while you're living it might be best to live from the source stuck inside of you . . . You are not going to worry about spondees, counts, or if the endings rhyme. You want to get it down, hard or crude or otherwise – any way you can truly send it through.'[60] One recalls the scene in the film *Dead Poets Society* when Robin Williams (who plays an English teacher in an elite New England preparatory school) instructs his students to rip out the section of their poetry texts dealing with metrical theory, so they can enjoy the visceral, direct, musical, ecstatic experience of great poetry unmediated by the interference of the technical jargon of verse form and prosody. Bukowski's relationship with the Webbs deepened in the following year, for in the summer of 1964 they came to visit him in Los Angeles.

Bukowski also composed an important story during this period, 'Murder', published in *Notes from Underground*, no. 1, in 1964 and subsequently retitled 'The Blanket'.[61] This swift, suspenseful tale illustrates Freud's idea of the *unheimlich*, or 'uncanny', as a blanket pursues a man, apparently intending to murder him. Freud traced the *unheimlich* theme in the German Romantic writer and musician E.T.A. Hoffman who 'brought into German literature the theme of *die Tücke des Objekts*, the malice practiced by inanimate objects which thwart and frustrate people, especially those of high intellect'.[62] Bukowski's unnamed narrator seeks answers to the riddle of existence: 'I am evidently a weak man. I have tried to go to the bible, the philosophers, to the poets, but for me, somehow, they have missed the point. They are talking about something else entirely.'[63]

The categories of sanity and insanity are also useless: 'Madness? Sure. What isn't madness? Isn't Life madness? We are all wound-up like toys . . . a few winds of the spring, it runs down, and that's it . . . and we walk around and presume things, make plans, elect governors, mow lawns . . . Madness, surely, what ISN'T madness?'[64]

Charles Rosen in *The Romantic Generation* – his study of Chopin, Liszt, Berlioz, Mendelssohn and Schumann – observed that in Hoffman's stories, 'the world of everyday reality coexists with a hallucinatory world of delusion which gives significance to the former: the "real" world has priority but it is unintelligible without the irrational and often absurd world of shadows, magic, and paranoia that is always present.'[65] Several of the stories Bukowski would compose over the next several decades would explore the irruption of the irrational into the supposed 'normality' of everyday, 'sane' experience. 'The Blanket' was probably in part an effort to exorcise the ghost of Jane's death, for at the conclusion the narrator wonders: 'Maybe that blanket was some woman who had once loved me, finding a way to get back to me through that blanket . . . Maybe the blanket had been this woman either trying to kill me to get me into death with her, or trying to love as a blanket and not knowing how . . . .'[66] It succeeds in evoking an eerie mood of intense psychological dread and marks Bukowski's gradual return to publishing fiction since the appearance of his three stories in *Harlequin* in 1957.

In 1964 Bukowski began a correspondence with the Canadian poet Al Purdy, and wrote a review of another Canadian, Irving Layton, in *Evidence*.[67] He also became acquainted with several younger poets including Douglas Blazek, William Wantling and Steve Richmond, a UCLA Law School graduate who was more interested in pursuing a career in literature than as a lawyer. They began to correspond in March 1965 and Richmond visited Bukowski at De Longpre. Richmond came from a wealthy family, which allowed him the free time to live on the beach at Santa Monica, indulge in drugs and women, and write. He opened a bookshop and published Bukowski in the broadside *The Earth Rose 1: Fuck Hate* in 1966. Due to its 'obscene' title and declaration: 'Whereby, on this day we able minded creators do hereby tell you, the Establishment: FUCK YOU IN THE MOUTH. WE'VE HEARD ENOUGH OF YOUR BULLSHIT', and the two Bukowski poems dealing with self-castration, 'true story' and 'freedom' – Richmond's bookstore was raided by the police.[68] This would be one of several episodes in which Bukowski confronted the authorities over censorship.

Bukowski also began a voluminous correspondence with Douglas Blazek, first writing to him on 28 October 1964.[69] He was one of the major forces in the 'mimeograph revolution' and printed his stapled publication *Ole* in Bensenville, Illinois. Three poems of Bukowski's were published in *Ole*, vol. 1, no. 1, in 1964, including the first appearance of the graphic 'freedom'. Blazek wanted poetry to be raw, and indeed this poem signals a new 'freedom' as well in Bukowski's style. Although he had been open with sexual matters previously, as the 1960s progressed he began to push further against any self-censorship. Bukowski's exchange with Blazek is particularly extensive and he would compose letters virtually every day, sometimes writing to two or more correspondents at a time. The letters are a joy to read: many launch into highly lyric prose which suddenly takes flight into poetry.

On 7 September 1964, Bukowski and Frances became the proud parents of a daughter they named Marina Louise (her middle name in homage to Gypsy Lou Webb). In his poem 'birth', which appeared in *Wormwood* (no. 19, 1965), he recounts that he was in the waiting room reading the *Dialogues* of Plato when he was called in to see his new daughter and the events surrounding Marina's arrival are described with joy and gentle humour.[70] In his first novel *Post Office* (in which Frances becomes 'Fay') Bukowski ('Henry Chinaski') narrates Marina's infancy against the background of the racial violence which rocked Los Angeles a year later in August 1965, following the mistreatment of a black man by white policemen –

Frances Smith with Marina Bukowski, 1966.

the Watts riots: 'Marina Louise, Fay named the child. So there it was, Marina Louise Chinaski. In the crib by the window. Looking up at the tree leafs and bright designs whirling on the ceiling. Then she'd cry. Walk the baby, talk to the baby. The girl wanted mama's breasts but mama wasn't always ready and I didn't have mama's breasts. And the job was still there. And now riots. One tenth of the city was on fire.'[71]

The sheer hard work and tedium at the Post Office began to exact its toll on Bukowski. As early as 1963 he was already writing about his torment in the striking poem 'Existence':

I huddle in front of this cheesebox of numbers
poking in small cards
addressed to non-existent
lives . . .
and I am old enough to die,
I have always been old enough to die,
and I stand before this wooden cage
and feed its voiceless insides,
this is my job, my rent, my whore, my shoes,
the sickening task of leeching color from my eyes . . .

A Jeffers echo follows: 'the street is so hard, at least / give me the walls I have paid a life for, / and when the Hawk comes down / I will meet him halfway.'[72] The capitalized 'Hawk' alludes to one of Jeffers's most famous poems, 'Hurt Hawks'. His struggle all along had been to preserve some inviolate part of his spirit from being consumed by the American work machine, to buy time for his writing at the price of poverty. His motto became to 'save what you can, don't give in'.[73] There is pathos in his suffering, for he had confessed in a letter to the Webbs on 31 October 1964: 'I used to have a theory that if I could just make one person's life happy or real that would have been otherwise, then my own life would not have failed.'[74]

He had long experienced problems with his teeth which fell out or broke in his hand. This was most likely due to his poor diet: vast quantities of booze, fried eggs, soft boiled eggs for hangovers, fried steak or fried chicken, mashed potatoes with gravy from the Pioneer Chicken fast-food restaurant. He suffered dizzy spells, insomnia, pain from his haemorrhoids, blackouts and was unable to raise his arms over his head. His letters throughout the 1960s are a litany of health and work complaints in which he compares his sufferings to those of Christ. He writes to Ann Menebroker on 27 May 1965: 'Christ is not the only bastard who was ever nailed to the wood'; to Ruth Wantling, 10 August 1965: 'and I get these pains in my neck and back and chest, I feel like screaming, "oh Christ, let's start the bloody Crucifixion!"'; to Ruth Wantling, 11 September 1965: 'yes, I prob. do carry around my little wooden cross of pain and wave it a bit too much, and even feel foolish defending it'; to Jon and Louise Webb, 8 March 1966: 'each bowel movement here a real crucifixion'.[75] It is understandable that Bukowski would identify with Christ, for he indeed often felt himself to be 'despised and rejected of men, a man of sorrows and acquainted with grief' (Isaiah 53:3).

As a relief from his Christ-like agonies, Bukowski periodically transformed himself into Dionysus: one safe harbour where he could blow his mind during this time of mental and physical torture was with John Thomas. Bukowski met Thomas during early 1965 and they would remain friends for nearly three decades.[76] After a depressing day of work at the Post Office, Bukowski relished being able to visit him at his house in Echo Park to drink, pop pills and converse. In his novel *Hollywood* (1987) he wrote: 'Big John Galt [Thomas] God damn, what a life-saver he had been. Working for the post office, I had gone over to his place . . . There was always this big bowl of speed sitting on the coffeetable between us. It was usually filled to the brim with pills and capsules . . . I would dip in and eat them like candy . . . I fed off Big John Galt when there was nothing else around.' He also composed an homage to Thomas, 'the strong man', in which he refers to him as 'my Buddha, my guru, / my hero, my roar of / light'.[77]

Amidst domestic tensions with Frances, on 5 March 1965 Bukowski travelled by train to New Orleans for a two-week stay visiting the Webbs, an experience he recounted in a column in *Open City*.[78] He wrote as many as fifteen poems a day, and the Webbs fed the good ones immediately into their letterpress printer at 1109 Rue Royale. Bukowski drank heavily and misbehaved. *Crucifix in a Deathhand* was published in April 1965; it is divided into three sections and contains 51 poems. Bukowski invokes Robinson Jeffers in his preface: 'But this is a tough age and a tough life, and Jeffers was more than right . . .'.[79] Bukowski thought the book was not as strong as *It Catches My Heart* because he was required to compose the poems on demand. The title poem is a history of Los Angeles: 'we are in the basin / that is the / idea. Down in the sand and the alleys / this land punched-in, cuffed-out, divided, held like a crucifix in a deathhand / this land bought, resold, bought again and / sold again, the ward long over, / the Spaniard all the way back in Spain / down in the thimble again, and now, and now / real estaters, sub-contractors, landlords, freeway / engineers arguing . . .'.[80] Christian imagery returns, now in relation to the conquering Spanish who began the Californian land rush which shows no sign of slowing down.

'A Report upon the Consumption of Myself' plays throughout with the double meaning of the word 'blue' – as both a lovely colour and American slang for sad or depressed, feeling 'blue':

> I am a panther corked out and bellowing in
> cement walls, and I am angry at blue
> evenings without ventilators
> and I am angry with you, and it will come
> like a rose
> it will come like a man walking through fire
> it will shine like an unseen trumpet in a trunk[81]

The repetitions of 'it will come', 'it will shine' are typical of Bukowski's anaphoric, incantatory style. It is a July evening in Los Angeles and 'the palms up on the cliff waving / waving in the warm yellow light'. The speaker enters a drugstore 'to buy toothpaste, / rubbers, photographs of frogs, a copy of the latest / Consumer Reports (50 cents) for I consume and / am consumed and would like to know / on this blue evening / just which razorblade it would be best for me / to use, or maybe I could get a station wagon or buy a / stereo or a movie camera, say 8mm, under $55 / or an electric frying pan'.[82]

Thus the earlier reference to 'a man walking through fire' and 'the dangling sex rope hangs' turn on a double meaning: 'just which razorblade it would be best for me / to use' – to either shave or commit suicide. So the title 'A Report upon the Consumption of Myself' now also turns double: to 'consume myself' in suicide, as well as the suicidal mass consumption of American society where everything is for sale, where there is a price on everything, and nothing has any value. *Consumer Reports* is an American magazine devoted to rating products for 'consumers' to choose which might be the best to purchase: thus he plays a clever inversion on the title: 'A Report upon' / 'Consumer Reports'.

Bukowski manipulates a pattern of apocalyptic imagery including 'walking through fire', 'an unseen trumpet in a trunk' (echoes of the Revelation of St John), 'like the silver head / of some god-thing after they drop the bomb BANG', and finally 'and / they've blown up the Y.W.C.A. like a giant balloon and / sent it out to sea full of screaming lovely lonely / girls'.[83] This is typical of the complexity of his early poems: they are allusive, ambiguous, metaphorical – very much like the poetry prized by the New Critics. As we have seen, Bukowski had enjoyed reading the *Kenyon Review*, *Sewanee Review*, and admired the sensuous and intellectually dense poetry of Conrad Aiken. In his 'Foreword' to *The Roominghouse Madrigals*, published in 1988, he remarked: 'The early poems are more lyrical than where I am at now. I like these poems but I disagree with some who claim, "Bukowski's early work was much better." . . . In my present poetry, I go at matters more directly, land on them and then get out. I don't believe that my early methods and my late methods are either inferior or superior to one another. They are different, that's all.'[84] During this time he also made a trip to see the Webbs again – this time in Santa Fe, New Mexico. Then in November 1965, he and Frances split, which he recorded in the poem 'on beer cans and sugar cartons', published in *Simbolica* in January 1966: 'woman and child moving out / Wednesday; . . .

death doesn't always arrive like a bomb / or a fat whore / sometimes death crawls inch-by-inch / like a tiny spider crawling on your belly / while you sleep.'[85]

Although Bukowski had been preoccupied with poetry for some time, he gradually began to turn his attention back to prose: he now composed a series of short stories, essays and book reviews. Blazek published Bukowski's seminal literary manifesto 'A Rambling Essay on Poetics and the Bleeding Life Written While Drinking a Six-Pack (Tall)' in *Ole*, the first substantial statement of Bukowski's aesthetics. He describes his outsider status, discovering great books in the library and again complains about the 'dullness' of poetry: the dirty poets of the streets must storm the shiny clean tall ivory towers of the literary Establishment.[86] During this time he also discovered new writers. For example, on 16 July 1965 Bukowski wrote to Jon and Lou Webb: 'I am reading *Journey to the End of the Night* by Celine, and for me, he's a better writer than the early Sartre, better than Camus, and certainly better than Genet, he can write, he can write, oh, how that baby can write!!!'[87] He wrote a week later to the book collector Jim Roman, on 23 July 1965: 'Finally reading Celine and it's about time. A master, no doubt of it.'[88] Céline's severe misanthropy and use as of argot, slang and obscenity pleased him. So too, Bukowski would fashion quite intentionally and artistically a scatological, sexual and colloquial style. He avoided Graeco-Latinate words and instead hewed to bedrock, simple Anglo-Saxon and frequently strict subject-verb-object syntax.

1965 was also significant for two important literary encounters. He received a letter dated 19 October 1965 from one John Martin, an office supplies store owner from Los Angeles: 'Jon Webb gave me your address recently, and said to go ahead and write to you. I want to ask you about some of your books, but first (and most important) let me say that I think you are a most important and marvelous poet.'[89] Martin would soon become the publisher of Black Sparrow books and the central figure in Bukowski's rise to

Bukowski and John Martin, 1985.

world fame. Henry Miller wrote to Bukowski saying he admired his
writing but cautioned him about his drinking. This comment must
have rankled since Bukowski referred to the incident several times
and it spurred him to compose the uncollected poem, published
in *Kauri* (November/December 1965), wittily titled 'I Am Afraid
That I Will Continue To Drink Myself To Death For These Small
Reasons Mentioned Here And For Other Reasons That Neither
Of Us Has Time For Because I Have Need To Get Drunk Now'.[90]

In addition to the contacts with Martin and Miller, another
significant breakthrough was in fiction: *Confessions of a Man
Insane Enough to Live with Beasts* (the coupling of 'beasts' with
primal madness recalls the title of his first chapbook *Flower, Fist
and Bestial Wail*) was published in 1965.[91] This work is significant
as Bukowksi's first extended autobiographical prose and is divided
into nine sections. It is also noteworthy because the name 'Chinaski'
appears here for the first time while earlier, in 'The Reason behind
Reason' (1946), he had been 'Chelaski'. In an interview, Bukowski
revealed the genesis of the name: 'The "Chin" part, if you must know,
was thrown in because of my chin. I was one of those guys able to

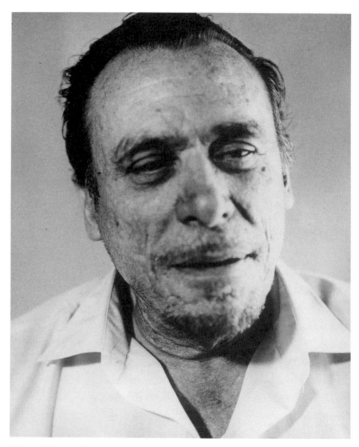

Bukowski, June 1967.

absorb a terrific punch. I was not a very good fighter but taking me
out was a great problem. I won a few by simply out-enduring the
stupid son of a bitch trying to do me in.'[92] And of course 'as' = 'ass'
– thus 'Chinaski' is a thoroughly embodied name to give to his
often wearily enfleshed anti-hero. *Confessions* opens provocatively:
'I remember jacking-off in the closet after putting on my mother's
high-heels and looking at my legs in the mirror, slowly drawing a

cloth up over my legs, higher and higher as if peeking up the legs of a woman.'[93] The narrative is not chronological, for we flash back and forth in time: he meets Jane and the next section returns to his adolescence and ordeal with *acne vulgaris*, then further into the future in section four to the charity ward near-death crisis. In section five, Bukowski's alter ego appears for the first time as he describes his application for work at a meat packing plant: 'Two days later I walked through the passgate into the wooden shack where I showed an old man my slip with my name on it: Henry Chinaski and he sent me on to the loading dock . . .'.[94]

As he attempts to carry the dead steer hanging from a hook, he muses: 'The shame of defeat taught me in American schoolyards as a boy told me that I must not drop the steer to the ground because this would prove that I was a coward and not a man and that I didn't therefore deserve much, just sneers and laughs, you had to be a winner in America, there wasn't any way out, you had to learn to fight for nothing, don't question . . .'.[95] To be 'a coward and not a man' reveals Bukowski's disgust with the American conception of 'masculinity': he was sometimes lambasted for endorsing the 'macho' stance of many of his male protagonists while he actually decried this attitude. You are either a 'winner' or a 'loser' – the competitive structure of life in the United States allows no deviation. In section nine, he tells us he worked 'as a shipping clerk for a place that sold overhead light fixtures' when he lived at Kingsley St.[96] He describes buying a 'second-hand Underwood' typewriter, drinking beer and beginning to write poetry, and concludes with a description of his meeting, marriage and separation from Barbara Frye. Thus *Confessions of a Man Insane Enough to Live with Beasts* is actually a mini-autobiography in nine sections, taking us from Bukowski's childhood up to 1957 and preparing the way for all his autobiographical fiction of the decades to come.

4

Age of Aquarius Dawning: A Dirty Old Man among the Beats and Hippies, 1966–1969

The mid-to-late 1960s were a significant phase in Bukowski's career as he began to divide his creative energies more equally between poetry and prose.[1] This period was also crucial in his evolution from a relatively unknown 'underground' author to international recognition in the literary world. His work reflected the zeitgeist: the driving, Dionysian impulse towards transcendence of the young and his relationship to the American counterculture – to key figures in Beat, hippy and artistic circles – intensified.[2] As we have seen, Kenneth Rexroth reviewed *It Catches My Heart in Its Hands* in 1964 in the *New York Times Book Review*. Bukowski himself wrote about Allen Ginsberg's volume of poetry *Empty Mirror* in 1966 in Douglas Blazek's *Ole*.[3] In his essay 'A Rambling Essay on Poetics and the Bleeding Life Written While Drinking a Six-Pack (Tall)' he referred to Ginsberg as 'the most awakening force in American poetry since Walt'.[4] He drew an affectionate portrait of Gregory Corso in his story 'I Just Write Poetry So I Can Go to Bed with Girls' and became friends with poets in the Beat orbit such as Harold Norse and Jack Micheline.[5] In addition, several of the major literary influences on the Beats – Dostoevsky, Pound, Céline – were also central figures for Bukowski. 'Reading and Breeding for Kenneth' recounts a poetry reading he gave to benefit Kenneth Patchen – an American poet of the counterculture who had been plagued with serious health problems.[6] Bukowski's poem 'Drawing of a Band Concert on a Matchbox' appeared in *Some/Thing* in 1966, with a cover designed by Andy Warhol.[7] Three of his poems also appeared in Warhol's *Intransit* in 1968, which Warhol edited with Gerard Malanga, who had asked for poems from Bukowski in 1962. An interview with Bukowski conducted by the American actor Sean Penn would appear in Warhol's *Interview* magazine in 1987.[8] He also published in many underground publications along with the Beats. For example, in 1966 he first appeared in Allen De Loach's *Intrepid* (published in Buffalo, New York), which had also published Timothy Leary, Gary Snyder, Ginsberg, Burroughs and Diane Di Prima.[9]

However, as he wrote in his poem 'The Beats', Bukowski was wary of their 'vanity' and 'posturing': they were photographed together and presumably conceived of themselves as a literary club (although Burroughs never thought of himself as a 'Beat'), whereas Bukowski took the stance of the heroic individualist, going his solitary way.[10] Bukowski's sense of social difference may have also been involved: all three of the major Beats had attended Ivy League universities – Ginsberg and Kerouac Columbia, and William S. Burroughs Harvard. As for the hippies, he mocked them in his poem 'the 60's': 'everybody was covered with beads / and was passing joints. / they stretched around on comfortable rugs and / didn't do anything. / I don't know how they made the rent.'[11] As he wrote to John Martin in 1993 about his job with the Post Office: '11 and ½ hour nights with only 2 or 3 days off a month. I was hardly a Flower Child.'[12] He was often quite dismissive of the more self-indulgent and deluded aspects of the youth culture. Although he shared their opposition to the Establishment, he did not think they were hardy enough: they were not steeled in poverty and despair as he had been. He would have agreed with Henry Miller who thought the tough ancient Gnostics made the hippies look like 'toilet paper'.[13] In *Nova Express*, Burroughs wrote: 'Listen to us. We are serving the Garden of Delights Immortality Cosmic Consciousness The Best Ever in Drug kicks. And *love love*

love in slop buckets. How does that sound to you boys? Better than Hassan i Sabbah and his cold windy bodiless rock? Right?'[14] Bukowski shared with Burroughs a scepticism about the 'love is all you need' chant of the hippies, a vision of reality at odds with his essentially Gnostic conception of planet Earth as a cosmic mistake.

Bukowski's outsider/'misfit' status meant that in some ways he had a closer affinity to those who were victimized by an unjust social system. To paraphrase Henry David Thoreau, those who have been imprisoned unjustly were often just men. One such figure was the American poet William Wantling (1933–1974) who had spent five years in San Quentin on drugs charges. Bukowski wrote to him on 9 July and they would have a close friendship which would, however, end unhappily.[15] Bukowski often expressed pride that prisoners wrote to inform him that his books were the most popular among the incarcerated.[16] Bukowski's thinking about art and 'criminality' was stimulated by his reading of Jean-Paul Sartre's *Saint Genet.* He wrote to Ann Menebroker on 25 October 1964: 'S.G. badly written for most part, but good shafts of light there, involuted, and somewhat fascinating like a little box of rusty razor blades . . . Genet, of course, was preceded as a robber-verse writer by Villon, who if I remember, was banned from Paris. Genet, more-like, has it made.'[17] Bukowski's explorations of rapists, prostitutes, murderers and the mad are in the French bad boy literary tradition from Villon to de Sade, Rimbaud, Verlaine, Baudelaire, Artaud, Céline, Genet and Bataille. Bukowski's stance also had much in common with that of Norman Mailer, who in his essay 'The White Negro' explored the existential mythology of 'hip' – the desire to liberate one's 'inner psychopath'; to push the body and psyche to their limits in quest of the Reichian orgasm; to live true to one's instinctive self in accordance with what D. H. Lawrence called the 'holy ghost'; to live and have one's being along the knife edge of insanity.[18]

On Saturday, 22 January 1966, John Martin came to visit Bukowski for the first time and Bukowski described the event in

'East Hollywood: The New Paris', a story published in 1981 in which Martin is 'Martin Johnson'. He says that he is starting a new press and asks if Bukowski has any poems he can look over: '"Open that door over there," I pointed at the closet. Martin Johnson got up, walked over, and pulled the door open. A mountainful of poems wavered a moment, then spilled forward onto the rug.'[19] In April 1966, Martin published the first poetry broadside of Bukowski, 'True Story'. In May he printed 'On Going out to Get the Mail'; in June 'To Kiss the Worms Goodnight'; in July, 'The Girls – for the Mercy Mongers' and in October 'The Flower Lover' and 'I Met a Genius', for which he paid Bukowski $30 each.[20] This would be the beginning of a mutually rewarding relationship, later humorously described by the two men as 'the meeting of Rolls and Royce'. Bukowski attributed their success to the practical, close-yet-distant nature of their partnership. He wrote to Martin in 1979: 'That's one of the best things I like about our relationship: you leave me alone and I leave you alone and we do what we have to do.'[21] Bukowski would become the best-selling author of Martin's Black Sparrow Press, and his work would later be published by Lawrence Ferlinghetti's City Lights and finally by HarperCollins/Ecco.

Following Céline, Bukowski discovered another Frenchman – Antonin Artaud. He wrote a laudatory review of *Artaud Anthology* which appeared in the 22 April 1966 issue of the *Los Angeles Free Press* and he told Joseph Conte in a letter two months later: 'Artaud wrote the iron line, like reaming fire through cement . . . Artaud is one of the few writers I look up to. Artaud, Dostoevsky, Céline . . . read Céline, Joe, this guy was laughing while they were killing him.'[22] Thus within two years, he had read Sartre, Céline and Artaud: fierce French rebellion against society seemed perfectly relevant to Bukowski during the mid-to-late 1960s when the American status quo was being threatened by the student revolution (Berkeley, 1964; Columbia, 1968; Harvard and Cornell, 1969), the escalating war in Vietnam, the demand for full participation in American society by blacks, Hispanics, Native Americans, women and homosexuals and the incipient environmental movement.[23] If we add Knut Hamsun to the trio of Artaud, Céline and Dostoevsky, we have Bukowski's Four European Horsemen of the Apocalypse in America.

In March 1966 he had to have his haemorrhoids removed and from this painful ordeal came Bukowski's first extensive prose of the period – *All the Assholes in the World and Mine* was published by Douglas Blazek and an excerpt also appeared in the November 1–15 issue of New York City's *East Village Other*, along with Andy Warhol's 'My True Story'.[24] Like *Confessions of a Man Insane Enough to Live with Beasts*, this is another foray into autobiographical fiction and is divided into thirteen numbered sections. Although the operation was actually agonizing, Bukowski as usual lessens the horror through laughter or, more precisely, he makes the horror itself seem humorous. This is his great skill as a comic writer. The doctor performing the operation speaks in a thick German accent: Bukowski's exaggerated, wild style shares many aspects in common with publications such as *Mad* magazine which featured caricatural, pointed and irreverent cartoon satires of American life and culture. Thus it is no surprise that later in the 1970s the comic book master genius of extreme estrangement, Robert Crumb, would illustrate Bukowski's work.

In addition to Blazek, Bukowski made contact with another dynamo of the mimeograph revolution, d.a. levy of Cleveland, Ohio, who published Bukowski's 'The Genius of the Crowd' in 1966.[25] The poem opens: 'There is enough treachery, hatred, / violence, / Absurdity in the average human / being / To supply any given army on any given day.' 'The Genius of the Crowd' has the fury of Robinson Jeffers's misanthropy as well as the wisdom of Lao Tzu's philosophy: 'AND The Best at Murder Are Those / Who Preach Against It. / AND The Best At Hate Are Those / Who Preach LOVE . . . / Those Who Preach PEACE / Do Not Have Peace'.

Bukowski's series of contraries echo Lao Tzu, who in the *Tao Te Ching* explored the paradox of how allegiance to abstract belief systems or ideologies prevent living in accordance with Nature, the Tao, the 'Way': 'The more prohibitions you have, / the less virtuous people will be. / The more weapons you have, / the less secure people will be.'[26] Bukowski would write two essays on levy, who was arrested by the police for publishing 'obscene' literature and committed suicide at 26, as well as an essay in support of Jim Lowell, whose Asphodel Bookshop in Cleveland was raided.[27] The fight for freedom of expression continued throughout the 1960s and Bukowski himself became an important participant in the struggle.

Bukowski became more daring during this period because movies, television, popular music and the censorship and obscenity debates over *Lady Chatterley's Lover*, *Lolita*, 'Howl', *Tropic of Cancer* and *Naked Lunch* had begun to loosen restrictions for writers.[28] In the masterful uncollected poem 'the faces are gnawing at my walls but have not yet come in . . .' which appeared in *Entrails*, edited by Gene Bloom in 1967, Bukowski precisely documents a visionary state of psychological dissociation: 'the yellow walls have faces divided into blocks and out / of ice-cube windows / the world wanders by – sticks and hints of world / in dress and in face / moving along the cement / stuck there, moving there, / people, heads arms eyes asses, / killers punks another madman another banker / a torturer of animals, / they go by . . .'.[29] The world has broken into fragments, bodies anatomized into discrete parts, observed silently by the poet through the window, recalling Hart Crane's lyric 'Legend' from *White Buildings*: 'As silent as a mirror is believed / Realities plunge in silence by . . .'.[30] The 'breakdown' of self in the poem suggests a kind of schizophrenic moment of illumination in which meaning implodes, in which names and the things in the world they signify are torn asunder. Furthermore by juxtaposing without break or comment 'killers', 'punks', 'another madman', 'another banker', 'a torturer of animals', Bukowski equalizes the 'high' and 'low' elements of society: bankers and killers are placed on the same level of perception.

Each of the following lines contains more specific images: yellow walls, an old woman, a butterfly, the mailman. As the poem progresses, normally taboo ideas surface: murder, oral sex, masturbation, rape. Previously Bukowski's imagination had not ventured so deeply into such transgressive realms. Yet violence, sexuality and madness are balanced by absurd humour: the speaker falls drunk into the fireplace naked while listening to Wagner and is suddenly magically transformed by soot into a black-faced Al Jolson singing his signature song 'Mammy'; he bleeds from the injuries caused by his accident, but 'I was laughing in my yellow walls'. He acknowledges that his 'health is so bad that my health doesn't give a / fuck', gets in the bathtub the following morning 'and I floated down in there / thinking, well, not everybody can do this and I am not / even in a madhouse, in fact, not anybody is even bothering / me, and then I rubbed soap on my cock, / dreamed a rape in my mindmovie and / jacked off.' The ungrammatical jarring 'not anybody is even bothering me' indicates the fragile relationship between self and external world: language splits incoherently during the descent into the unconscious. The poem charts the liminal ground between several binary 'oppositions' – legal and criminal, health and illness, sanity and madness, comedy and tragedy, white and black, permissible and forbidden sexuality – simultaneously. Although Bukowski had not read Michel Foucault, he charts the same transgression across the liminal borders of contested power relations in society which preoccupied the French philosopher: the criminal, the insane, racial 'minorities' and the sexually 'deviant'. Indeed, Bukowski's search for the *sacred* demands precisely this full acknowledgment of the *profane*: he must interchange the binary elements. As Foucault wrote in 1963: 'Profanation in a world which no longer recognizes any positive meaning in the sacred – is this not more or less what we may call transgression? . . . transgression prescribes not only the sole manner of discovering the sacred in its unmediated substance, but also a way of recomposing its empty form, its absence, through which it becomes all the more scintillating.'[31]

At the close of the poem, Bukowski refers to creating a 'mind-movie', a perfect phrase to describe the psychedelic, hallucinogenic 1960s. Indeed there is a narcotic-induced-like phantasmagoria in some of his work during this period. And while Bukowski, as we have seen, preferred alcohol, he did experiment with drugs. John Thomas records giving him Dexaml, LSD, Dexedrine as well as DMT, which is the alkaloid in *ayahuasca*, or *yagé* (the extremely powerful hallucinogenic plant from the Amazonian rainforest William S. Burroughs described in *The Yage Letters*).[32] It is probable that the fantastic imagery of Bukowski's work from the mid-to-late Sixties derived partially from these experiences. Aldous Huxley's famous book on the consciousness-expanding effects of mescaline, *The Doors of Perception*, was published in 1956 and reprinted in 1963, just as the psychedelic movement began to gather force.[33] Huxley took his title from William Blake: 'If the doors of perception were cleansed everything would appear to man as it is: infinite.'[34] Bukowski had sought ecstasy through writing, classical music, sexual love, alcohol and solitude. Yet the difference between Bukowski and the transcendentalist effort to reach nirvana is that he always remains firmly on planet Earth, wounded, rambunctious, shrieking, stunned, making a 'mindmovie' in his bathtub. It is this combination of lyrical language which spills out of the self into fantastic realms of the subconscious with the down-to-earth 'obscene', 'vulgar', wounded yearnings of the body which defines his originality.

Bukowski now made contact with Carl Weissner, then living in Heidelberg, who had discovered his work in March 1966 in the

Carl Weissner, 1978.

British magazine *Iconolatre*.[35] Weissner, astonished by this prolific, unknown genius, would feature him in his magazine *Klactoveedsedsteen* (the name is from a tune by Charlie Parker), ultimately becoming his most important German translator. Bukowski also began to appear in other publications of the German underground, including *Acid: Neue Amerikanische Szene*, as well as John Bennett's *Vagabond*, edited in Munich.[36] Bukowski's friendship with Harold Norse – who had been active in the 'Beat Hotel' in Paris with Burroughs and Brion Gysin – also began and he composed a tribute to Norse entitled 'The Old Pro' for *Ole*.[37] Bukowski's personal and professional life became increasingly connected – both in the United

States and Germany – to the dawning of the 'Age of Aquarius', as the musical *Hair* hopefully intoned.

In 1967 Bukowski again met John Bryan, who proposed that he write a weekly column for his underground newspaper *Open City* entitled 'Notes of a Dirty Old Man'. It is probable that this was intended as an allusion to Dostoevsky's *Notes from Underground* (which had been the title of Bryan's earlier magazine) for indeed many of Bukowski's anti-heroes in the series recall the crazed, misanthropic central character in one of the Russian writer's greatest works. The first column – dealing with how policemen might best handle drunk drivers – appeared in the 12–18 May 1967 issue.[38] This would launch a turning point in his career: Bukowski composed hundreds of columns over the next eight years for *Open City*, as well as *NOLA Express* of New Orleans and the *Los Angeles Free Press* and later in the 1980s for *High Times*. John Bryan said of Bukowski: 'He had endless energy and style. He could produce unimaginable quantities of first-rate prose and poetry at a single sitting. He had a certain loathsome charm.'[39] 1967 also opened another door for Bukowski: he appeared for the first time in *Evergreen Review*, published by Barney Rosset of Grove Press. The magazine featured a roster of renowned international authors including Samuel Beckett, Václav Havel, Jean Genet, Nicolás Guillén, Eugène Ionesco and William Burroughs.[40]

In launching the 'Notes of a Dirty Old Man' column, Bukowski was finally given the journalist job he had always desired. He was free to contribute whatever he chose: stories, poems, essays, interviews, even a series of cartoons concerning one 'Clarence H. Sweetmeat'. He gave free rein to his wild, fecund imagination. One column from 1967 (which, as we shall see, was cited by the FBI in their investigation of Bukowski) begins:

> I was going over my old Racing Forms, having a beer and a
> smoke, really hungover, shaky, depressed; gently thinking suicide

but still hoping for a lucky angel when there was a knock on the door . . . IT WAS A WOMAN, and what a woman in the 9 p.m. rain – long red hair all down the back, jesus: tons of red miracle. And the face, open with passion, like a flower ripped open with the fingers from the bud, a kind of fire-cheating, and the body, the body was nothing but sex, sex still jumping singing looking flowing humming in the 9 p.m. rain saying, 'Bukowski, Charles Bukowski?' and I said, 'come on in,' and she did . . .[41]

This blend of wish-fulfilment and realistic detail (red hair, 9 p.m., rain and the lovely simile 'like a flower ripped open with the fingers from the bud') is typical of Bukowski's excursions into dreamlike fantasy. They have sexual intercourse, he goes to the bathroom and, upon returning, his night angel has suddenly disappeared. He takes a match and burns one of her long red hairs he finds on the chair. Several of his columns evoke this uncanny mood of free-floating lust: mysterious chance encounters with women occasion a crack in the veneer of 'civilization' and suddenly expose the sexual electric charge of naked instinctual desire.

On 7 April 1967 Black Sparrow published the chapbook *Two Poems* containing 'a little atomic bomb' and 'family, family'. 'a little atomic bomb', later collected in *Play the Piano Drunk Like a Percussion Instrument until the Fingers Begin to Bleed a Bit* (1979) is an ironic ballad describing the increasing militarization of America during the 1960s: 'o, just give me a little atomic bomb / not too much / just a little / enough to kill a horse in the street / but there aren't any horses in the street.'[42] Bukowski often reflected on the madness of the arms race as the US increased its military might against the 'Communist threat' throughout the Cold War period and during the escalation of the war in Vietnam by President Lyndon Johnson. Yet he also sometimes felt that humanity had become so unredeemable that it might be best to start over and begin afresh. As he confided to William Wantling on 9 July 1965: 'I . . . think it's time they dropped the god damned hydrogen bomb and got everything over with.'[43]

John Martin published Bukowski's first Black Sparrow book – *At Terror Street and Agony Way*, containing 40 poems – in April 1968 in an edition of 800 paperback and 75 hardbound copies.[44] The title has spiritual resonance – 'terror' and 'agony' possess both existential and Christian overtones and these moods accompanied him daily as he confessed in the uncollected poem 'Who Killed Charles Bukowski?' from 1966: 'I go to the kitchen and drink water and / feel the terror again / the terror of starving in alleys; / the terror of the landlord, the empty belly'.[45] The manuscripts of the poems of the book had been lost but Bukowski's friend John Thomas was able to reconstruct the texts by transcribing them from a tape recording that had been made.[46] One of the finest poems – 'beerbottle' – was first published in *Wormwood Review* in 1964:

> a very miraculous thing just happened:
> my beerbottle flipped over backwards
> and landed on its bottom on the floor,
> and I have set it upon the table to foam down[47]

If William Carlos Williams could muse about cold plums in the refrigerator, Bukowski certainly had poetic license to praise a beer bottle in flight. After this casual and humorous opening, the poem turns to more serious matters: 'what sets / the blackbird in the cat's mouth / is not for us to say, or why some men / are jailed like pet squirrels / while others nuzzle in enormous breasts / through endless nights – this is the / task and the terror, and we are not / taught why.' 'The task and the terror' echoes the volume's title, for Terror Street and Agony Way form the dread crossroads of existential choice and determined fate. As William Blake wrote in 'Auguries of Innocence': 'Some are born to sweet delight / Some are born to endless night.'[48] But we do not know why this injustice prevails. The poem concludes by returning to the miracle of the bottle's upright landing and the good luck it portends for the evening: 'and perhaps tomorrow my nose will be longer; / new shoes, less rain, more poems.' It is deftly accomplished: the enjambed lines moving deliberately forward as they circle in a motion mirroring the beer bottle turning over itself and landing upright – shifting from an unexpected lucky event to philosophical questioning and back to the hope that the luck will hold – as if Bukowski is performing a poetic act of legerdemain for us, ending the poem in full circle with the word 'poems'. The poem is what it does.

Several other selections illustrate Bukowski's range of subject matter. 'i wanted to overthrow the government but all i brought down was somebody's wife' returns to his time in San Francisco in the early 1940s when he had an affair with an Italian Communist's wife following a political discussion: 'a tottering dynasty myself, always drunk as possible, / well read, starving, depressed, but actually / a good young piece of ass would have solved all my rancor, / but I didn't know this; / I listened to my Italian and my Jew / and I went down dark alleys smoking borrowed cigarettes / and watching the backs of houses come down in flames.'[49] Another poem, 'poverty', portrays a fully instinctive man's perceptive eyes caught momentarily as he lowers his hands lighting a cigarette: they resemble the clear eyes of a tiger.[50] The human who is most animal-like is the most fully human: we remember Annable's advice in D. H. Lawrence's *The White Peacock*: 'be a good animal'. The poems of *At Terror Street and Agony Way* were recorded by Barry Miles who had proposed including Bukowski in a poetry series on the Zapple label (a subsidiary of Apple Records) to Paul McCartney and the Beatles, who agreed to the project.[51]

In 1968 *Poems Written Before Jumping Out Of An 8 Story Window* was published by Poetry/X/Change in Glendale, California. It contains '86'd', first published in *Blitz* in 1965, which reflects Bukowski's hard-bitten wisdom about the dangers of mob behaviour and the lost human race: 'it is fairly dismal to know that / millions of people are worried about / the hydrogen bomb / yet / they are already / dead.'[52] 'mostpeople' (as e.e. cummings would have it) do not fully live and simply do as others around them are doing, never breaking out of what Martin Heidegger called *das Man* – the mass behaviour of 'the They' or 'One' – into authentic selfhood. The book supplied the title for a selection of poems published as *Gedichte die einer schrieb bevor er im 8. Stockwerk aus dem fenster sprang* (1974) which sparked Bukowski's rise to fame in Germany. For this volume Weissner chose poems from *Poems Written Before Jumping, The Days Run Away Like Wild Horses Over the Hills, At Terror Street and Agony Way*, as well as a selection of poems from various magazines and letters.[53]

In March 1968 the FBI began to investigate Bukowski. The FBI file indicates that they had questions about his 'common-law wife' – this was clearly Frances Smith – who 'has been reported to have attended a number of Communist Party meetings in the Los Angeles area'.[54] This page of the report continues, indicating 'that one Charles Bukowski, poet, was the author of an article appearing on page 43 of the June, 1963, issue of *Mainstream*.' Also singled out is the 'March [1968] edition of the *Underground Digest, The Best of the Underground Press* . . .'. It is clear that the FBI was trying to fathom Bukowski's political commitments as well as to build a case against him in which a dossier of his 'obscene' writings for the underground press would be cited as evidence.[55]

In August 1968 Carl Weissner travelled from Germany to meet Bukowski and left a memorable account of his visit to his apartment:

I went in. The door squeaked a little. I remained standing and looked around. The shades were pulled down, it smelled of cigarette butts, rancid socks and old beer stains on the rug.

A ripped up couch with the stuffing falling out. A set of auto-mobile tires in the corner. Shelves full of books, boxes full of books, newspapers, magazines. Photos and newspaper clippings on the wall; descriptions of shootings, robberies, sex murders; one big sheet of wrapping paper with complicated calculations and diagrams – a mysterious system for horse betting, based on all the results of the horse races at Santa Ana, Santa Anita, Del Mar and Hollywood Park over the last three years. In front of the window towards the street a huge work desk with a very large old Remington and a thick stack of typing paper.[56]

In addition to his links with the German underground through his friendship with Weissner, Bukowski in 1968 also had three poems in *Intransit: The Andy Warhol–Gerard Malanga Monster Issue*: 'That's Where They Came From', 'It's Very Good to Know when You're Done' and 'Poem for Brigitte Bardot'.[57]

1969 was a thrilling *annus mirabilis* for Bukowski: *Penguin Poets 13* (in which he appeared along with Harold Norse and Philip Lamantia), *A Bukowski Sampler*, *Notes of a Dirty Old Man* and *The Days Run Away Like Wild Horses Over the Hills* were all published. He began editing *Laugh Literary and Man the Humping Guns* with Neeli Cherkovski. The cover of the first issue proclaimed: 'In disgust with Poetry Chicago, with the dull dumpling pattycake safe Creeleys, Olsons, Dickeys, Merwins, Nemerovs and Merediths'.[58] Yet there were troubles in his personal life: he was warned about his absenteeism at the Post Office and he was also anxious during this period because Frances was travelling about the country with their daughter Marina. In *Notes of a Dirty Old Man* he wrote: 'with him it wasn't dying that mattered. With him it was the unsolved and loose parts left behind – a four-year old daughter in some hippy camp in Arizona . . .'.[59]

Notes of a Dirty Old Man was published on 24 January 1969 in an edition of approximately 28,000 copies by Essex House, a small

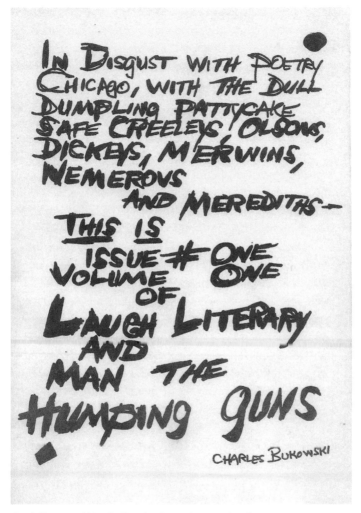

Laugh Literary and Man the Humping Guns, vol. 1, no. 1 (1969).

publisher of erotica in North Hollywood.[60] The book contains a variety of essays and stories concerning boxing matches, horse races, sexual encounters, politics. The first page begins appropriately with a fight – a scene Bukowski returns to in 'Dirty Old Man Confesses' as well as *Ham on Rye* – between himself and his buddy 'Elf', probably Robert Baume, his literary friend from college. The story opens with a single, non-stop sentence which occupies the entire paragraph. Elf

> wrote too much like Thomas Wolfe and, outside of Dreiser, T. Wolfe was the worst American writer ever born, and I hit Elf behind the ear and the bottle fell off the table (he'd said something that I disagreed with) and as Elf came up I had the bottle, good scotch, and I got him half on the jaw and part of the neck under there and he went down again, and I felt on top of my game, I was a student of Dostoevski and listened to Mahler in the dark, and I had time to drink from the bottle, set it down, fake with a right and lend him the left just below the belt and he fell against the dresser, clumsily, the mirror broke, it made sounds like a movie, flashed and crinkled and then Elf landed one high on my forehead and I fell back across a chair and the thing flattened like straw, cheap furniture, and then I was in deep . . .[61]

The prose is swift and assured, striking a balance between narrative chutzpah and sly humour, with the typical Bukowski wry lyricism thrown in the mix: 'I was a student of Dostoevski and listened to Mahler in the dark'.

Bukowski also makes trenchant comments on the political scene of the period. During the crisis year of 1968, when both Martin Luther King, Jr and Robert Kennedy were assassinated and the Chicago Democratic Convention was besieged by protests, Bukowski described the events in a thoughtful essay:

It's one thing to talk about Revolution while your belly is full of another man's beer and you're traveling with a sixteen-year-old runaway girl from Grand Rapids; it's one thing to talk about Revolution while three jackass writers of international fame have you dancing to the ooooooooooMMM game; it's another thing to bring it about, it's another thing to have happen. Paris, 1870–71, 20,000 people murdered in the streets, the streets as red with blood as with rain, and the rats coming out and eating at the bodies, and the people hungered, ravaged, no longer knowing what it meant, coming out and yanking the rats off the corpses and eating the rats. And where is Paris tonight? And what is Paris tonight?[62]

Bukowski pokes fun at Allen Ginsberg who led chanting of the Buddhist mantra 'Om' in the streets of Chicago as well as Jean Genet and William Burroughs who also participated in the anti-war marches in August 1968. The reference to the Paris Commune of 1870–71 as America was rioting in the streets again illustrates an underappreciated fact about Bukowski: that he was more historically and politically knowledgeable than his critics imagine. Bukowski saw the choices facing Americans in 1968 as very grim: 'we can choose between Nixon and Humphrey and Christ and be fucked anyway we turn'.[63] The ultimate goal, Bukowski tells us, is to become 'more real and more human' – as lyrical a definition of the utopian dreams of the young as one might wish. The book has been extremely successful, remaining in print over the past 40 years and attracting several well-known fans including Raymond Carver and Tom Waits.[64]

The Days Run Away Like Wild Horses Over the Hills contains work from Bukowski's first four volumes of poetry.[65] As we have seen, the book is dedicated to Jane and includes several moving poems dedicated to her memory: 'remains'; 'Uruguay or hell'; 'I thought of ships, of armies, hanging on'. 'remains' tells us 'and her photographs are stuck onto a painting / by a dead German and she too is dead'. The 'dead German' here must be Ernst Haeckel, one of whose paintings Bukowski had inherited from his parents.[66] As the war in Vietnam escalated, Bukowski expressed his anguish in 'Poem for the Death of an American Serviceman in Vietnam'.[67] He also composed a deeply felt poem about the Buddhist monks in Vietnam who killed themselves by self-immolation, 'on the fire suicides of the buddhists': 'you sophisticates / who lay back and / make statements of explanation, / I have seen the red rose burning / and this means more'.[68]

It was Harold Norse who had been responsible for introducing Bukowski's work to the London editor Nick Stangos at Penguin Books, and the relationship between the two poets began to flourish. Norse described Bukowski during this time as

> misshapen – a big hunchback with a ravaged, pockmarked face, decayed nicotine-stained teeth, and pain-filled green eyes. Flat brown hair seemed pasted to an oversized skull – hips broader than shoulders, hands grotesquely small and soft. A beer gut sagged over his belt. He wore a white shirt, baggy pants, an ill-fitting suit, the kind convicts receive when released from prison. He looked like one, down and out.[69]

Their friendship would cool considerably over the years and, as we shall see, Bukowski wrote an acid portrayal of Norse in his story 'The Day We Talked About James Thurber', depicting him as a fop with a French name.[70]

Bukowski gave his first public poetry reading at The Bridge, a bookstore off Hollywood Boulevard, on 19 December 1969 and read again the following night.[71] He designed a poster announcing the event: 'Bukowski will give his first public demolition poetry readings here Dec. 19+20 9:30 PM – Different Rantings Each Nite. One $!'[72] He greatly feared giving readings, perhaps partially rationalizing his anxiety by claiming art was to be created in private and had nothing to do with declaiming before audiences. In this he resembled the great Canadian pianist Glenn Gould who also despised playing in public and retired from the stage at 32.

Bukowski's mood in the late 1960s is reflected in 'Absence of the Hero', a prose piece Weissner published in *Klactovedsedsteen*. It opens with a surreal, expressionist passage which curiously recalls Bertolt Brecht's *Baal*: 'I walked out into the street and the green trees stuck their yellow teeth out at me. And their rubber cocks. I was a dead gagging finger in a sexless sky.'[73] In *Baal*, Brecht writes: 'the willows are like rotten stumps of teeth in the black mouth of the sky', thus also making the striking connection between trees, rotting teeth and the sky.[74] While the narrator is trapped in the nightmare of his daily, anguished existence, the major event of 1969 has happened: America is on the moon. The contrast between the quotidian and the cosmic is emphasized by his dismissive reaction upon reading in the newspaper 'some shit about men landing on the moon . . .'.[75]

Bukowski's absenteeism at work and his writings for the underground newspapers had not gone unnoticed by the Post Office hierarchy. One of his fellow employees apparently alerted them to the fact that he was publishing material unbecoming a postal worker. The FBI continued its surveillance file on him, placing as 'exhibits' three of the 'Dirty Old Man' columns he had begun writing for *Open City*, including one about Henry Beckett collected in *Notes of a Dirty Old Man*; one about LeRoi Jones (collected in *Absence*); and one (described above) concerning a sexual encounter with a redheaded woman.[76] The chronology of events then becomes ambiguous. The usually accepted narrative has been that John Martin offered Bukowski $100 a month to write full-time and they determined his monthly expenses would be '$35 for his rent, $20 for groceries, $5 for gas, $15 for beer and cigarettes, $10 to pay the telephone bill and $15 for Marina's child support.'[77] Bukowski agreed and Martin would publish his work. Martin did not tell

Los Angeles, Calif.
Oct. 3, 1969

HEMORRHOIDS

hello Pradip Choudhuri:
    I don't recall receiving a letter from you, although I might have, or others might
have written me, but I have been busy gambling, drinking, working, going crazy, fighting
men and women, sleeping, eating, shitting.... so forth. Besides, I have laid aside
the poem and am working on the short story for a bit. So, it isn't MOODS with me
that keep me from answering all my mail; it's just that I get too much mail--mail from
lonely women, hard-up women; mail from poets, mail from editors, mail from India,
Germany, France, Belgium and England--and today one from Beruit, wherever that
is. I am also editing a magazine--LAUGH LITERARY AND MAN THE HUMPING GUNS, and
so I also get a lot of shit in the mail that people call writing. Besides this, there
are my ulcers, hemmhorhoids, dizzy spells, use of reds, mary, meth, yellows, hash, beer,
whiskey, wine, cigarettes and cigars, and an occassional jackoff now and then. Plus
light bills, gas bills, phone bills, tax bills, flat tires, toothache, insomnia,
a loose universal joint on my ten year old car, and an affliction of anxiety anuerosis,
a heavy affliction, plus a healthy jolt of parnoia. Plus this, my five year old
daughter comes down now and then from San Francisco and takes over--everything stops--
except what she wants to do. I am hooked on her too. Also they are talking of removing
me from the job I hate because of too much absenteeism...

    so it's moods, yes, too, but simply it is because there is not enough of me to
go around for what there is to do.

    yes, you have permission to use my poem, whatever it is that Carl gave you.
I don't have any photographs, god save me, and all my stupid books are out of
print. A letter from Germany today from a publisher... he wants to know...

    well, shit, hope this reaches you in time. If I get in your thing, mail me a
copy. I'd like to find out what I have written.

                    hold,

                    Charles Bukowski

Letter to Pradip Choudhuri, 1969.

his wife Barbara at the time, since this represented a considerable financial risk for him.

But this version – that John Martin approached *him* with the idea of writing full-time – may be incorrect, since the evidence points towards the reverse situation. Knowing that he was about to be terminated from the Post Office, Bukowski came to Martin. According to Sounes, Bukowski – not telling Martin about the threatened dismissal – proposed: 'If you get me out of the post office, I'll write more books than you can publish.'[78] Bukowski's leaving the Post Office reminds us of Henry Miller's dramatic exit from the 'Cosmodemonic Telegraph Company' – the symbolic severing of the artist from slavery to the capitalist machine. And although Bukowski was undergoing many perturbations of the body and spirit during this period, he retained his creative strength and *joie de vivre*. Barry Miles came to visit him in 1969 to make the recording of his poetry for Zapple records. He arrived at De Longpre and found a fiery spirit: 'Buk stood filling the doorway, a large man with thin hair, a grey face, ravaged and pock-marked from severe acne in childhood, and colourless lips which broke into an expressive smile. He was vital, friendly, humorous; he seemed to burn with life.'[79]

5

A Professional Writer and the Dogs from Hell, 1970–1978

As the new decade arrived, Bukowski's world had changed radically. The dream he had nourished for so long – to attempt living exclusively by his pen – had finally been realized. Yet the prospect which lay before him was frightening. The old cliché – be careful what you wish for because you might get it – in this case proved perfectly apt. However much he had vilified the Post Office and Uncle Sam, they had provided one *sine qua non*: a reliable, steady source of income. John Martin's offer of monthly $100 payments had at least allayed his concerns about child support and alimony, but he had yet to prove himself a marketable author. When Martin suggested he tackle a novel – since fiction sells significantly better than poetry – Bukowski took immediate action. He sat before his typewriter each evening at precisely the same time he used to begin work at the Post Office: 6:18 p.m. He fuelled his typing with beer, Scotch (Cutty Sark pints), 'cheap cigars', classical music on the radio: he awakened in the mornings hungover to find pages scattered on the floor. He revelled in the creative struggle: 'It was the good fight, at last. My whole body, my whole spirit, was wild with the battle.' Nineteen days later he phoned Martin and said: 'It's finished.' Martin asked, 'What?' Bukowski replied, 'The novel. Come over and pick it up.' When Martin later asked Bukowski what compelled him to complete the book so swiftly, he responded: 'fear'.[1] Martin's instincts about the potential of a novel were sound: published on 8 February 1971, the book has been translated worldwide and remains one of his most popular.

Post Office opens 'It began as a mistake', which is an allusion to the first line of Céline's *Voyage au bout de la nuit*: 'Ça a débuté comme ça', 'It began like that.'[2] The novel is divided into short chapters – a technique he learned from John Fante – while the picaresque plot follows our lower-class protagonist Hank Chinaski from one misadventure to another. Chinaski appears to be unwise but is in actuality the secret possessor of the paradoxical, contradictory truths of existence. He is a 'holy fool', a trope which recurs repeatedly in Bukowski's work.[3] The book telescopes various periods in Bukowski's life, returning to the early 1950s when he worked as a mail carrier: snarling dogs; sexual encounters with lonely women; the struggle to memorize postal codes. Bukowski also indicts the American economic system which is founded on the illusion that buying things will bring happiness. One of the women on his route complains that he only brings her bills and Chinaski muses: 'It wasn't my fault that they used telephones and gas and light and bought all their things on credit. Yet when I brought them their bills they screamed at me – as if *I* had asked them to have a phone installed, or a $350 t.v. set sent over with no money down.'[4]

The novel exposes the authoritarian and hierarchical us postal system, which becomes a microcosm of American working-class life, a theme Bukowski would explore more fully in his second novel *Factotum* (1975). Indeed, Bukowski was prescient: between 1986 and 2010 there were several incidents of violence in post offices throughout the country and the phrase 'going postal' has entered the American colloquial dictionary to describe a person who suddenly becomes murderously enraged.[5] *Post Office* resembles Kafka's arbitrary bureaucratic world in which orders are given for no apparent purpose yet are slavishly followed by the employees. For example, the boss 'Purple Stickpin' orders employees to stop putting their belongings on top of a cabinet – for no logical or practical reason. Of course the best way to dismantle power is humour, and the painful and comic aspects of Chinaski's life are finely balanced: the novel is very funny indeed. Chinaski is a zany character, yet his rebellion is an affirmation of the human spirit. In his review of the novel, Valentine Cunningham explained our identification with Chinaski: 'But it's a sympathy that, despite one's outrage, Bukowski makes the reader share. Pressed in by Post Office bureaucrats and their heaps of paperwork, the misfit looks frequently like an angel of light. His refusal to play respectability ball . . . can make even this ribald mess of a wretch seem like a shining haven of sanity in the prevailing Los Angeles grimnesses.'[6] Chinaski is indeed a 'ribald misfit', yet he is ultimately 'angelic' – the ancient Greek word for messenger is *angelos* and Chinaski, if not an actual angel, brings along with his mail a message of light in the darkness.

With the publication of *Post Office*, Bukowski officially made his *Abschied* to the Terminal Annex. He now had considerable free time on his hands and the life of a writer on De Longpre would be full of adventures. In his story 'East Hollywood: The New Paris', he described his environment:

> East Hollywood sits in the smog in front of the purple mountains. It begins at Hollywood Boulevard and runs east of Western Avenue down to Alvarado Street, bordered by Santa Monica Boulevard on the south. Here you will find the greatest contagion of bums, drunks, pillheads, prostitutes per square foot, in Southern California.[7]

Bukowski was surrounded by oddballs and freaks whose tales he listened to with great interest. As he told John Thomas: 'You can get some good stories out of ordinary people, because they don't try to tell them with, you know, aplomb or anything.'[8] Some of these tales found their way into his own work. In 'The L.A. Scene', a 'Dirty Old Man' column from 1972 collected posthumously in *Portions*, he describes many of the characters such as Red Strange whom he encountered during this period.[9]

In order to supplement his income, Bukowski had to overcome his distaste for giving poetry readings: he continued to tread the boards for more than a decade. On 15 May 1970 he appeared at the University of New Mexico and on 30 May at Bellevue Community College in Washington State. The story 'I Just Write Poetry So I Can Go to Bed with Girls' is an engaging account of his time in Santa Fe when he met Gregory Corso and reveals the new Bukowski of the 1970s: an obstreperous Dionysus spouting poetry, pursued by eager maenads.[10] He now appeared as the modern incarnation of the sublime lyric of Archilochos: 'I know how to lead off / The sprightly dance / Of the Lord Dionysos / the dithyramb. / I do it thunderstruck with wine.'[11] In addition to his performances, he was aided financially by the sale by John Martin of an archive of his literary papers to the University of California at Santa Barbara for $5,000 in 1970.[12]

Because of his increasing notoriety as author of the 'Dirty Old Man' series and greater visibility around Los Angeles, Bukowski began to attract more female attention. He once recalled that 'I must have been crazy from 1970 to 1977' and his first major love was Linda King – a young, voluptuous sculptress and budding poet whom he met in the summer of 1970.[13] This relationship would blossom into the most intense he had experienced since Jane. Linda, who had been married previously, had been institutionalized for mental illness and subjected to shock treatments. Their affair was marked by constant fighting, jealousy (Bukowski claimed she was always flirting with other men and he was less than faithful himself) and violence: on one occasion he broke her nose. Bukowski also began in 1970 to contribute to adult magazines such as *Adam*, *Pix*, *Knight* and *Fling* in order to supplement his income. This began a pattern which would continue to the end of his career as he would ultimately submit stories to *Oui, Penthouse, Hustler* and the German edition of *Playboy*. He remarked that he would throw in some sex in order to sell the story to the magazines, but then weave an interesting plot around the gratuitous eroticism.[14]

In 1971 Bukowski began a fruitful association with the editor of the *New York Quarterly*, William Packard.[15] Packard was a strong advocate of his work and they became frequent correspondents. Bukowski's supposed 'anti-formalism' still came in for criticism but in an essay entitled 'Notes on The Bukowski' for the *Small Press Review* Packard asserted: 'Hell, he's technically to the point of making you think he has no craft at all, which I suppose is the ultimate technique, is the ultimate craft. Bukowski's craft is the poem as poem. And the story as story. I mean, he has a gut notion of what a poem and story should be.'[16] Bukowski's gift was making the difficult – the creation of seemingly effortless writing – seem easy. Bukowski returned the admiration, writing to Packard: 'But I'll tell you, there have been three miracles in my life: *Loujon Press, The Black Sparrow Press* and *The New York Quarterly*.'[17]

In 1972 he and Linda King collaborated on a chapbook entitled *Me and Your Sometime Love Poems*. Bukowski illustrated it with his funny drawings and contributed eleven poems.[18] The romantic highs and lows of their affair continued, leading to constant break-ups and reconciliations. Their passionate love letters are replete with declarations of love and delight in sexual experimentation: Linda encouraged Bukowski to perfect his skills at oral sex. She had been working on a sculpture of Bukowski's head and during their arguments he would return the bust to her doorstep: it became a pawn in their battles. Yet Linda remained seduced by his energy, intensity and brilliance: 'he was very funny. He had a way of living, making each moment real. Sometimes he would be real stubborn and not talk at all, but for the most part, if you were around him, you felt this aliveness.'[19]

As their relationship became increasingly tempestuous, Bukowski became involved with another woman: Liza Williams worked in the entertainment business and wrote a column for the *Los Angeles Free Press*.[20] The director Taylor Hackford now began work on a Bukowski documentary for public television which recorded this developing triangular romantic melodrama. The one-hour black-and-white movie depicts Bukowski in his bungalow, going to the liquor store, recounting his time as a postal worker as well as his performance in San Francisco at the City Lights Poets Theatre, where on 4 September 1972, with much trepidation and after vomiting several times, he stepped out onto the stage to confront a huge and rowdy audience. He drank beer from a refrigerator located handily nearby and engaged in animated repartee with the overflow crowd. At the party following the reading in Ferlinghetti's apartment where Bukowski was staying, a violent fight erupted between Bukowski and Linda: the following morning, there was a section of a door kicked out, a broken window and the floor was strewn with empty bottles.[21]

During this period Bukowski met Robert Crumb at a party at Liza's house. Later Crumb would illustrate the stories *Bring Me Your Love* (1983), *There's No Business Like Show Business* (1984) as well as the posthumously published journal *The Captain is Out to Lunch and the Sailors Have Taken Over the Ship* (1998). In an interview, Crumb revealed that he admired Bukowski's writing and identified with his sense of 'alienation'.[22] Crumb's art catches exactly the German Expressionist extremity of emotion in Bukowski as well as his absurd humour, emphasizing through his wild caricatures the anxiety-ridden horror of life expressed in his desperate vision.

Mockingbird Wish Me Luck (1972) was Bukowski's first substantial poetry collection since *The Days Run Away* (1969) and contains early as well as more recent poems. 'consummation of grief' had originally appeared in *Sun*, no. 8 (1962) and is a melancholy poem containing an image of the slowness of time which will recur in the poem 'the crunch' in *Love is a Dog from Hell*: 'and the sadness becomes so great / I hear it in my clock . . . what counts / is waiting on walls / I was born for this / I was born to hustle roses down the avenues of the dead.'[23] This concluding line echoes the Mexican *dia de los muertos* invoked in Tennessee Williams's *A Streetcar Named Desire*. In Scene 9 of the play, a blind Mexican woman 'in a dark shroud' enters and cries repeatedly: 'Flores. Flores. Flores para los muertos. Flores. Flores.'[24] So too Bukowski's image unites flowers, death and avenues: it is his fate to 'hustle roses' through the moribund streets of the city.

The volume also contains several of Bukowski's best-known poems, including 'The Mockingbird' which culminates in the death throes of the bird caught by a cat:

> yesterday the cat walked calmly up the driveway
> with the mockingbird alive in its mouth,
> wings fanned, beautiful wings fanned and flopping,
> feathers parted like a woman's legs,
> and the bird was no longer mocking,
> it was asking, it was praying
> but the cat
> striding down through the centuries
> would not listen.[25]

The poem rewrites Robinson Jeffers's 'Hurt Hawks', which also spins long, precisely descriptive lines and connects death and femininity: 'The broken pillar of the wing jags from the clotted shoulder, / The wing trails like a banner in defeat . . . What fell was relaxed, / Owl-downy, soft feminine feathers; but what / Soared: the fierce rush . . .'.[26] Bukowski often grieved the death of animals he saw dead in the streets of Los Angeles: like Jeffers, he also believed humans were the inferior breed. In 'The Broken Balance', after describing hawk, weasel, heron and woodpecker, Jeffers contrasts animals with humans: 'These live their felt natures; / they know their norm / And live it to the brim; they understand life. / While men moulding themselves to the anthill have choked / Their natures until the souls die in them; / They have sold themselves for toys and protection: / No, but consider awhile: what else? Men sold for toys.'[27] The authentic person, however, defines him-/herself against this abdication of selfhood: they have not 'sold themselves for toys and protection', but rather they have what Bukowski called 'style', as he defines it in his famous poem: 'style is the answer to everything / a fresh way to approach a dull or a / dangerous thing . . . 6 herons standing quietly in a pool of water / or you walking out of the bathroom naked / without seeing / me'.[28] 'Style' is the mark of inventive originality, the refusal to become like everyone else, the determination to live life artistically and with 'class'.

'the shoelace', another well-known poem, argues that madness is caused not by a large tragedy but rather by a small piling up of trivial events which gradually becomes the proverbial 'straw that broke the camel's back'. The continuing barrage of life's irritations becomes comical: 'rickets or crickets or mice or termites or / roaches or flies or a / broken hook on a / screen, or out of gas / or too much gas'.[29] One recalls the funny sequence of surreal images in Bob Dylan's 'Subterranean Homesick Blues'.[30] Dylan breaks customary logic and links the quotidian with the larger world in a comical fashion. So does Bukowski: 'the sink's stopped-up, the landlord's drunk, / the president doesn't care and the governor's / crazy'. The hepped-up rhythms and repetitions create a ballad-like poem which connects the surreal lyricism of Dylan and Bukowski. The ending of the poem is typical Bukowski:

> with each broken shoelace
> out of one hundred broken shoelaces,
> one man, one woman, one
> thing

enters a
madhouse
so be careful
when you
bend over.[31]

The final joke is a frequent Bukowskian trick: writing a serious poem and then surprising the reader with an absurd or comic ending.

In the spring of 1972 the American short story writer Raymond Carver invited Bukowski to read in Santa Cruz. Carver's poem 'You Don't Know What Love Is' memorializes Bukowski's lively performance and rejoinders with the audience.[32] The two men drank all night and went to breakfast the next morning. Carver could not eat anything, so Bukowski ate his own breakfast as well as Carver's.[33] According to Carol Sklenicka, Carver saw Bukowski as one of his 'heroes' and both writers wrote about working-class life, alcoholism and created a pared-down, hammered-out, Hemingwayesque style.[34] But Bukowski remarked in an interview that 'I never got much out of Carver and still can't quite see what the fuss is all about.'[35]

Bukowski was excited by his next project; he wrote to Carl Weissner in February 1972: 'I'll try to get the City Lights book to you when it comes out. I do think the stories fouler (better) than Notes of a D.O Man. Instead of calling it Bukowskiana (not my idea), I have retitled it Erections, Ejaculations, Exhibitions and General Tales of Ordinary Madness. At the printer's now, says L.F. [Lawrence Ferlinghetti] He calls it a great book. I agree. I don't think that since Artaud or Nietzsche there has been anybody as joyfully mad as I am.'[36] *Erections, Ejaculations, Exhibitions and General Tales of Ordinary Madness* was published two months later in April, a titanic 478-page, 64-story collection of Bukowski's 'Dirty Old Man' columns for *Open City*, *NOLA Express* as well as work from *Knight, Adam, Pix* and *Evergreen Review*.[37] Many of the selections had no titles when they appeared in the 'Dirty Old Man' series so they were supplied by the editor, a practice later followed by John Martin in his collections of the columns. It was later divided into two separate volumes by City Lights: *Tales of Ordinary Madness* and *The Most Beautiful Woman in Town*.

The book continues Bukowski's practice of savaging his friends and acquaintances in a sharply satirical manner. One of the stories, 'The Birth, Life and Death of an Underground Newspaper' deeply offended John Bryan, for in it he becomes a witless 'Joe Hyans'. Bukowski describes the birth of *Open City*, the inception of his 'Dirty Old Man' column, police busts and the eventual demise of the paper, and brags 'my columns continued to be good, but the paper itself was half-ass'.[38] Another story – 'The Day We Talked About James Thurber' – takes Harold Norse as its target, portraying him as 'some great French poet who was now living in Venice, California'.[39] 'Andre' wrote 'his shitty little immortal poems and he had two or three sponsors who sent him money'.[40] Bukowski proceeds to make fun of Norse's relationship with the Beat Hotel in Paris: 'He knew Corso, Burroughs, Ginsberg, kaja. He knew all that early hotel gang who lived at the same place . . .'.[41]

The volume also contains several stories which cross into transgressive domains. 'The Fuck Machine' describes a device which provides ecstatic sexual experiences and explores the Baudrillardian concept of virtual versus 'real' reality which would inform many Bukowski stories: the men prefer the machine woman to a real one.[42] 'The Fiend' portrays the middle-aged Martin Blanchard's rape of a small girl. The violation is graphically described, and at the close Blanchard turns himself in to the police. The story created a scandal: Bukowski defended himself saying that his job as a writer was to 'photograph' reality and that the role of writer and moralist were separate categories.[43] 'The Copulating Mermaid of Venice, Calif.' involves necrophilia, again charting the liminal territory beween fantasy/real relationships which would preoccupy

Bukowski as he examined the complexities of sexual longing and frustration.[44] Several stories and essays in the book continue his exploration of the counterculture. In 'The Big Pot Game', he pokes fun at both the supposed 'new' language of the hippies – 'groovy', 'man', 'like it is', 'the scene', 'cool' – which was not new to him since he says he heard it first in 1932 at the age of twelve, and sarcastically observes 'in the 1830's Gautier's pot parties and sex-orgy parties were the talk of Paris. That Gautier wrote poetry on the side was also known. Now his parties are better remembered.' Lester Bangs, the noted rock journalist, wrote in his review for *Creem*: 'what I principally admire Bukowski for is his prose. It's spare, to the point, dirty, abusive, violent and self-mocking.'[45]

Bukowski was awarded a grant from the National Endowment for the Arts from 1 June 1973 to 31 May 1974: he had applied several times for various fellowships – including a Guggenheim – but had been turned down, so this was a welcome development. In July 1973 he went with Linda King to Utah on the annual trip to her home state which he humorously documented in *Women*. Bukowski the city man had particular trouble navigating the forests and mountains: he got lost and required Linda to help him find his way out.[46] From February to July Bukowski moved to 2440 Edgewater Terrace with Linda. In August they separated and he moved to 151 S Oxford Avenue, #24, a modern, sterile, claustrophic apartment building which he loathed.[47] A sign of Bukowski's increasing fame was the broadcast on 26 November 1973, of Taylor Hackford's documentary *Bukowski* on Channel 28, the Los Angeles public broadcasting station KCET. The film had been screened a month earlier on 19 October 1973 at the Barnsdell Park Arts Center.[48]

On 17 December 1973 Black Sparrow Press published *South of No North*, a collection of 27 stories including his columns for the *Los Angeles Free Press* as well as the longer works previously published by Doug Blazek, *Confessions of a Man Insane Enough to Live with Beasts* (1965) and *All the Assholes in the World and Mine* (1966).

Sections from his abandoned novel *The Way the Dead Love* were also published. The title *South of No North* suggests the direction-lessness of many of his characters: they have no way to orient themselves. As in post-structural thought, there is no connection between the signifier and an absent signified while humans are merely counters in a system of supposedly stable meaning which is constantly dissolving into nothingness. As he wrote in a 6 February 1979 letter to Carl Weissner: 'Shit, my characters seldom evolve. They are too fucked up. They can't even type. I like to let it go free and sometimes there is nothing to explain about them, they are just jagged edges of something.'[49]

In one story, 'No Way to Paradise', miniaturized men are used by a woman as a means of sexual satisfaction.[50] Bukowski, like Krafft-Ebing, gives us a kind of *Psychopathia Sexualis* and many of the stories veer into the fantastic, into Lacan's 'the Real'. As in one of the episodes in Rod Serling's thoughtful science fiction television series *The Twilight Zone* in which an attractive woman is found at the end to be a robot, there is often a moral at the end of these fantastic allegories in which reality is found to be replaced by a weird simulacra of itself. Bukowski was again exploring territory similar to Jean Baudrillard, who also saw 'virtual reality' replacing conventional 'reality'. As Vladimir Nabokov once wrote, 'reality' is a word which must always have quotation marks around it.

Bukowski also returned to his engagement with literary precursors. 'Class' depicts a fight with Hemingway and may be compared with the story 'The Night Nobody Believed I Was Allen Ginsberg' in which Ginsberg is comically invoked. Bukowski sometimes engages in a version of Harold Bloomian *agon* with his 'strong' predecessors or contemporaries: Hemingway as his prose rival and Ginsberg as his competitor in poetry.[51] He names them, pulls them into his humorous narratives in order to at once admit yet defuse the rivalry by sending it up in a tongue-in-cheek way. Another story, 'Bop Bop Against that Curtain', describes the burlesque shows Bukowski attended as an adolescent, while 'This is What Killed Dylan Thomas' recounts his trip to San Francisco and his sudden thrust into the limelight.[52] Chinaski is now worried he will be destroyed by success. On the plane towards San Francisco, 'the drinks arrived. I had poetry, and a fine woman. Life was picking up. But the traps, Chinaski, watch the traps. You fought a long fight to put the word down the way you wanted. Don't let a little adulation and a movie camera pull you out of position. Remember what Jeffers said – even the strongest men can be trapped, like God when he once walked the earth.' The allusion is to Jeffers's poem 'Shine, Perishing Republic': 'There is the trap that catches noblest spirits, that caught – they say – God, / when he walked on earth.'[53] The story derives its title from Kenneth Rexroth's well-known poem about the death of Dylan Thomas entitled 'Thou Shalt Not Kill' (1953) in which Rexroth indicts society for the death of the great Welsh poet: 'And all the birds of the deep sea rise up / Over the luxury liners and scream, / "You killed him! You killed him. / In your Goddamned Brooks Brothers suits, / You son of a bitch."'[54] So too Bukowski imagines his own death, but rather ironically following his poetry reading at the hands of American 'success': 'Well, it was over. They came around. Autographs. They'd come from Oregon, L.A., Washington. Nice pretty girls too. This is what killed Dylan Thomas.'[55]

Bukowski was able to move out of his dreaded apartment on Oxford Avenue in June 1974. He found another place 'just off of Hollywood and Western' on Carlton Way near his old apartment on De Longpre in East Hollywood which was suitably déclassé, as he tells us in one of his 'Dirty Old Man' columns: 'It is my kind of neighborhood – massage parlors and love parlors are everywhere; taco stands, pizza parlors, sandwich shops . . . whores night and day; black pimps in broad hats with their razor-sharp noses . . .'.[56] Although Charles Baudelaire was not among Bukowski's favourite poets, it is clear that the American Charles found the philosophy of

Bukowski at Carlton Way, 1976.

Les Fleurs du mal congenial. Here he had his books, his magazines, his shelves full of his own publications, his writing table under which he kept barbells to do periodic exercising.[57] His favourite liquor store, the Pink Elephant, was nearby.

He became friendly with his neighbours Brad and Tina Darby: Brad was the owner of a porn shop while Tina danced as a stripper. The two appear in several of Bukowski's works, including the story 'The Ladies Man of East Hollywood' in which Brad is portrayed as 'Tod', a compulsive womanizer, while the Bukowski character observes him with a combination of envy and disgust.[58] Tod's perpetual sexual romping meets a bad end. Again, we are reminded that Bukowski referred to himself as a 'Puritan' and that for all his attempts to do so, he found it difficult to disassociate sexual passion from deeper feeling – hence the narrator's disapproval of Tod's 'swinging' behaviour.[59] And for the romantic Bukowski, the aftermath of his love affair with Linda King was bleak. He wrote to Ann Menebroker on 28 June 1974: 'I don't know if I ever want to get back into a strong affair again. I am too emotional; when the games begin – the hard games men and women play against each other, I am lost.'[60]

On 25 November 1974, Bukowski read in Santa Cruz with Ferlinghetti, Snyder and Ginsberg. The event was memorialized by Ric Reynolds who described Bukowski's drunken encounter with the author of 'Howl' at a party:

A man of genius, the first poet to cut through light and consciousness for two thousand years and these bastards don't even appreciate it. Have a drink Allen . . . God, it's good to see you Allen, really. I don't care if you are a fake. Did you hear that folks? Washed up. Everybody knows that after *Howl* you never wrote anything worth a shit. How about that folks, a vote. Has Allen written anything worth a shit since *Howl* and *Kay'dish*?[61]

The *Berkeley Barb*, xx/21 (6–12 December 1974).

In vino veritas. It is a humorous moment, yet also fraught as Ginsberg then attempts to correct Bukowski's pronunciation: 'Kah'dish'.[62] It is clear that Bukowski was now feeling his oats, strutting his stuff with the big boys and enjoying himself immensely in his chosen role of *enfant terrible*.

Due to his increasing notoriety, during the 1970s he began to give more interviews and revealed various aspects of his methods of composition. Writing was for him a kind of ritual accompanied by four necessary accessories: alcohol, classical music, the sound of the typewriter, tobacco. He described the act of writing as a kind of seizure:

I feel a tightness . . . Actually, I feel bad – like I'm about to get into a fight, sort of. Then I play footsy with the goddamn chair and typewriter and table. Finally, I sit down, drawn to the machine as if by a magnet, against my will. There's absolutely no plan to it. It's just me, the typewriter and the chair. And I always throw the first draft away, saying 'that's no good!' Then I enter into the act with a kind of fury, writing madly for four, five, even eight hours. Next day I'll write for two or three. Then I'm spent and exhausted and won't touch the typewriter again for at least a week, when the whole cycle starts over.[63]

He also describes this trance-like state in the poem 'room service'. His lady enters the room as he is typing. He leaps up from his chair and screams as she hands him a snack on a plate. He thanks her but confesses her intrusion has thoroughly frightened him: 'you know, / when I'm at this / typer / I'm gone / around / some corner'.[64]

Bukowski's reputation in Germany expanded during this period. Benno Kasmyr published *Gedichte die einer schrieb bevor er im 8. Stockwerk aus dem Fenster sprang* in April 1974: it sold 50,000 copies, which was unprecedented for a book of poetry.[65] This was the key moment in Bukowski's breakthrough in Europe. Weissner attributes his success to the fact that young people were weary of the primarily political focus of contemporary German literature and found in Bukowski the direct, honest, hip, personal voice they were seeking. *Stories und Romane* – known in Germany as 'The Blue Book' because of its dark blue cover graced with a portrait of Bukowski by Robert Crumb – would appear three years later in 1977, containing *South of No North, Factotum, Notes of a Dirty Old Man* and *Post Office*, and sold nearly 100,000 copies.[66] This pattern of substantive fame and royalties in Europe accompanied by lesser visibility in America would continue over the years.

Burning in Water, Drowning in Flame appeared in June 1974, a retrospective volume containing major selections from *It*

Bukowski's Olympia SG-1 typewriter which he used 1975–83.

Catches, Crucifix, At Terror Street as well as new poems from
1972–3 such as 'on the circuit', describing his violent fight with
Linda King at the San Francisco reading, and 'out of the arms',
hymning his merry-go-round-like romantic life.[67] 'we the artists'
tells the story of an 80-year-old landlady Bukowski encountered
during the early 1940s in San Francisco who is named 'Mama
Fazzio' in a wonderful story from 1968. Indeed, poem and story
were frequently connected in Bukowski's vast autobiographical
oeuvre and he would reuse the same plot in both genres. As he
told Douglas Howard in 1975: 'Yeah, I get my natural kicks writing
short stories, a relaxer; then I go back to the poem; I jump back
and forth. One helps the other.'[68] He claimed that the difference
between the two genres was that the stories required little revision:
'they just come straight on out. I'll change a word or two that's
awkward. I revise poems much more. Stories, they just come out.'[69]

In 1975 Bukowski's second novel *Factotum* was published. The composition was laborious: it required four years, while *Post Office* sprang forth in just nineteen days. *Factotum* was inspired by both Knut Hamsun and George Orwell. In an interview Bukowski revealed: 'I got the idea, kind of, from *Down and Out in Paris and London*. Ran into it by accident. I read that book and said, "This guy thinks something has happened to him? Compared to me, he just got scratched." Not that it wasn't a good book, but it made me think I might have something interesting to say along those same lines.'[70] The novel opens with Chinaski's arrival in New Orleans carrying 'a cardboard suitcase that was falling apart', which alludes to Hamsun.[71] He is accosted by 'a high yellow' woman: '*Hey, poor white trash!*' She mocks him as he observes her: 'she had her legs crossed high and she kicked her feet; she had nice legs, high heels, and she kicked her legs and laughed.' He begins to approach to investigate her sexual offer but upon seeing a black man's face behind the curtain, he 'backed down the pathway to the sidewalk'.[72] This opening scene unfolds the entire novel in microcosm: the poor labourer who goes from city to city, sometimes accepting sexual provender if it appears, at the lowest rung of the social hierarchy, navigating each existential choice as he attempts to survive.

After wandering the country, he returns to his parents in Los Angeles, then moves out. His next trip is to New York City as he crisscrosses the country: New Orleans, LA, New York, Philadelphia, St Louis, LA, Miami. Bukowski again takes the elements of his life and transforms them for his autobiographical fiction. His jobs are meaningless: dog biscuit factory, putting posters on subways, shipping clerk in a ladies' dresswear shop, auto parts warehouse, fluorescent light fixture company, an automobile brake parts company, the 'Coconut Man' in a baking shop, a store specializing in Christmas items such as 'lights, wreaths, Santa Clauses, paper trees'.[73] The tasks are absurd: each worker is locked Sisyphus-like into a tiny niche performing mechanical actions unconnected to any deeper significance. Chinaski's one sure escape, as always, is alcohol: 'So I stayed in bed and drank. When you drank the world was still out there, but for the moment it didn't have you by the throat.'[74] Galen Strawson makes an astute comment on Bukowski's style: 'Sometimes it seems just too mannered in its bluntness. But it's also funny and sharp, observant, clever with details, and honest. When Bukowski describes someone, one's sure he's seen that person.'[75] Richard Elman in the *New York Times Book Review* wrote: 'A few years back in more prosperous times Bukowski may have passed for a crank. With a sizable percentage of the population more or less permanently unemployed he seems more like a prophet . . . Not since Orwell has the condition of being down and out been so well recorded in the first person.'[76]

Bukowski's romantic life continued on its roller-coaster course when on 10 November 1975, a young woman named Pamela Miller arrived on the scene. She had a friend named Georgia Peckham-Krellner who was a Bukowski fan. Since it was Georgia's birthday, Pamela conceived the notion of telephoning him to see whether she and her friend could visit. At 2 a.m. she found his name in the phone book, called, and thus began the affair Bukowski would memorialize in his short story 'Workout' (1977) in which Pamela becomes 'Nina':

Nina was 24, small, but with a near-perfect body and long hair that was the purest of reds. She had gone the route: borne a child at 16, then had two abortions, a marriage, a slight run at prostitution. Barmaid jobs, shackjobs, benefactors, unemployment insurance, and food stamps had held her together. But then she had a great deal left: that body, humor, madness, and cruelty . . . Nina was a rifleshot into the brain of the psyche: she could kill any man she wanted to. She had almost killed me. But so had some others.

The story depicts a triangular relationship between the narrator, Nina and Karyn, and the inevitable break-up of the affair.[77] As he would cynically (or realistically) declare in John Dullaghan's documentary *Born into This*: 'Love is a fog that burns with the first daylight of reality.'

The following year, in 1976, Bukowski met Linda Lee Beighle. Born near Philadelphia in 1944, she had run away from home and was active in the counterculture. She admired his work and had been to several of his readings when she came to see him at the Troubadour on 29 September 1976. He called her a few days later and visited her at her health food restaurant the Dew Drop Inn, where she 'made him an avocado melt and a smoothie'.[78] She was deeply involved in spiritual matters, had travelled to India and was a follower of the guru Meher Baba, becoming particularly committed to the plight of the Tibetans. She responded to 'the deeply philosophical Bukowski . . . he would talk about the inner world, spiritual things, sometimes for hours'.[79] Linda persuaded him to switch from beer to good wine and to improve his diet through vitamins and health foods. He ate less red meat, began to enjoy crab and lobster more often instead of Pioneer Fried Chicken, fried steak and fried eggs.[80] Bukowski had been drinking heavily during this period. The poem '240 pounds' memorably describes his titanic intake of beer, wine, vodka, Scotch, whiskey and gin, his belly hanging over the belt which cut into his flesh, his fattened face, red eyes and pitted, unhealthy skin.[81] Linda arrived just in the nick of time.

In October 1976 he gave a poetry reading in Vancouver, and began an affair with a woman named Jane Manhattan (who would become 'Iris Hall' in *Women*) who said of him: 'He was funny all day every day. A great love of life, and an enjoyment – always to be seeing the funny thing, and making a comment. He was a comedian.'[82] One is reminded that Franz Kafka – usually imagined as a rather lugubrious writer – was said to have been quite entertaining in

Apo 29, 1975

Hello Nancy:

    you really react to some of my poems.

     but you see, I write ####poems about men and women and
me and things and sometimes something is recorded, and I often
come out short... dwarfed, frizzled...myself. it's all in the
matter.

     I think the women might become truly liberated if they realize
that some women can be shits, at times, just as some men can be.
to simply defend women as women,no matter, that can only be
self-defeating. and you know this.

     I'm no woman-hater. They've given me more highs and magics
than anything else. but I'm also a writer, sometimes. and
there are variances in all things.

     good symphony music on tonight. drinking beer, smoking
these little imported cigars some good soul sent me through
the mail. many people are good to me. they mail me things.
cookies, yeah. photos. sounds. drawings. many hate me.
but there are some out there who know that I'm truly some kind
of simple soul caught in a wild gamble. they know me. they
know that I sit between these walls. they know I've been burned.
and that I still laugh. and send out my little #####messages.
and they prefer Bukowski to Mailer because Bukowski is not a
professional anything.

     I'm glad you still like me. it's all in the matter. like
being able to tell hatred from photography.

XO

Letter to Nancy Flynn, 1975.

Bukowski with Linda Lee, 1977.

person. So too, Bukowski, although his work often sounds the *de profundis clamavi* note. In addition to his romantic successes, Bukowski achieved a major national breakthrough with a long interview in *Rolling Stone* magazine. He was also visited during this time by Joan Levine Gannij who took a sequence of photographs of him standing by his refrigerator, beer bottle in hand, with Georgia Peckham-Krellner, the friend of Pamela Miller. They were published, as well as others taken during this session, as *The Cruelty of Loveless Love* (the title is from Bukowski's poem 'Carson McCullers': 'all her books of / terrified loneliness / all her books about / the cruelty / of loveless love') in a lavish edition by Kunst Editions in New York in 2001.[83] Photography began to play an increasing role in the marketing of Bukowski: the German Michael Montfort began to regularly take pictures of him, Gerard Malanga included his portrait of Bukowski in his book *Screen Tests* and of course Robert Crumb's brilliant drawings helped promote the 'Bukowski brand' worldwide.

Bukowski began to enjoy the jet travel that went along with his national poetry performances. He wrote to Jojo Planteen on 19 March 1976: 'Just back from Univ. of Pitt. Reading in New York June 23, San Fran on Nov. 19. Survival process.'[84] He wrote to Joan Jobe Smith about 'a gig in Pitt[sburgh] for one grand plus air [fare]. Luckily, I was on and the crowd response was high-pitched and continuous . . . one of my better warblings. Next stops Tallahassee, Iowa City and N.Y. City . . . the best part about readings is FLYING there and back, stoking up on vodka 7's and living in old hotels, new motels . . . free ice and morning madness. Maybe I'm a fucking trouper after all. I just lift a beer bottle and the crowd goes crazy.' At this University of Pittsburgh reading, the singer Tom Waits had been the opening performer on the evenings of 12 and 13 March. A wild, hilarious and sexually explicit short story, 'The Big Dope Reading', in which a drunken and marijuanaed Chinaski frolics with Holly, Kali, Alacia and Zana, memorializes a reading in Florida.[85]

Bukowski with his daughter Marina at Venice Beach, 1977.

His next book, the poetry collection *Love Is a Dog from Hell*
(1977) marks a critical juncture in Bukowski's poetic development.
It chronicles his erotic adventures during this period, in particular
with the bosomy Pamela Miller (whom he nicknamed 'Cupcakes',
apparently due to her bountiful *poitrine*). He is at his most raw
and tormented in his cycle of poems about their affair, which had
previously been published as a separate collection entitled *Scarlet*
(1976).[86] In the copy of *Scarlet* he dedicated to Pamela he wrote:
'For the girl who made me write these poems, for the girl who
made me feel that feeling which comes so seldom in a lifetime.'[87]
The spirit of Catullus' great distich, poem 85, hovers over the
volume: '*Odi et amo. quare id faciam, fortasse requiris? / nescio, sed*

fieri sentio et excrucior.' 'I hate and I love. You wonder, perhaps, why I'd do that? / I have no idea. I just feel it. I am crucified.'[88] Bukowski was re-reading Catullus during this period. In a letter to John Martin of 22 January 1976, he asked: 'Have you ever read Catullus? There's a translation by Carl Sesar via Mason & Lipscomb, seems full of butter, fire and laughter. Too bad Cat seemed to have drifted off into homosexuality. That may be a standard literary trait but it always discourages me. Anyhow, he could lay down a line, and he was dead around the age of 30.'[89] Bukowski responded to Catullus' absolute directness and hip contemporaneity: 'Yeah, that Catullus was too much. He was more modern then than the moderns now.'[90] He describes the symptoms of Catullan desolation in 'the crunch': 'there is a loneliness in this world so great / that you can see it in the slow movement of / the hands of a clock / people so tired / mutilated / either by love or no love. / people just are not good to each other / one on one . . . or the terror of one person / aching in one place / alone / untouched / unspoken to'.[91] The *rallentando* of 'in the slow movement' followed by the dragging anapaests of 'of the hands of a clock' mirrors time's stillness during the anguish of love's dark night of the soul, while the line 'people just are not good to each other' recurs as a haunting refrain.

In early 1977 Bukowski's life began to move into yet another direction. Linda Lee recalls:

> Hank got a call from Barbet Schroeder asking if he could come over and talk to him about writing a screenplay. Hank said, 'Oh maaan, that's not my thing. I gotta go to the track, write my poems. You do a movie, you get everybody else's hands in there, it ends up it's not your writing any more.' But Barbet came, they hung out and talked. He was a great storyteller who'd had some unbelievable experiences in life, and he talked Hank into it. And once Hank made a commitment, he was true to Barbet: he had great loyalty that way.[92]

Schroeder (*b*. 1941), a former assistant to Jean-Luc Godard, contacted Bukowski because he admired his writing: thus began a long and arduous process to make a film based on his life, culminating ten years later in the movie *Barfly*.

Bukowski also began work on a manuscript originally titled *Love Tale of a Hyena* (it would retain this title in the German edition: *Das Liebesleben der Hyaene*). The name was changed to *Women* and the novel was published on 15 December 1978, in an edition of 7,257 copies.[93] *Women* is a prose companion volume to *Love is a Dog from Hell*, returning to similar themes and dramatis personae. Many of the women with whom Bukowski had relationships during this period found their way directly into the novel. Linda King is Lydia Vance; Pamela O'Brien is Tammie; Liza Williams is Dee Dee; Linda Lee is Sara; Amber O'Neill is Tanya; Joanna Bull is Mercedes; Ruth Wantling is Cecilia; Jane Manhattan is Iris Hall. Bukowski had read Boccaccio's *Decameron* and he often remarked that he wanted to duplicate the author's vision of love and sex as ridiculous.[94] There are no other major male characters, thus focusing the entire narrative on Henry Chinaski's erotic mayhem. It is finely balanced, veering between absurd humour and profound anguish.

Bukowski's excitement over the composition of *Women* is apparent in his urgency to see it appear in print: in a letter to John Martin he complained about delays in publication. Bukowski was joyous about what he had accomplished. As he wrote Martin: '*Women* is my proudest and best book . . . I await *Women* unlike I've ever awaited any other book. As I wrote it I could feel it happening – that certain carving into the page with certain words in a way that you feel the power and the magic and the luck.'[95] He had achieved a tight unity of form and content through an episodic structure and created a sustained, hard, mad, tragic comedy. He also foregrounded sex more intensely than previously: the mechanical repetetiveness of work and jobs in *Post Office* and *Factotum* was now replaced by a constant merry-go-round of women available for sex. Bukowski seemed to want to live purposely on the edge, perhaps to gather material for his writing but also because he knew no other way to live than instinctively, violently, passionately, even if it led him into the labyrinth. As he acknowledged in two letters in 1972: 'my energy is going where my feelings are'; and 'You know, the writing must come out of the living, the reaction to living. If I get a little scorched now and then, it's for the good of the barbecue.'[96] John Thomas reports that Bukowski 'would say that great creative genius had some kind of positive connection to cowardice and fear. And that brave men were stupid men . . . This was something he liked in Céline: Céline's fears, his terrors. And there was some remark Céline made, I forget where: "You can't be frightened enough."'[97] Indeed, any pretensions of Chinaski to triumphant, phallic malehood are deflated since during his many beddings of women he is frequently unable to achieve an erection and he constantly exposes his fear, vulnerability and impotence: he is often too drunk to perform.

Yet there is something Dionysian and ritualistic about *Women*, about Chinaski always prepared with his beer, Scotch or bottle of wine, the sequence of events rhythmically and hypnotically repeated, awaiting with fear and trembling anticipation the arrival of the next female. As Walter Burkert wrote: 'Ritual is something atavistic, compulsive, nonsensical, at best circumstantial and superfluous. But at the same time something sacred and mysterious.'[98] Bukowski synthesizes here the Dionysian themes of passion and irrationality which he had begun to explore more intensely in the 1960s. Indeed, the ancient Greek god seems to form a constant point of conscious and unconscious reference for him, symbolizing connections between sexuality, alcohol, blood, madness and the life force. Burkert observes that 'the association of wine and blood, with wine being described as the blood of the vine, is ancient and widespread.'[99] Chinaski in many ways incarnates (in an often weary and comical way) the Dionysian elemental attitude towards the universe of archaic man.

The addictive nature of his sexual compulsions – in obvious ways the complement to his love of drink – is suggested by the novel's ending. He has just answered the phone and hung up on a girl named Rochelle who identifies herself as 'a cute chick'. He congratulates himself on his precarious strength to resist her charms and not give in to temptation: 'I hung up. There I had done it – that time.' And the novel closes:

I walked into the kitchen, opened a bottle of vitamin E, 400 I.U. each, and downed several with half a glass of Perrier water. It was going to be a good night for Chinaski. The sun was slanting down through the venetian blinds, making a familiar pattern on the carpet, and the white wine was chilling in the refrigerator.

I opened the door and walked out on the porch. There was a strange cat out there. He was a huge creature, a tom, with a shining black coat and luminous yellow eyes. He wasn't frightened of me. He walked up purring and rubbed against one of my legs. I was a good guy and he knew it. Animals knew things like that. They had an instinct. I walked back inside and he followed me.

I opened him up a can of Star-Kist solid white tuna. Packed in spring water. Net wt. 7 oz.[100]

It is a brilliant ending, with the emphasis on the amounts of 'individual units' in the vitamin E and the weight of the tuna can, hopefully anchoring the fragile Chinaski in the mathematical facts of daily life and his touching encounter with his doppelgänger – a tomcat.

Bukowski had been invited by the Hamburg poet Christoph Derschau to give a reading in Germany and he wrote to Carl Weissner on 22 February 1978 about his upcoming trip:

Linda Lee and I will be leaving L.A. May 8th at 8:15 p.m. and will arrive at Frankfurt May 9th at 3:20 p.m . . . I think one reading is enough. Linda Lee says she looks forward to meeting you. There are some changes. We are off the beer, just drink wine, German, mostly white and only eat fish and poultry, no red meat. I have come down from 223 pounds to 196 but drink more than ever. We should try to slow down just a bit in Germany, though.[101]

Michael Montfort, who had been photographing Bukowski for several years, proposed that they do a book together about his European trip which would become *Shakespeare Never Did This*. Bukowski was astonished to find his audience of 1,200 people at the Markthalle in Hamburg (many were turned away and just 300 had showed up a few months previously to hear Günter Grass) responding to him in the most intense way for the first time.[102] In Germany he and Linda, accompanied by Montfort, went to Heidelberg, Mannheim, Hamburg and Andernach but Bukowski had little interest in castles, museums, cathedrals, mountains, lakes and forests: he preferred remaining indoors with large quantities of German red or white wine.

He and Linda returned to Paris in November 1978 to appear on the famous French literary talk show *Apostrophes* hosted by Bernard Pivot – the topic was 'Writers on the Margin' and the event became a *succès de scandale*.[103] His fellow panelists were Gaston Ferdière, the psychiatrist of Artaud; the writer Catherine Paysan; and François Cavanna, editor of *Charlie Hebdo*. Bukowski drank several bottles of wine and was clearly uncomfortable with the pretentious proceedings. The proper Pivot was unable to control his barbaric American guest, and Bukowski ended up leaving the stage. Afterwards, he pulled his knife on a security guard.[104] The next day, the reviews of his appearance were laudatory. Bukowski's books flew off the shelves of French bookshops and when he travelled to Nice the next day with Linda, a group of six waiters acknowledged his heroic status by lining up and simultaneously bowing to him.[105]

Bukowski on the French TV programme *Apostrophes*, 1978.

His trip was an unqualified success, but later he would have one regret. Bukowski recalled: 'And the saddest thought of all, when I was in Paris and Sartre sent word that he'd like to meet me and I said, no. Horrible, horrible, horrible . . .'.[106] But back in America things were not looking horrible as Bukowski's situation began to markedly improve. His publisher City Lights received $44,000 for the rights to film stories from *Erections* – later to become *Tales of Ordinary Madness*.[107] He was doing so well financially that he was advised to make some major purchases to offset the taxes he would be required to pay. He and Linda began to look for houses in Topanga Canyon and as far north out of Los Angeles as Bakersfield, and decided finally on the harbour town of San Pedro: in October they bought a house and moved in November 1978.[108]

6

Turning Sixty in San Pedro: 1979–1986

As Bukowski began his new life in San Pedro, he turned a small room on the second floor overlooking the harbour into a studio and installed the essential paraphernalia for his nightly writing ritual: radio tuned to classical music; wine bottle and glass next to the typewriter (later, in December 1990, he switched to a word processor); a supply of Mangalore Ganesh beedies – the Indian cigarettes rolled by lepers of which he had become fond because, he said, 'they contain no chemicals and no nicotine, and they go very well with red wine'; ashtray; photographs of a German First World War Fokker triplane and Louis-Ferdinand Céline on the wall.[1] The former owners of the house had left behind a lucky piece of furniture, as he would note in his novel *Hollywood*: 'there was an old desk left in there, a huge ugly old thing. Now, after decades, I was a writer with a desk.'[2] He kept his working area in disarray: a messy crucible which replicated the many dishevelled rooms in which he had composed over the past three and a half decades. Typically Bukowski would write from 10 p.m. to 2 a.m. with several cats roaming the house or sitting at his feet. He continued to be prolific, shifting constantly between story, poem, novel and essay.

As we have noted, due to his increasing financial success, Bukowski was advised to make some major purchases in order to minimize his tax liability. In June 1979 he entered a BMW dealership: the salesman ignored his unprepossessing client, but Bukowski surprised him by paying $16,000 cash for a black BMW 320i.[3] He also began to drink finer quality wines: over the next several years his work began to contain references to German Bernkasteler Riesling, Cabernet, Concannon Petite Sirah and Côte de Nuits-Villages Louis Jadot.[4] His poetry recorded the incongruity of his present lifestyle. In 'the recess bells of school', he describes his presumably regular, stable, affluent present circumstances: 'I telephone plumbers and lawyers, / I get towed in from freeway breakdowns, / I get my teeth cleaned . . .'. But even though one might assume that he has left his tormented past behind, he concludes that 'everywhere / it's all the same'.[5] He has merely exchanged one absurdity for another; now it is just a higher class of pointlessness. But he had evolved an enjoyable modus vivendi: he would typically rise late in the morning and head to the track where his car was valet parked. He would return and eat with Linda (occasionally they would dine at the famed Hollywood restaurant Musso and Frank's), spend time in the jacuzzi, watch some television and then retreat upstairs to write.

The horse races at Santa Anita, Del Mar and Hollywood Park continued to be a *sine qua non*. He had told John Thomas in the 1960s that he dreamed one day he might be able 'to play the horses in the day time and write at night! To make it both ways! I think it can be done! Man, I'd be like an electric current, baby, Jesus!'[6] His fantasy had come true: he was now a gambler by day and a literary man by night. Bukowski gave some advice to neophyte horse race enthusiasts in his 1975 essay 'Picking the Horses: How to Win at the Track or at Least Break Even':

First let's begin with some don'ts:
Mental clarity is a must. Don't arrive at the races after fighting last-minute traffic. Either arrive early and settle down easily to your business or arrive around the second or third or fourth races. Get yourself a cup of coffee, sit down and inhale and exhale a few times. Realize that you're at no dreamland, that no money

Bukowski's hands holding a racing form, 1982.

is being given away and that beating the horses is an art and that there are very few artists around.

Bukowski was constantly evolving new, complex systems of betting which he took quite seriously and elaborated with the mathematical precision and intensity of an earnest cosmologist explaining his latest theory concerning the origin of the universe.

Using his black felt-tip pen, he would cover his racing form with abstruse markings and symbols.[7] He required peace and quiet to concentrate: he was resentful if fans would come up and disturb him while he was absorbed in the race. Bukowski was an irreligious man, and the racetrack continued to be his substitute temple – the place where he could feed his muse, observe humanity at its lowest common denominator worst, and thus reacquaint himself with the brutal facts of reality and return prepared to tell the truth at his typewriter.

Bukowski began to tackle new genres as he entered his final creative phases, including a travel book, detective novel and journal. *Shakespeare Never Did This* (1979) is a swiftly paced travelogue composed of 25 sections in which Bukowski telescopes his two trips in May 1978 to Germany and the October trip to Paris for his appearance on *Apostrophes*. The volume is illustrated with photographs by Michael Montfort who had become a close friend.[8] When he visited tourist spots, his reactions were typically contrarian. In section 21 he writes that the cathedral in Köln

almost made me wish I could accept the Christian God instead of my tiny 17 gods of protection because one big God would have helped me through a lot of muck and terror and pain and horror, it would have been easier and maybe even more sensible . . . I was not a thinking man, I went by what I felt and my feelings went to the crippled, the tortured, the damned and the lost, not out of sympathy but out of brotherhood because I was one of them, lost, confused, indecent, petty, fearful and cowardly; unjust, and kind only in small flashes and even though I was fucked-over, knowing it didn't help, it didn't cure it, it only solidified it.

The Big God just had too many guns for me. He was too right and too powerful.[9]

Bukowski and Michael Montfort, 1980s.

The 'gods' – here 'my tiny 17 gods of protection' – are for Bukowski analogous to the ancient Greek pantheon – symbols of internal psychological and external natural forces – as well as the Romans' *Lares et Penates*, the household gods of protection. The 'righteous', punishing, savage, jealous, annihilating, judgmental, vengeful, terrible Judaeo-Christian 'Big God' was too similar to the monstrous father Bukowski had spent his life attempting to forget. In Bukowski's universe, God the Powerful Father was to be avoided rather than worshipped.

Bukowski's life would take yet another unexpected turn as he entered the world of Hollywood. Barbet Schroeder, who had first contacted Bukowski in 1977, convinced him to write an autobiographical screenplay and, early in 1979, he began work on *The Rats of Thirst*, later entitled *Barfly*.[10] In a letter to Hank Malone on 15 October 1979 he reported: 'Finished a screenplay called *Barfly* for Barbet Schroeder and he claims he's going to do it, although at the moment he's only pulled in $200,000 for production and it takes maybe 5 times that but he's good at that sort of thing.'[11] As he worked on the script, Bukowski asked John Fante for advice, who responded on 6 February 1979:

> Your French director who stands over your shoulder measuring the screenplay at one minute per page sounds like a kook to me. It seems to me that subject matter determines style and time. Maybe you might want to break some rules . . . You need limitless horizons and distances. You cannot be bound by the Frenchman's rules. You are the writer, so write a unique, an unorthodox screenplay.[12]

Bukowski returned to his life at the famous bar in Philadelphia in the 1940s and his subsequent meeting with Jane in Los Angeles for material, thus telescoping two periods of his life. As we have seen, there is no evidence that he ever read Bertolt Brecht's early play *Baal* (1919) but *Barfly* also features a drinking, philosophizing, lyrical and sexually voracious poet with a marked *nostalgie de la boue*.[13]

Published in 1979, *Play the Piano Drunk Like a Percussion Instrument until the Fingers Begin to Bleed a Bit* is the shortest of his major collections. '40,000 flies', another poem about writing a poem, teases about the ease of inventing imaginative lines and concludes: 'it's so easy to be a poet / and so hard to be / a man'.[14] We can hear an echo of Pablo Neruda's 'Walking Around': 'I'm tired of being a man.'[15] Although Bukowski did not speak of Neruda as an influence, it is probable that he found his long, rich, surreal lines, surprising metaphors and Whitmanian lists appealing. Neeli Cherkovski remembered Bukowski's excitement when Neruda won the Nobel Prize in literature. 'Outside of myself, I don't know anyone with such a clean line. When he says "blue" he means blue. The problem is when he becomes political. That is his weakness.'[16]

In an interview in 1975, Ben Pleasants asked Bukowski whether 'a writer can be political and artistic at the same time' and received this response:

Bukowski: I was going to answer that Neruda got away with it.
Also, there was this guy in Germany who wrote the song
'Mack the Knife.' I've heard his stuff over the radio. He has
such a powerful clean line, and he's talking about things that
are happening during the day: it gets very good and then he
throws in, can I say, Marxist lines, and it just deadens me. I say,
why did he do that?

Pleasants: Because he's a Marxist.

Bukowski: It's like a guy with one ball, finally, to me. I think you
can improve life without being political.[17]

Bukowski here resembles Vladimir Nabokov, who notoriously
objected to 'ideas' and 'ideology' in literature. Some of the names
on Nabokov's roster of disliked writers – Faulkner, Mann, Dreiser,
Malraux – overlap with Bukowski's own list.[18] In this sense he was
an aesthete, committed to 'style' and preferring like Nabokov that
literature remain free of 'general ideas' as well as 'commitment' of
the 'ideological' or 'political' kind.

Yet Bukowski often registered moral outrage at injustice, even
if he felt there were no possible political solutions to the lack of
heart and soul in humanity. Bukowski's poems about old age and
death span his entire career, beginning with 'Old Man, Dead in a
Room'. 'the proud thin dying' from *Play the Piano* is a poignant
depiction of the elderly – poor, emaciated, and unable to afford
proper food – roaming in that prime symbol of American abun-
dance, the supermarket. They will starve, die alone and be removed
from their rooming houses 'by young blond boys with long hair'.
There is no justice: 'it's the order of things: each one / gets a taste
of honey / then the knife.'[19] This empathy for the downtrodden is
as significant a side to Bukowski as his much more publicized tough
side. This sweetness is also on display in a tender love poem to
Linda Lee (the book is dedicated 'for Linda Lee Beighle, the best'),
'mermaid', in which he observes her in the bathtub: 'you were not

only the essence of that / moment / but of all my moments /
up to then / you bathing easily in the ivory / yet there was nothing
/ I could tell you'.[20]

In October 1979 Bukowski flew to Vancouver to give a reading
at the Viking Inn and on 31 March 1980 gave his final reading at
the Sweetwater in Redondo Beach during which he engaged in
constant, lively repartee with his audience: this wild jousting con-
test was memorialized in the recording *Hostage*.[21] Barbet Schroeder
now came to live in Venice to continue his work on *Barfly*. This
period is chronicled in the story 'My Friend, the Gambler' in which
Schroeder becomes 'Jean Sasoon' and Linda Lee 'Cristina'.[22] Steve
Cosmos, a French gambler who is a kind of doppelgänger of the
narrator, gets into serious legal trouble, is put in prison in France,
yet is portrayed sympathetically. Bukowski effectively uses
exchanges of letters to develop the plot and reveal character and
demonstrates his skill at crafting a technically flawless long piece
of fiction late in his career.

The film *Barfly* would ultimately take seven more years to reach
the screen. It was a slow struggle to secure financing and select
actors: Tom Waits, James Woods and Kris Kristofferson all were
considered for the lead role.[23] Bukowski now met the French
director Jean-Luc Godard for whom he wrote the English-language
titles for *Every Man for Himself* (*Sauve qui peut (la vie)*), which was
released in 1980.[24] In the film Isabelle Huppert plays a prostitute
who recites lines from a Bukowski story. Another film project
also saw fruition: in 1981, the film *Tales of Ordinary Madness* was
released with Ben Gazzara – who plays 'Charles Serking' – Ornella
Muti, Susan Tyrell and Tanya Lopert. Directed by Marco Ferreri,
it is based on Bukowski's story 'The Most Beautiful Woman in Town'
in which the narrator becomes involved with a self-destructive
woman who commits suicide. Bukowski disliked the film intensely
and screamed at the screen during the premiere at the Encore
Theatre in Hollywood, memorialized in the story 'Mad Enough'

(in which the film is parodied as 'Songs of the Suicide Man') included in *Septuagenarian Stew* (1990).[25]

In 1981 he published *Dangling in the Tournefortia* which opens with 'the lady in red', returning us to memories of the famous outlaws of the 1930s: 'Pretty Boy Floyd, Baby Face Nelson, Machine Gun Kelly, Ma / Barker, Alvin Karpis, we loved them all.'[26] Bukowski ranges about his life during every period, and some of the poems deal with his new life in San Pedro. He begins to play curious variations on earlier themes as in 'fear and madness': 'barricaded here on the 2nd floor / chair against the door / butcher knife on the table / I type my first poem here / switchblade in pocket / I type this for my tax accountant / . . . I am broke again / I own ¼ of this house / I have a pear tree / I have a lemon tree / I have a fig tree / everybody is worried about my soul now / I am worried about my soul now.'[27]

As he became more successful, he had to deal with questions about whether he would remain 'faithful' to his former lifestyle and subject matter. In 'the secret of my endurance', he humorously tells us that when people who are down and out write to him, they probably don't realize where their letters arrive: 'well, they are dropped into a box / behind a six-foot hedge with a long driveway leading / to a two-car garage, rose garden, fruit trees, / animals, a beautiful woman . . .'.[28] In 'guava tree' he considers his escape from the world of work: 'I lay with my white belly up to the sun under the pineapple / guava tree while other people's children are at school / and my woman is at work and it is quiet and I am alone with the / birds and I count eleven of them on the wire overhead / and there's nothing to do here.' The opening is finely controlled, the long lines giving a sense of rest and calm as clear immediate images flow forward: white belly, sun, pineapple guava tree. Los Angeles has many tropical trees and plants; the guava invokes a prelapsarian world in which the speaker basks in the sun. He goes on to remember the jobs where he was used to make profit for others, his former colleagues who 'liked me because they thought I was crazy / and the foremen were puzzled because I worked hard / but with disdain'. He celebrates his escape and his soothing return to the nurturing body: 'I turn on my belly, spread both arms wide feeling like / the wolf who got out of the trap but without gnawing a / leg away. / they got something, of course, that's why I'm still / resting, but it's the parts that are left that I'm / celebrating under this pineapple guava tree just / before noon.'[29] His belly and arms are intact – two sites of suffering during his post office days – and he revels like a cat stretching out its limbs after sleep celebrating his new-found freedom.

'bad fix' describes his cat Butch, one of a cycle of poems about felines Bukowski would compose during his final phase. Butch has been 'neutered' and has almost chewed off his owner's hand at feeding time. But Butch remains tough: 'at night / I hear him mauling and / running other cats through / the brush. / Butch, he's still a magnificent / old cat, / fighting / even without it.' Butch is a survivor: he 'retains / endures'. The seven stanzas, broken into lines of one to seven words each, conclude magnificently and emphatically: 'peering at me with those / evil yellow eyes / out of that huge / undefeated / head', the insistent, thumping trochaic rhythm of 'evil yellow eyes' answered resolutely by the final trochaic 'undefeated / head'.[30]

Bukowski began work on his fourth – and what many consider to be his greatest – novel, *Ham on Rye* in 1980. Although he completed it a year later, it was not published until 1983. He had perhaps held off composing the work because it required that he revisit his horrifying childhood spent at 2122 Longwood Avenue, 'The House of Horrors'. In a letter to Carl Weissner, 29 May 1982, he confessed: '*Ham on Rye* was hard to sit down to, to write the first word down. After that, it got easier. I think I had the distance to bring it off. I thought about it a month or so before I began. After all, who wants to read childhood stuff? It brings out the worst kind of writing. I hoped to bring in the sense of the ridiculous and some humor. My parents were strange.'[31] Like Henry Miller, who set out in 1928 to write his life story by making a chart which would carry him through the writing of *Tropic of Cancer*, *Tropic of Capricorn* and *Sexus, Nexus* and *Plexus*, Bukowski would also end up covering his life in autobiographical fiction, but not in a chronological fashion. Rather, the novels criss-cross his life back and forth approximately from various periods: *Post Office*, 1950–69; *Factotum*, 1942–50; *Women*, 1970–77; *Ham on Rye*, 1920–41; *Hollywood*, 1978–87; and *Pulp* his final years.

The title has triple resonance: since *Ham on Rye* describes the trials of his youth and adolescence, it carries an homage to J. D. Salinger's (a writer he admired) famous novel of teenage angst *The Catcher in the Rye*; there is a pun on the American expression 'ham' – for a comedian – and on 'rye' – meaning rye-whiskey; and finally the boy is like a piece of ham sandwiched between the two slices of rye-bread parents.[32] The terrors of his childhood are chillingly recorded:

> Then the first blow of the strop hit me. The sound of the strop was flat and loud, the sound itself was almost as bad as the pain. The strop landed again. It was as if my father was a machine, swinging that strop. There was the feeling of being in a tomb. The strop landed again and I thought, that is surely the last one. But it wasn't. It landed again. I didn't hate him. He was just unbelievable, I just wanted to get away from him. I couldn't cry. I was too sick to cry, too confused. The strop landed once again. Then he stopped. I stood and waited. I heard him hanging up the strop.
> 'Next time,' he said, 'I don't want to find any hairs.'[33]

The passage is one of the most emotionally wrenching in the novel, achieved through the regular thudding repetition of the word 'strop', as well as the carefully modulated alternation of longer and shorter sentences: 'But it wasn't. It landed again.' Bukowski hammers out a perfectly controlled prose with which to depict the ritual violence of his terrorized childhood.

Chinaski begins to evolve a nihilistic philosophy. In one scene as he sits on the beach surrounded by sand, surf, sun and lithe California girls: 'I closed my eyes and listened to the waves. Thousands of fish out there, eating each other. Endless mouths and assholes swallowing and shitting. The whole earth was nothing but mouths and assholes swallowing and shitting, and fucking.'[34] This awareness of the world as slaughterhouse recalls Bukowski's admiration for Arthur Schopenhauer. In *The World as Will and Representation*, Schopenhauer asserted that life is just 'momentary gratification, fleeting pleasure conditioned by wants, much and long suffering, constant struggle, *bellum omnium*, everything a hunter and everything hunted, pressure, want, need and anxiety, shrieking and howling; and this goes on *in saecula saeculorum* or until once again the crust of the planet breaks.'[35] If Schopenhauer exposed the illness, D. H. Lawrence diagnosed the cure to life's absurdity: 'There was no sense to life, to the structure of things. D. H. Lawrence had known that. You needed love, but not the kind of love most people used and were used up by. Old D. H. had known something.'[36] But the usual balm for a child – love – is unavailable: 'We all came from Depression families and most of us were ill-fed, yet we had grown up to be huge and strong. Most of us, I think, got little love from our families, and we didn't ask for love or kindness from anybody.'[37]

Chinaski then discovers alcohol and literature: as we have seen, the narrator employs the word 'magic' to describe their effects. They transform his world, allow him to escape from his tortured life and find solace. Furthermore, he is now joining his own emotional, spiritual and intellectual life to the secret society of writers who provide a constant frame of references for his own experiences.

Life and Art shape, transform, and comment upon each other. As Paul Ricoeur has observed: 'A life is no more than a biological phenomenon as long as it is not interpreted. And in the interpretation fiction plays a considerable, mediating role.'[38] *Ham on Rye* thus becomes both autobiography and *Künstlerroman*: a novel describing the genesis of his artistic vocation. For example, in chapter 48 when he beholds with disgust his father jamming spaghetti and meatballs and French bread into his mouth he 'remembered what Ivan had said in *The Brothers Karamazov*: "Who doesn't want to kill the father?"', and later in the same chapter he wonders how he might approach girls in the library, and muses: 'What would Maxim Gorky have done under such circumstances?'[39] Later references to Thurber, Saroyan and Irwin Shaw further underscore the role of literature in his self-creation.[40] His own life is constantly interpreted through literature so that he at once observes his experiences through a kind of literary screen and redefines his life in terms of literature.

Chinaski makes periodic trips to Skid Row in order 'to get ready for my future'.[41] The Japanese bomb Pearl Harbor, and his friend Becker, who is about to go overseas, reveals suddenly that he is an orphan. Chinaski says to him after he punched him on the shoulder, 'You're the best I've known.'[42] The novel concludes as he ends up playing a boxing game at the Penny Arcade with a Mexican boy: his toy figure is wearing blue boxing trunks and the Mexican boy's red. The figures box: 'Then blue trunks dropped again, hard, making the same iron clanking sound. I looked at him laying on his back down there on his little green velvet mat. Then I turned around and walked out.'[43]

Bukowski in his sixties was no less volatile than Bukowski at twenty. He often carried a knife with him, and threatened the waiters with it at a wedding reception at the Polo Lounge at the Beverly Hills Hotel (as he had the security guards at *Apostrophes*).[44] In this, he again resembled William S. Burroughs, who was never without a gun and also possessed a variety of knives. And in yet another connection between these two otherwise dissimilar authors, Bukowski's house began to fill up with cats. Linda's influence was quite positive for she got him to drink less hard liquor, however their relationship between 1981 and 1984 was marked by several break-ups and reunions.[45]

Hot Water Music was published in 1983. John Martin collected 36 stories, the majority of which were columns from the 'Dirty Old Man' series written in the early 1970s to which he added titles, as with *South of No North*. Russell Harrison in his book *Charles Bukowski: Against the American Grain* mistakenly assumed these stories were recently composed and hence claims they are stylistically superior to their predecessors:

> Bukowski was able to distance himself from his material, through an increased control of language (most noticeable with respect to diction and sentence structure). His handling of plot also became more assured. The clearest measure of his increased confidence, however, was his increased use of the third person. There was no longer the need to 'vouch' for the authenticity of his material by writing in the first person.[46]

Yet in point of fact these stories were written at the same time as his earlier ones, but published fourteen years later. Gay Brewer in his *Charles Bukowski* repeats the error, claiming 'gone is the artificial spontaneity that marred the early short prose'.[47]

One story, 'Scream When You Burn', which actually first appeared in *NOLA* in 1971, opens: 'He poured a drink and looked out the window at the hot and bare Hollywood street. Jesus Christ, it had been a long haul and he was still up against the wall. Death was next, death was always there.'[48] The narrator's girlfriend calls and they fight over his drinking. Then in typical Bukowski fashion, his continual literary obsession makes an appearance:

He picked up Camus' *Resistance, Rebellion and Death* . . . read some pages. Camus talked about anguish and terror and the miserable condition of Man but he talked about it in such a comfortable and flowery way . . . his language . . . that one got the feeling that things neither affected him *or* his writing; in other words, things might as well have been fine. Camus wrote like a man who had just finished a large dinner of steak and french fries, salad, and had topped it with a bottle of good French wine. Humanity may have been suffering but not him. A wise man, perhaps, but he preferred somebody who screamed when they burned.[49]

Unlike Artaud and Céline, Camus (although Bukowski admired *L'Étranger*), did not 'scream when he burned'. Other stories return to transgressive, fetishistic territory: in 'Not Quite Bernadette' a man fantasizes about 'Bernadette' while having intercourse with a vase which breaks and causes him to visit the doctor to whom he tells the story of their relationship; in 'The Man Who Loved Elevators', Harry is afflicted by the compulsion to have sex only in elevators. Other stories return to the literary life: poetry readings, aspiring writers, and 'How to Get Published' which comically describes Bukowski's relationship to the Webbs – here transformed into 'H.R. Mulloch and his wife, Honeysuckle'.

Bukowski continued his relationship with the dying John Fante during this period. A long short story later published in two parts in *Oui* entitled 'I Meet the Master' is his homage to Fante and recounts the visits which he and Linda had made to his bedside at the Motion Picture Hospital in Hollywood in 1979 and to Malibu in June 1980 and finally his funeral on 11 May 1983 at Our Lady of Malibu Church.[50] Bukowski composed several poems in homage to Fante, including 'a great show', 'epilogue', 'fante', 'the passing of a great one', 'suggestion for an arrangement', 'result' and 'the wine of forever'.[51] Bukowski had been instrumental in having Fante's work republished by Black Sparrow and hence rediscovered by a new generation of readers and, in his preface to *Ask the Dust*, he again paid homage to the 'Master'.[52]

Bukowski had always been a master of the apothegm, and he contributed 32 clever sayings to *High Times* magazine in February 1983, published as 'Ecce Hetero: Bukowski's Thoughts to Live By'. Among the most witty: 'Human relationships do not work'; 'I have never met a nonimmaculate cat'; 'Religion is not the Opium of the People. It is a peanut-butter sandwich. On white bread'; 'A whore is a woman who takes more than she gives. A man who takes more than he gives is called a businessman'; 'When the agony of all the people is heard, nothing will be done'; 'The best people are the ones you never meet'; 'Check your ass for the shining candle'; 'It's exactly as good as it's ever going to get'; 'That's enough. See you in Dresden.'[53]

War All The Time (1984) invokes Hobbes and Heraclitus: *bellum omnium contra omnes*, and *polemos panton men pater esti* (πόλεμος πάντων μὲν πατήρ ἐστι). If Bukowski can be said to have a 'late style', its beginnings can be discerned here in his increased attention to death, to his literary heroes, to his cats, to a new metaphysical, stripped-down and often tender lyricism. He also explores his seemingly long ago past in 'overhead mirrors', which describes his time in East Hollywood when he was drinking Scotch, beer and sniffing cheap cocaine. He became increasingly depressed and told his neighbour Brad Darby who brought him something in a pink bottle to settle his nerves. During the night he became severely agitated and 'at times I / got up / and walked around / turned the radio off and on, flushed the toilet / now and then, ran all the faucets in the place, / then shut them off, turned the lights off and / on, got back on the bed, rested but not too long, / got up, sipped water out of the tap, / sat in a chair and took some coins / out of my pocket and counted them: 25, 26, 27 / cents . . .'.[54] The poem vividly captures a state of nervous exhaustion and panic and his frenetic

Nov. 16, 1984

Hello Thorsten, Schwarz:

You are near good old Andernach, it's a beautiful little town. My old uncle died there a couple of years ago (my mother's brother) but I got to see him on both of my trips to Europe. He lived to be a few years past 90. I'll never last that long.

It's all right to be a policeman. Without some kind of law, many of the people would be at each other's throats.

I still write and drink and gamble. My editor publishes about a book a year. I always had the need to write but never thought I'd be this lucky.

Now don't get shot, and go easy on the drunks.

Yes,

Bob

Letter to Thorsten Schwarz, 1984.

activity seems a way to keep in motion so that he will not collapse into insanity. The next night he visits his neighbours, drinks beer, vodka, takes 'one little / yellow pill' and listens to music, smokes 'two bombers / drank 18 or 19 beers' and returns home. He sleeps and awakens without vomiting, walks the streets, buys a newspaper and returns to 'read it / fascinated, finally, with what the / other people / were doing'.[55] The poem is a kind of *saison en enfers*, but he returns to the living, finally able to read about other people's madness now that he has safely emerged from the labyrinth of his own.

In 1984 *Barfly the Screenplay* was published and Schroeder completed a documentary he had begun in 1982, *The Charles Bukowski Tapes* – four hours of 52 brief scenes of Bukowski reading poems, drinking, laughing, driving down Hollywood Boulevard, showing the house where he grew up ('The House of Horrors') talking about Nature, Elizabeth Taylor, Zoot Suiters, Henry Miller, Skid Row and why he likes women's legs. These were subsequently shown on French television at the close of each broadcast day.[56] It is likely the French were curious about the *enfant terrible* who had walked out on *Apostrophes* six years previously. When we place the *Bukowski Tapes* next to *Barfly*, the documentary emerges triumphant, for we get the power of *l'homme soi-même*: his verbal virtuosity, instantly coining metaphors on the spot, improvising, landing perfectly on his feet with a perfect line or joke. Bukowski wrote to Stephen Kessler on 15 January 1985 to decline his request to meet him, saying that he had 'talked for sixty hours for a video. I believe it began showing on National TV in France, prime time, this Jan. 7 or 8. It is supposed to run in segments of from 3 to 6 minutes for a great many nights, depending on how long it takes somebody to bomb the station. What I'm trying to say here is that *I'm sick of talking about myself.*'[57]

In late 1984 Linda and Bukowski reconciled and planned their marriage. Linda became quite ill on the wedding day, but gathered her forces and the wedding went forward as planned: they became husband and wife on 18 August 1985. They were married at the

Philosophical Research Society – an organization devoted to eso-
teric wisdom – by the head of the Society, Manly P. Hall, author of
The Secret Teachings of All Ages. Linda's mother Honora and sister
Jhara, Marina and her boyfriend Jeff Stone, John Martin – the best
man – and his wife Barbara, Michael Montfort and his wife were
in attendance. There was a reception at a Thai restaurant which
included Gerald Locklin, Steve Richmond and John Thomas during
which Bukowski was highly animated, dancing at one point with
Linda's wedding hat on.[58]

A month later, on 23 September, the newlyweds appeared at a
party celebrating the birthday of Michael Montfort's wife Frances
Schoenberger at Spago, Wolfgang Puck's restaurant near Sunset
Boulevard. Several other Germans and Austrians were present at
the affair including the actress Hildegard Knef and Arnold Schwarzenegger with his wife Maria Shriver. As the evening progressed,
Bukowski became increasingly inebriated and obstreperous, telling
the cigar-smoking Schwarzenegger: 'You little piece of shit! You
and your big shitty cigar, who do you think you are? Just because
you make these shitty little movies, you're nothing special, you
megalomaniac piece of shit . . .'. According to Gundolf Freyermuth, Schwarzenegger looked startled and listened helplessly.[59]

You Get So Alone at Times that It Just Makes Sense (1986) contains
one of Bukowski's masterpieces, 'quiet'. It is typical of his later work
in which theme, form and style are deftly fused, in which daily,
simple events point subtly to psychic depths. He writes the poem by
hand, he tells us, to avoid disturbing his wife who is not feeling well.
As his cat arrives in the room and comes to lie between his feet, he
remarks that 'we are both / melting / in the same / fire'.[60] He begins
to muse about his difficult past, his continued creation of poetry and
his ability even at age 65 to 'run rings / around / those pamby / critics', Li Po, drinking, and then sees the reflection of his head smoking
a cigarette in the window.[61] As he turns back to his writing, he is
aware 'there is never / a final / grand statement / and that's the /

Charles and Linda Bukowski's wedding, 1985.

fix / and the trick / that works / against us'.[62] At this moment, his attention focuses again on his cat:

> he has a
> splash
> of white on his
> face
> against an
> orange-yellow
> background
>
> and then
> as I look up
> and into the
> kitchen

I see a bright
portion
under the overhead
light

that shades into
darkness

and then into darker
darkness and
I can't see
beyond
that.[63]

Throughout the 30 stanzas, he skilfully varies the lines from one to six syllables: his wife alone in the other room, the lovely cat arriving, the light in the kitchen beckoning him to some revelation which the poem has just concluded is beyond human reach. There are several vectors of relationship set up: husband to wife, man to cat (they are both 'melting in the same fire'), man to the 'darker darkness' which is at once the inscrutable future and death itself.

'no help for that' also explores the depths of existential aloneness:

there is a place in the heart that
will never be filled

a space
and even during the
best moments
and
the greatest times

we will know it[64]

The lines gap, leaving a space precisely to demonstrate the interior spaces which cannot be made whole. Like Pascal, who said '*les espaces infinis m'effraient*', so too Bukowski is startled into silence, made mute by the mystery of our remote location. Our fate is simply to 'wait / and / wait / in that space', like Lucky and Pozzo in Beckett's *Waiting for Godot*.[65] Bukowski often writes – like Beckett – about spiritual emptiness and his people, like Beckett's, are the bums, prostitutes, the forlorn and forsaken, the poor – the fallen world. The spiritual hunger of the defeated is his constant theme. As Matthew Arnold lamented in 'Dover Beach': 'We are here as on a darkling plain / Swept with confused alarms of struggle and flight, / Where ignorant armies clash by night.' 'sunny side down' alludes to Hemingway's great short story 'A Clean, Well-Lighted Place' – the setting as in Hemingway is a café: 'NOTHING. Sitting in a café having breakfast. NOTHING. The / waitress, / and the people eating.'[66] The word NOTHING is repeated at intervals five more times in capital letters, recalling Hemingway's repetition of 'nada' in the electrifying 'our nada who art in nada' passage in the story and, as in Hemingway, the diner here becomes a microcosm of the lonely human struggle for meaning.

Bukowski continued to steadily write short stories during his late phase and 'The Invader' (1986) deals again with the incursion of the absurd and violent into daily life.[67] The main character and his wife are having a quiet evening when a monkey comes into their house. This leads to tragic consequences as the 'wild' cannot be assimilated by the 'civilized' and the plot reaches a horrific climax. Bukowski also wrote an essay in 1986 entitled 'Looking Back at a Big One' for an Ezra Pound *Festschrift* entitled *What Thou Lovest Well*. The essay is noteworthy for its discussion of the importance of Pound's poetry and politics in Bukowski's own creative development: 'But I was able to read certain portions of the Cantos, and although I wasn't always sure of what I was reading, I had to admire how, in some fashion, he made those lines ride the paper in a high and fine style. Pound was to poetry what Hemingway was to prose: they each had a way of inciting and exciting when there really wasn't much of that about.'[68]

Meanwhile, the drama over *Barfly* continued, as Sean Penn became interested in the film. He offered to play the role of Bukowski in the film for $1, but this would hinge on Dennis Hopper directing the film. A meeting was arranged with Penn, Hopper and Schroeder at Bukowski's house but Bukowski was unimpressed with Hopper so Schroeder would continue to be in the director's chair.[69] Mickey Rourke and Faye Dunaway were set to play the leads in the film. However, the funding of Menahem Golan and Yoram Globus, the owners of Cannon films, was threatened. Faye Dunaway writes in her autobiography that she 'offered to work for no money up front, to forgo my salary in exchange for a deferment or a percentage of the profits. With that offer, Cannon found the money somewhere and gave Barbet his deal, and we went into production.'[70] *Barfly* would reach the silver screen after all.

7

Journey to the End of the Night: Late Style, 1987–1994

The new year began with the filming of *Barfly* on 19 January 1987 in the ten blocks around MacArthur Park and at the Maryland Royal Palms at 360 South Westlake, next to the Aragon where Bukowski and Jane had lived. To add an air of verisimilitude to the proceedings, actual barflies were cast in supporting roles.[1] Bukowski collaborated intensely in the production and Schroeder emphasized that the author would have total control over his script: not one word would be altered without his approval. The striking black-and-white photography by German cinematographer Robby Müller recalls a dark, intense expressionist film about an anguished loner which Bukowski much admired – David Lynch's *Eraserhead*.[2] Indeed Jack Nance, lead actor in *Eraserhead*, plays the role in *Barfly* of the detective seeking information about the reclusive poet Henry Chinaski.

The film opens with the neon-lit signs of various Los Angeles bars against the driving rhythm and blues of Booker T and the M.G.'s: The Sunset, The Hollyway, Kenmore, Oasis, Crabby Joe's, Snug Harbor, Silver Platter, Side Show, Catalina, Ski Room, Smog Cutter, The Golden Horn. Music by Mozart, Handel, Scriabin, Mahler, Stamitz, Beethoven and Terry Riley is effectively used throughout. There are several memorable scenes, including a cameo appearance of Bukowski himself, sitting at the bar drinking a beer and turning to observe Mickey Rourke as he strides to meet Wanda for the first time, observing in the present his earlier self; an elderly drunk at the bar whose one hand shakes so badly he rigs up a pulley cord to raise his other hand to bring the glass to his mouth; a dog snarling in a car window and Chinaski saying to it: 'Beautiful. Hate, the only thing that lasts'; Henry bending down bloodied to drink water pulsing from a fire hydrant in the middle of the night or intentionally running into the bumper of the phony Californian kissing couple in front of him at a stoplight; the stately upward strains of a Handel *Concerto Grosso* playing as he drives up the hill to Tully's house.

Barfly, for all its supposed provocative sexuality, 'vulgarity' and violence is a film about poetry, about the assault upon the sensitive individual by an ugly society. Three poems are featured with accompanying music as the verses are recited through a voice over. 'Humanity, you never had it from the beginning' from 'those sons of bitches' (*Mockingbird*); 'nothing but the dripping sink / the empty bottle / euphoria / youth fenced in, / stabbed and shaven / taught words / propped up / to die' from '2 p.m. beer' (*It Catches*); and 'this thing upon me is not death . . . it is not death / but dying will solve its power' from 'Old Man, Dead in a Room' (*It Catches*). The thematic unity of death, poetry, love, violent estrangement, solitude, alcohol and the ecstasy of classical music is thus subtly emphasized throughout the film. *Barfly* premiered at Cannes in May 1987 and the publicity surrounding its release on 16 October 1987 led Bukowski to be interviewed by mass circulation magazines such as *People*:

> Beer in hand, the potbellied old boozer shuffles around his living room. His face is a topographic road map of pockmarks and warts. A tiny self-portrait hangs near the front door. He jeers at it. 'Tough guy,' he says with a W.C. Fields rasp. 'I think I'm Bogart.' . . . His name is popping up in gossip columns. He dines with Norman Mailer, takes Sean Penn to the racetrack and gets visits from Madonna. 'Why,' his next-door neighbor asks, 'would Madonna come to see you, Hank?'[3]

Bukowski's circle of friends and acquaintances expanded: Shel Silverstein, the well-known author of poetry for children, came to visit. However, Bukowski was allergic to the publicity machine and refused to appear on television programmes such as *20-20*, *60 Minutes* and *The Johnny Carson Show*.[4] *Barfly* pleased him, although he objected to Rourke's exaggerated portrayal of his younger self and was less than enthusiastic about Dunaway's performance.[5]

Bukowski was following the precedent of Eugene O'Neill's *The Iceman Cometh* and Saroyan's *The Time of Your Life* in choosing to set much of the action in a bar. Wanda remarks: 'I can't stand people. I hate them', and Henry responds: 'Yeah.' Their ensuing witty dialogue echoes a scene in Saroyan's great play *The Time of Your Life* (1939):

> Henry: I think I'll ask you the same damn thing people are always asking me.
> Wanda: Like?
> Henry: Like, what do you do?
> Wanda: I drink.[6]

When Joe and Mary meet for the first time in Saroyan's *The Time of Your Life*, the exchange is similar:

> Mary: What do you do?
> Joe: Do? To tell you the truth, nothing.
> Mary: Do you always drink a great deal?
> Joe: Not always. Only when I'm awake. I sleep seven or eight hours every night, you know.
> Mary: How nice. I mean to drink when you're awake.[7]

Bukowski's world of dream and fantasy, the magic bar where he finds love in the person of Jane, where the world's misfits huddle for protection recalls Saroyan's San Francisco Bar: Nick's Pacific Street Saloon, Restaurant and Entertainment Palace.

Another film based on Bukowski's life and work – *Crazy Love*, or *Love is a Dog from Hell* was released in 1987 and directed by the Belgian Dominique Deruddere. Bukowski enjoyed the film and it was reviewed by Walter Goodman in the *New York Times* who called it 'funny, tender, surprising'. It is based on 'The Copulating Mermaid of Venice, Calif.', as well as scenes from *Ham on Rye*; Harry Voss is the central character. Goodman observes that 'the episodes are no more than anecdotes, really, but rich in incident, and the writing, photography (by Willy Stassen) and direction fill them with conviction.'[8] Perhaps brought on by the brouhaha attending *Barfly* and its aftermath, Bukowski became ill during the winter of 1987. The doctors could find no specific cause and he was instructed to stop drinking.[9] A retrospective collection *The Roominghouse Madrigals: Early Selected Poems, 1946–1966* was published in 1988 and contains a preface in which Bukowski explores the differences between his early and present work.[10]

Bukowski now turned his attention to writing a satirical *roman-à-clef*, *Hollywood*, which he completed in autumn 1988 and published in 1989.[11] The novel describes the making of *Barfly*, entitled here *The Dance of Jim Beam*. Bukowski disliked movies and he had only a small, select list of admired films: *Eraserhead* (his favourite), *One Flew Over the Cuckoo's Nest*, *The Elephant Man* and *Who's Afraid of Virginia Woolf?*[12] He also enjoyed Ray Milland's performance in *The Lost Weekend* (1945) – about a desperate alcoholic. Bukowski abhorred 'the film industry' and *Hollywood* afforded him the opportunity to vent his spleen. The people he encountered during the creation of *Barfly* make barely disguised appearances: Barbet Schroeder / Jon Pinchot; Norman Mailer / Victor Norman; Werner Herzog / Wenner Zergog; Sean Penn / Tom Pell; Jean-Luc Godard / Jean-Luc Modard; Timothy Leary / Jim Serry; Mickey Rourke / Jack Bledsoe; Faye Dunaway / Francine Bowers; Roger Ebert / Rick

Talbot; David Lynch / Manz Loeb; Madonna / Ramona; Dennis Hopper / Mack Austin. Old friends also appear: Carl Weissner / Karl Vossner; Michael Montfort / Michael Huntington; John Thomas / John Galt. Of course Bukowski knew of the tradition of famous authors such as Aldous Huxley, William Faulkner and John Fante getting entangled in the cesspool of Hollywood.[13] However, he refused when offered to continue writing scripts. He told Pamela Cytrynbaum in the *New York Times Book Review*: 'I guess I never believed Hollywood – I heard it's a horrible place – but when I went there, I found out how really horrible, horrible, horrible, horrible it was, black and cutthroat . . . Somehow when you get it on paper, tell it, it gets it out of your mind. It keeps you from jumping out a window or cutting your throat.'[14]

The novel is deft, fluent, entertaining and commences *in medias res*: 'A couple of days later Pinchot phoned. He said he wanted to go ahead with the screenplay.'[15] The theme of class division is sounded at the outset as our scriptwriter Chinaski goes to meet with the backers of the film at Marina del Rey. Observing the wealthy on their sailboats in the harbour, he observes: 'Such were the rewards of the Chosen in the land of the free.'[16] Chinaski experiences anxieties as he crosses class boundaries: 'Yes. I felt the fear, the fear of becoming like *them*.'[17] 'Them' – again *das Man*, 'the They', the Other, the comfortable, smug, spiritually empty American bourgeoisie he had abhorred. His wife Sarah remarks at the opening: 'Your greatest strength . . . is that you fear everything', and he responds, 'I wish I had said that.'[18] As the novel progresses, he enters the enclaves of the 'elite': The Beverly Hills Hotel, the Château Marmont, far removed from his dingy rooming houses.

The book charts a trajectory from his former poor East Hollywood to the 'real Hollywood', and in Baudrillardian terms, Bukowski reverses the equation, revealing the phoniness of the 'real'. As he enters the Beverly Hills hotel, he remarks: 'A magic world. I liked it because I hadn't seen anything like it before. It was senseless and perfect and safe.'[19] This recalls the scene in *Barfly* when Henry climbs the hill in a fancy sports car with Tully to the soaring strains of a Handel *Concerto Grosso* to her luxurious home: he tells her that she lives in 'a cage with golden bars'. The fact that it is 'perfect and safe' and 'magic' makes it 'senseless'. Again, the 'real' and 'unreal' are counterpoised: the real is blood, poverty, death, struggle, madness – the unreal is Hollywood. There is ambivalence at the root of this: on one level he desires his work to become known, yet this recognition, or 'success', pulls him precisely into the world to which he has always been an outsider and to which he has set himself in opposition. Thus the novel works on two levels: it explores Chinaski's reactions to this world of Hollywood illusions and it is also a dark comedy depicting the incredible machinations involved in bringing his script to the screen.

Yet the 'gods' are on Chinaski's side: it is payback time for hard karma. After being compensated for his work on the screenplay and then negotiating another deal for his books which are being translated in Germany, he reflects: 'Within an hour I was 45 thousand dollars richer. 30 years of starvation and rejection were starting to kick in.'[20] He is saved from doom by his wife Sarah: 'The gods had sent me Sarah to add ten years to my life. The gods kept driving me to the blade, then, at the last moment, lifting my head off the block. Very strange, these gods.'[21] In one scene, he explains to Sarah why he retells the same tales about his life: 'but somehow, the telling of old stories, again and again, seems to bring them closer to what they were supposed to be'.[22] Here, in a seemingly throwaway line, he reveals how the artist takes the raw material of his life and through constantly reworking and re-examining it, tries to bring it closer to truth, to what it was 'supposed to be'.

When the movie is completed, the publicity machine commences with photographers taking pictures of the stars, and parties to celebrate. Opening night is comically reported: he and Sarah are seated in the first row so the faces on the screen appear elongated and the dialogue is garbled.[23] The novel ends with Chinaski responding to his wife's question about what he will do; he says he will write a novel 'about writing the screenplay and making the movie' and she asks what he will call it:

'Hollywood.'
    'Hollywood?'
    'Yes'
And this is it.[24]

Here, in a quick, literary sleight of hand, Bukowski self-referentially reprises the ending of *Post Office.*

Bukowski's health problems returned: on 6 July 1988, he wrote to Carl Weissner that he had '2 skin cancer burnoffs so far'.[25] After finishing *Hollywood* in the early autumn of 1988, Bukowski contracted a fever and his weight dropped to 168 lb.[26] He felt tired and weak and consulted several expensive doctors in Beverly Hills, none of whom could diagnose his illness.[27] Then he took one of his cats to the veterinarian who told Bukowski that he should be checked for tuberculosis and it transpired that he had indeed 'probably contracted the disease as a child' from one of his uncles.[28] He stopped drinking during his treatment. There was, however, joy in his life the following year: his daughter Marina married Jeffrey Stone on 7 October 1989.[29]

This struggle with death is reflected in a taut story Bukowski composed entitled 'The Other'.[30] He meets his 'double', his alter ego, and engages in an intricate dance of death and wills with him, including a hair-raising pursuit on the endless freeways of Los Angeles. Previously Bukowski had owned a 1958 Plymouth, a 1962 Comet and a blue 1967 Volkswagen Beetle, but now that he owned powerful German cars, he could drive as swiftly as he desired. In a letter to Steve Richmond of 1 March 1984 he writes: 'You should see me tooling that BMW at 80 mph on the curves of the Pasadena freeway, idiotic and I know it, but fuck it . . .'.[31]

In 1990 Black Sparrow published *Septuagenarian Stew* (a companion volume of poems and stories, *Betting on the Muse*, was published posthumously in 1996). In his later works Bukowski begins to deal for a final time with the writers who had meant the most to him. William Saroyan would be remembered in a cycle of poems and in the short story 'Action' in which he is named 'Henry Baroyan', thus combining in his name Bukowski's own actual given name.[32] Baroyan gambles, drinks, has tax troubles, marries twice – as did Saroyan – thus writing, drinking, gambling, luck and problems with women are connected in Baroyan's life as they were in Bukowski's. Several of the poems are also homages to writers. One of the poems, 'the burning of the dream', is in memory to the LA Public Library where Bukowski first encountered many of the writers he admired.[33] 'nowhere' laments the lack of great writers such as Miller, Céline and Jeffers.[34] In 'birthday party' he remembers his meeting with Norman Mailer at the Château Marmont and that they both drove black BMWs: '"tough guys drive black / BMW's", / I tell / him.'[35]

For Christmas 1990 Linda presented her husband with an Apple Macintosh IIsi.[36] He even took a course in how to use it, humorously recounted in 'computer class': 'control panel. / find file. / select all. / show clipboard. / hide ruler. / insert header.'[37] He also composed 'an animal poem' published posthumously in *The Night Torn Mad with Footsteps*: 'I've got two kittens who are rapidly becoming / cats and at night / we share the same bed . . . this is the last poem / tonight, there's / one glass of wine left / and both of the cats / are asleep on my feet. / I can feel the gentle weight of them / the touch of their fur / I am aware of their breathing: good things do happen and I know that as / armies everywhere march out to make / war / the kittens / at my feet / know more . . .'.[38] Bukowski tells us in the poem that it is his 'first cat poem' and it would be followed by

Bukowski and one of his cats, 1980.

many more. Linda and he adopted a fleet of stray felines which they christened with a variety of fanciful names including Craney, Ting, Ding, Patches, Beeker, Bhau, Feather, Beauty, Bleeker and Blob. He told Sean Penn: 'My cat, Beeker, is a fighter. He gets mauled up a bit sometimes, but he's always the winner. I taught him it all, you know . . . lead with the left, set up with the right.' In 'exactly right', he praises his cats for they are 'smart, spontaneous, self- / absorbed, naturally poised and awesomely / beautiful'. They teach us humans, for 'when you are feeling down, very down, / if you just look at a cat at rest, / at the way they sit or lie and wait, /

it's a grand lesson in persevering . . .'.[39] In addition to a house full of cats, in 1990 Bukowski also bought an Acura Legend and prettified the house: he installed a lap pool, security system, jacuzzi, and new furniture.[40]

Bukowski spoke repeatedly during this period of his sense that his writing had continued to evolve. He told Donald McRae in 1991: 'Inside I feel the same – only stronger with the writing getting better as I get older.'[41] He felt his inspiration had deepened: 'I am being fed from different sources.'[42] Bukowski's 'late style' begins with an increasing interiority – his many poems about death, 'the gods', his cats, and his pared-down, gnostic style – his concerns and approach shifted as he entered his final creative phase. There is a relentless experimentation with form and style as he composed poems, a journal, stories, essays and a weird final novel, *Pulp*. In a letter to Stephen Kessler of 29 January 1993 he declared: 'A writer should get better as he gets older: there's more to work with, a larger canvas. But most writers get lucky too early, then get the fat head, get greedy, get dull, fall apart. They are short distance runners. Too bad. That's why we have so much crappy literature about . . .'.[43]

While it is impossible to make generalities about the late periods of artists, there may be an effort to sum up, to try to bring to conclusion some of the disparate strands which have been lifetime obsessions. D. H. Lawrence's late poems come to mind, such as 'The Ship of Death'. In Lawrence's final poems there is an increasing emphasis on the 'self' as an inviolate sacred space which must be honoured. So too, in Bukowski's 'late period' works, he summarizes and brings to a higher level of expression the major themes of his entire career. In several poems such as 'no leaders, please', the emphasis is on self-salvation: 'be self-taught. / and reinvent your life because you must; / it is your life and / its history / and the present / belong only to / you.'[44] Bukowski himself changes his 'tone and shape' so that they cannot 'categorize' him. The threat of the 'they' remains, and each individual must fight against being like 'they' are. 'nobody but you' exhorts, 'nobody can save you but / yourself'; 'the laughing heart' counsels, 'your life is your life. / don't let it be clubbed into dank / submission. be on the watch. / . . . the gods will offer you / chances. / know them, take them. / you can't beat death but / you can beat death / in life, / sometimes. / and the more often you / learn to do it, / the more light there will / be'. 'roll the dice' also celebrates this quest for authenticity: 'if you're going to try, / go all the way. / there is no other feeling like / that. / you will be alone with the / gods / and the nights will flame with / fire. / do it, do it, do it. / do it. / all the way / all the way. / you will ride life straight to / perfect laughter, it's / the only good fight / there is.'[45] One must risk, gamble – 'roll the dice' – in order to achieve originality, 'style', to make the existential choices to create one's own life. In this entire sequence of poems, the repetition of key lines urges the reader to accomplish the 'fight' of true being, and 'the gods' will help one, 'laughter' will accompany the struggle, and 'death in life' will be triumphed over, if only 'sometimes'.

There now appeared another sign of Bukowksi's increasing recognition following the success of *Barfly*: Neeli Cherkovski's biography entitled *Hank* was published by Random House in 1991. Over the next several years, four more biographies were published, again demonstrating that Bukowski's audience had now grown far beyond the confines of the underground and that his work was beginning to gain widespread appreciation and acceptance.[46] During this period, Marcus Grapes, the editor of the literary magazine *OntheBus* asked him 'to keep a journal I could publish in installments'.[47] The journal entries were collected and published posthumously as *The Captain is Out to Lunch and the Sailors Have Taken Over the Ship* (1998). The entries extend from '8/28/91 11:28 PM' (each section is dated and timed) to '2/27/93 12:56 AM' and are illustrated by superb Robert Crumb drawings. In the entry for '8/29/91 10:55 PM' he explodes with joy over Mahler's music and

Robert Crumb, illustration for *The Captain is Out to Lunch and the Sailors Have Taken Over the Ship* (1995).

wonders why he is still so obsessed with writing; it would be better if he were 'to go to sleep or look at your 9 cats or sit with your wife on the couch. You're either at the track or with your Macintosh . . .'.[48] Apparently, Bukowski took his own advice to spend more time with his wife, because a few months later, on 11 November 1991, he took Linda to Disneyland.[49]

The Last Night of the Earth Poems (1992), a massive 405-page volume, is Bukowski's last major volume of poetry and the first book he composed on the computer. His characteristic obsessions receive a final recapitulation: the race track, music, writers, apocalypse. 'the beggars' reminds us why he went to the track: to witness the human drama, 'the beggars of the grandstand', to encounter the horror that 'as race after race / unfolds / they are routinely / sucked of / money and / hope'.[50] The magnificent 'Dinosauria, we' invokes the end of the world: 'we are born into a government 60 years in debt / that soon will be unable to even pay the interest on that debt / and the banks will burn / money will be useless / there will be open and unpunished murder in the streets'. When the human race disappears, 'there will be the most beautiful silence never heard / born out of that'.[51] But these dark prophecies are balanced by the gentle love poem to his wife Linda, 'confession', which end with the moving words: 'and the hard / words / I ever feared to / say / can now be / said: / I love / you'.[52]

This often tender emotional nakedness marking the late period is evident in 'the bluebird': 'there's a bluebird in my heart that / wants to get out / but I'm too tough for him, / I say, stay in there, I'm not going / to let anybody see / you'.[53] Bukowski has found the perfect metaphor to disclose his hidden vulnerabilities, and the gap between his outer image and his wounded heart: 'there's a bluebird in my heart that / wants to get out / but I'm too clever, I only let him out / at night sometimes / when everybody's asleep'. The ballad-like repetitions of 'bluebird in my heart' increases the emotional impact of the poem, ending in the wrenching 'and we sleep together like / that / with our secret pact / and it's nice enough to / make a man / weep, but I don't / weep, do / you?'[54]

Several poems were written on an IBM electric while his computer was being repaired, such as 'sitting with the IBM' in which he muses about the Brahms symphony on the radio, his five cats who 'sit outside under the cool juniper bushes / listening to me / type'.[55] This is a typical late Bukowski poem, in which he weaves in music, composing poetry, his cats, the hot summer night, his wife, a reference to Henry Miller. He allows all the disparate aspects of awareness to find their way into the poem and leaves the inconclusiveness as conclusion: 'as the cats wait under the juniper / bushes and I pour more wine, more wine, / more wine'.[56] The Chinese poet Li Po, about whom Bukowski wrote a brief sketch in 1986, hovers over these late, effortless, wine-soaked poems which Bukowski floats and burns down the river of time.[57] He has reached into the mystery of consciousness, observing each simple, daily moment as it arrives and honouring it with a Zen-like philosophical detachment as it departs.

Against these moments of peaceful contemplation, Bukowski did not fail to notice world events. The streets of Los Angeles again erupted in violence and bloodshed following the verdict in the Rodney King case, an African-American man who had been severely beaten by the police during his arrest. The beatings were caught on videotape but at the conclusion of the trial the officers were exonerated. On 29 April 1992, the rioting began and continued for six days, ending on Monday 4 May: 53 people died and thousands were injured. Bukowski composed a poem entitled 'riots' which chronicles the fact that he has witnessed two riots in his lifetime – the first in Watts in 1965 – and 'nothing was corrected last / time. / nothing will be corrected this / time. / the poor will remain poor. / the unemployed will remain / so. / the homeless will remain / homeless / and the politicians, / fat upon the land, will live / very well.' And in 'the con job', he sarcastically notes the beginning of the first Iraq War: 'the ground war began today / at dawn / in a desert land / far from here / and the Blacks, Mexicans / and poor whites / were sent there / to fight and win / as on tv / the fat white rich newscasters / first told us all about / it'.[58] In both the Los Angeles riots and the first invasion of Iraq, the American underclass continued to be victimized.

Bukowski also wrote two important essays about his poetics during this period, including 'Basic Training' and 'Playing and Being the Poet'. In 'Basic Training' he asserts that he was driven by the need to write in his own way: 'I hurled myself toward my personal god: SIMPLICITY. The tighter and smaller you got it the less chance there was of error and the lie. Genius could be the ability to say a profound thing in a simple way.'[59] And in 'Playing and Being the Poet', he explores the source of his inspiration:

> Poetry comes from where you've lived and how you've lived and from what makes you create it. Most people have already entered the death process by the age of 5, and with each passing year there is less of them in the sense of being original beings with a chance to break through and out and away from the obvious and the mutilating. Generally, those who do have had life experiences and continue to have life experiences that set them aside, isolate them in such a manner that they become beautiful freaks, visionaries with their own visions.[60]

In the summer of 1992 Bukowski underwent an operation for cataracts. He also began to write his final novel *Pulp*, which was published posthumously on 22 April 1994.[61] As Jules Smith observes, he was influenced by his friend Gerard Locklin's novel *The Case of the Missing Blue Volkswagen* which parodies in very brief, sometimes just one-to-two-paragraph long chapters, all the clichés of the detective genre.[62] Bukowski also enjoyed the BBC series *The Singing Detective* when he was ill in 1989.[63] *Pulp* is

Bukowski's send-up and homage to Dashiell Hammett and Mickey Spillane and 'is dedicated to bad writing'. It is also his *Abschied* – his farewell – to life itself, as the novel recapitulates his marriages, John Martin and Black Sparrow Press, his relationship to Céline and to literature, horse racing, bars, sex and women.

Pulp has the edgy, mad gaiety of a late Beethoven piano bagatelle. The opening chapter sketches out swiftly the themes: sex, literature, death, waiting. We meet Nick Belane, a 'private dick' in Los Angeles who has been given the task by 'Lady Death' to find Céline. He must also find the 'Red Sparrow' (a play on Black Sparrow Press – John Martin becomes 'John Barton' and there is an obvious reference as well to *The Maltese Falcon* of Dashiell Hammett). A string of in-jokes for those familiar with Bukowski's life follow: we meet Red Koldowsky, the owner of a bookstore (this is Shalom 'Brooklyn Red' Stodolsky, the quick-tempered owner of Baroque Books on Hollywood Boulevard who was a great promoter and friend of Bukowski's). And the theme of identity is introduced: 'Was Celine Celine or was he somebody else? Sometimes I felt that I didn't even know who *I* was.'[64] A volley of more inside plays on Bukowski's life follow: Barton says 'If you find the Red Sparrow I will give you a hundred dollars a month for life', as well as allusions to classical music – Eric Coates and Scarlatti.[65] There is also a series of literary references – to Céline, Faulkner, Thomas Wolfe, McCullers, Mann, Hemingway, Dante, Fante. Fante's famous novel even gets a nod-within-a-nod in a comic exchange between Dante and Fante: '"Tossed the jock coming out of the gate," said Fante. "You're kidding." "I'm not kidding. Ask the dust."'[66]

There is an absurd, existential edge as Belane makes portentous statements which recall a comedian Bukowski admired – Woody Allen: 'Existence was not only absurd, it was plain hard work.'[67] The quest for meaning is parodied: the detective becomes the hermeneut attempting to interpret the clues but life finally cannot be shaped into a coherent narrative. He reaches this non-conclusive conclusion:

'I mean, say that you figure that everything is senseless, then it can't be quite senseless because you are aware that it's senseless and your awareness of senselessness almost gives it sense. You know what I mean?'[68] And recalling Beckett's view of the human condition in *Waiting for Godot*, 'we were all just hanging around waiting to die and meanwhile doing little things to fill the space.'[69] The in-jokes continue in chapter 38 when outer space alien Jeanne Nitro meets Lady Death at the bar with Belane – this recalls the triangle scene in *Barfly* when Wanda and Tully meet with Henry, but now told again in the voice of Woody Allen: 'Here, basically, I was sitting between Space and Death. In the form of Woman. What chance did I have?'[70] Finally, apocalypse appears in chapter 39: 'The earth. Smog, murder, the poisoned air, the poisoned water, the poisoned food, the hatred, the hopelessness, everything. The only beautiful thing about the earth is the animals and now they are being killed off, soon they will be gone except for pet rats and race horses. It's so sad, no wonder you drink so much.' And our hero responds: 'Yeah, Jeannie. And don't forget our atomic stockpiles.'[71] The novel concludes with Belane dying in a blaze of yellow, Bukowski's favourite colour.

Bukowski attended a U2 concert with Linda in November 1992: the singer Bono dedicated the performance to the couple. Afterwards, Bukowski drank heavily and when he arrived home fell on the steps leading into the house, gashing his head and injuring his head, knee, back and right hand.[72] Even with all the *Sturm und Drang* of his life, however, Bukowski did not lose his zany sense of humour. On 2 January 1993, he wrote to William Packard:

Dear NYQ:

I am a native Albino who lives with a mother with a wooden leg and a father who shoots up. I have a parrot, Cagney, who says, 'Yankee Doodle Dandy!' each time he excretes, which is

4 or 5 times a day. I once saw J.D. Salinger. Enclosed are my
Flying Saucer Poems. I have an 18 year old sister with a body
like you've never seen. Nude photos enclosed. In case my
poems are rejected, these photos are to be returned. In case
of acceptance, I or my sister can be reached at 643-696-6969.

sincerely yours,

Byron Keats[73]

Not only did he appear in the *New York Quarterly* regularly, but
Bukowski now began to be accepted by the Establishment which for
so long had ignored him. He had several poems accepted in the
redoubtable *Poetry Chicago* which he had so frequently criticized.[74]
He published in the *American Poetry Review*, while the famous *Prairie
Schooner* published 'the laughing heart' and 'a new war', a poignant
farewell to life which recalls Mahler's *Das Lied von Der Erde*.[75]

Bukowski was soon brought down by a serious illness, diagnosed
as myelogenous leukaemia in early 1993.[76] He wrote to John Martin
on 14 March 1993: 'Some rough days ahead in chemotherapy.'[77] He
spent 64 days in the hospital, undergoing blood transfusions and
treatment with antibiotics.[78] Carl Weissner came to visit him in the
hospital for several days. Bukowski's mood was likely lifted in early
May 1993 when John Martin edited *Run with the Hunted: A Charles
Bukowski Reader*, which was published by HarperCollins.[79] In August,
however, the leukaemia returned and on 25 August Bukowski began
practising the Ayurvedic method to deal with his illness.[80] On 19
September he began meditating: 'had my first TM session today' and
the disease went into remission but then returned.[81] Linda recalled
that 'we went up to Malibu, to a transcendental meditation center.
Then afterwards we'd go to Gladstone's on the beach and have a big
crab dinner. But he got into it . . . he would sit 20 minutes a day,
twice a day, and mediate . . . Even in the hospital, when he was going

Bukowski's funeral at Green Hills Memorial Park, 1994.

through chemo, he would sit in his room and mediate 20 minutes a day, twice a day.'[82] Sean Penn recalled, 'they called me one day saying they were in the Malibu area, and I went down there and we had a late lunch . . . That was the last time I saw him. Things went south.'[83] He contracted pneumonia and his immune system was weakened by cancer. Charles Bukowski died at 11:55 p.m. on 9 March 1994.[84] The funeral was held at Green Hills Memorial Park where Buddhist monks officiated at the ceremony.[85] According to Philomene Long, 'on the night of his funeral Linda told me she had "the image of Hank as a Tibetan Lama."'[86] And Long makes the Buddhist connection: 'Hank's favorite color *was* yellow, the color of Buddhist monks' robes, and often he would say how he hated to see suffering.'[87]

Bukowski's passing was mourned in his homeland. Willi Winkler wrote in *Die Zeit*, 18 March: 'On Wednesday of last week, the German poet Heinrich Karl Bukowski died of leukemia at age 73.'[88] In America, he was remembered fondly by his friend Ruben

Rueda, a bartender at Musso and Frank's: 'Did you ever hear his laugh? He didn't laugh from here (his mouth), he laughed from here [his belly]. A loud, deep laugh. Very rare . . . There will never be another like him.'[89] His wife Linda recalled:

> His voice was very soft and very sweet and he had a center. His center was something that was as sturdy as a mountain. He had an inside central awareness, a conscious spirituality – he wouldn't want to say that – but a profound inner center that never wavered no matter what was going on in the world outside – whether he was winning at the race-track or not winning at the race-track. He didn't like to think of himself outwardly as a so-called 'spiritual' person but he was one of the most spiritual human beings that I've ever known in my life.[90]

During the past eighteen years, Bukowski has not been forgotten. Black Sparrow issued posthumous volumes yearly between 1995 and 2001. In May 2002 John Martin retired and sold the rights to Bukowski's (as well as Paul Bowles's and John Fante's) works to Ecco, a division of HarperCollins, which began publishing Bukowski regularly in 2005.[91] John Dullaghan's full-length documentary *Born Into This* appeared in 2003.[92] Camille Paglia wrote about his love poetry in her book of essays *Vamps and Tramps*.[93]

Meanwhile, Bukowski – the prototypical marginalized outsider – began to become increasingly central. Jim Harrison, in his review in the *New York Times Book Review* of *Pleasures of the Damned*, a collection of Bukowski's poetry from 1951 to 1993, predicted his canonization: 'It is ironical that those who man the gates of the canon will rarely if ever make it inside themselves. Bukowski came in a secret back door.'[94] David Lehman officially canonized him in the *Oxford Book of American Poetry*, Garrison Keillor in three anthologies, and his work appeared regularly in *The Best American Poetry* anthologies.[95] He is included in guides to 'Cult Fiction',

Linda Bukowski at Bukowski's gravesite, 1994.

featured in literary reference books such as *Who's Who in Twentieth Century Literature* and *501 Great Writers* and his places of residence noted in Beat guidebooks for those seeking to trace the visionary company's itineraries.[96] His novels, stories, poems, essays and interviews are translated into Hebrew, Bulgarian, Icelandic, Turkish, German, Italian, Serbo-Croatian, Czech, Slovenian, Swedish, Danish, Norwegian, Hungarian, Greek, Russian, Finnish, Portuguese, Dutch, Catalan, Polish, Farsi, Spanish and Japanese.

Bukowski continues to influence popular culture: Matt Groening has alluded to him on *The Simpsons*; Bob Dylan reads his poems on his *Radio Hour*; the poem 'The Laughing Heart' has been used in a marketing campaign by Levi Strauss jeans; groups such as *The Fugs* and rappers base their songs on his writings; a musician recites his poems to the accompaniment of J. S. Bach; young people tattoo his image and quotations from his works on their bodies; his books rank as the most highly stolen from bookshops.

In 2006 Linda Lee Bukowski bequeathed his literary archive to the Huntington Library in San Marino, California. This magnificent institution, on acres of stately manicured grounds and botanical gardens, holds – among many other treasures – a Shakespeare First Folio, Galileo's *Dialogo sopra i due massimi sistemi del mondo*, the Ellesmere manuscript of Chaucer's *Canterbury Tales*, the original autograph manuscripts of Langston Hughes, Jack London and Henry David Thoreau's *Walden*. To many it is a matter of some pleasurable amusement that Bukowski's literary legacy is now housed in this cathedral of culture which is located not far from his own preferred temple – the Santa Anita racetrack where he spent so many happy days and evenings.

References

Frequently cited works are abbreviated as follows:

Works by Charles Bukowski

Absence	*Absence of the Hero: Uncollected Stories & Essays, 1946–1992*, ed. David Stephen Calonne (San Francisco, 2010)
'Aftermath'	'Aftermath of a Lengthy Rejection Slip', in *Portions*
Burning	*Burning in Water, Drowning in Flame* (Santa Barbara, CA, 1978)
Erections	*Erections, Ejaculations, Exhibitions and General Tales of Ordinary Madness* (San Francisco, 1972)
Ham on Rye	*Ham on Rye* (Santa Barbara, CA, 1982)
It Catches	*It Catches My Heart in Its Hands* (New Orleans, 1963)
Last Night	*The Last Night of the Earth Poems* (Santa Rosa, CA, 1992)
Living on Luck	*Living on Luck: Selected Letters 1960s–1970s Volume 2*, ed. Seamus Cooney (Santa Rosa, CA, 1995)
Love is a Dog	*Love is a Dog from Hell* (Santa Barbara, CA, 1977)
Mockingbird	*Mockingbird Wish Me Luck* (Los Angeles, 1972)
Notes of a Dirty Old Man	(San Francisco, 1973)
Play the Piano	*Play the Piano Drunk Like a Percussion Instrument until the Fingers Begin to Bleed a Bit* (Santa Barbara, CA, 1979)
Portions	*Portions from a Wine-Stained Notebook:*

	Uncollected Stories and Essays, 1944–1990, ed. David Stephen Calonne (San Francisco, 2008)
Reach	*Reach for the Sun: Selected Letters 1978–1994 Volume 3*, ed. Seamus Cooney (Santa Rosa, CA, 1999)
Roominghouse	*The Roominghouse Madrigals* (Santa Barbara, CA, 1988)
Screams	*Screams from the Balcony: Selected Letters 1960–1970*, ed. Seamus Cooney (Santa Rosa, CA, 1993)
The Days Run Away	*The Days Run Away Like Wild Horses Over the Hills* (Santa Barbara, CA, 1969)
You Get So Alone	*You Get So Alone at Times that It Just Makes Sense* (Santa Rosa, CA, 1986)

Other Works

Sunlight	*Sunlight Here I Am: Interviews & Encounters 1963–1993*, ed. David Stephen Calonne (Northville, MI, 2003)
Who's Big in the 'Littles'	Debritto, Abel, *Who's Big in the 'Littles': A Critical Study of the Impact of the Little Magazines and Small Press Publications on the Career of Charles Bukowski from 1940 to 1969*, PhD thesis (Universitat Autonoma de Barcelona, 2009)

1 Deutschland, Vaterland, The Name of the Father: 1920–1943

1 Howard Sounes, *Locked in the Arms of a Crazy Life* (Edinburgh, 2010), p. 8. Also see Neeli Cherkovski, *Hank: The Life of Charles Bukowski* (New York, 1991), pp. 12–14; Bukowski, letter to John William Corrington, 14 January 1963, *Screams*, p. 55.

2 *Germany: A Phaidon Cultural Guide* (Englewood Cliffs, NJ, 1985), p. 35; James Bentley, *Blue Guide: Germany* (London, 1987), p. 211.

3 'Aftermath', p. 2. Bukowski's success in Europe is due to the fact that the Germans, French, Spanish and Italians see him as a European. As Andrea Pinketts has observed, 'Charles Bukowski e uno die piu grandi scrittori dell letterature europea, pur essendo Americano.' See Paolo Roversi, *Charles Bukowski: Scrivo racconti e poi ci metto il sesso per vendere* (Rome, 2010), p. 11.

4 Sounes, *Locked in the Arms of a Crazy Life*, p. 8.

5 Cherkovski, *Hank*, pp. 12–13.

6 *Ham on Rye*, p. 11.

7 Ibid., p. 9.

8 'Emily Bukowski', *You Get So Alone*, p. 154.

9 *Sunlight*, p. 40.

10 Sounes, *Locked in the Arms of a Crazy Life*, p. 9.

11 Bukowski, 'Notes of a Dirty Old Man', *Open City*, 16–22 June 1967

12 Bukowski, 'German', in *The Flash of Lightning Behind the Mountain* (New York, 2004), p. 3.

13 *Screams*, p. 55.

14 'Ah, Liberation, Liberty, Lilies on the Moon', *Absence*, pp. 75–6.

15 Bukowski in *Life Magazine*, December 1988. Quoted in James A. Haught, *2000 Years of Disbelief* (New York, 1996), p. 293. See also Neil Schiller's excellent essay 'Social Mechanics and American Morality: The Meanings of Nothingness in the Prose and Poetry of Charles Bukowski', *Bukowski Unleashed: Essays on A Dirty Old Man, Bukowski Journal*, I, pp. 30–89.

16 'London', in *William Blake*, ed. Michael Mason (Oxford, 1988), p. 274.

17 Theodore Roethke, 'The Lost Son', in *Contemporary American Poetry*, ed. A. Poulin, Jr (Boston, 1975), p. 311. On punitive German child-rearing practices, see Susan Griffin, *A Chorus of Stones: The Private Life of War* (New York, 1992). Griffin quotes from 'the advice of German

child-rearing experts from this and the last century. *Crush the will*, they write, *Establish dominance. Permit no disobedience. Suppress everything in the child'* (p. 120).

18 *Ham on Rye*, p. 39.

19 Charles Bukowski, 'the recess bells of school', in *The Continual Condition* (New York, 2009), p. 15. On trauma and creativity, see Edmund Wilson, 'Philoctetes: The Wound and the Bow', in *The Wound and the Bow: Seven Studies in Literature* (Athens, OH, 1997). Also see Maria Damon, *The Dark End of the Street: Margins in American Vanguard Poetry* (Minneapolis, MN, 1993), chapter 3, 'The Child Who Writes/The Child Who Died'.

20 *Ham on Rye*, p. 27.

21 On the Depression see Alfred Kazin, *Starting out in the Thirties* (New York, 1980); Harvey Swados, ed., *The American Writer and the Great Depression* (Indianapolis, 1966); Howard Zinn, *A People's History of the United States: 1492–Present* (New York, 1999), chapter 15, 'Self-Help in Hard Times', pp. 377–406.

22 Barry Miles, *Charles Bukowski* (London, 2005), p. 28.

23 Charles Bukowski, *Beerspit Night and Cursing: The Correspondence of Charles Bukowski and Sheri Martinelli 1960–1967*, ed. Steven Moore (Santa Rosa, CA, 2001), p. 221

24 *Sunlight*, p. 198.

25 Sounes, *Locked in the Arms of a Crazy Life*, p. 13.

26 Franz Kafka, 'In the Penal Colony', in *The Complete Stories*, ed. Nahum N. Glatzer, foreword by John Updike (New York, 1971), pp. 140–67.

27 Nikos Kazantzakis, *The Saviors of God: Spiritual Exercises*, trans. Kimon Friar (New York, 1960), p. 5.

28 *Ham on Rye*, p. 95.

29 Ibid., p. 96.

30 On writers and alcohol, see Thomas B. Gilmore, *Equivocal Spirits: Alcohol and Drinking in Twentieth-Century Literature* (Chapel Hill, NC, and London, 1987); Tom Dardis, *The Thirsty Muse: Alcohol and the American Writer* (New York, 1989).

31 *Notes of a Dirty Old Man*, p. 190

32 'we ain't got no money, honey, but we got rain', *Last Night*, p. 281

33 'waiting', *Last Night*, pp. 107–8.

34 'my old man', *Love is a Dog*, pp. 292–4.

35 *Mockingbird*, p. 78; See also *Notes of a Dirty Old Man*, pp. 190–93.

36 *Portions*, p. 89.

37 'I Meet the Master', *Portions*, p. 208. On Bukowski and Fante, see
    Stephen Cooper, *Full of Life: A Biography of John Fante* (New York,
    2000), pp. 309–10. Also see David Stephen Calonne, 'Two on the
    Trapeze: William Saroyan and Charles Bukowski', *Sure: The Charles
    Bukowski Newsletter*, 5/6 (1992), pp. 26–35.

38 *Portions*, p. 208

39 Ibid., pp. 208–9.

40 *Ham on Rye*, p. 152

41 Ibid., pp. 152, 153.

42 *Notes of a Dirty Old Man*, p. 86.

43 Cited by Larry Smith in 'The American Working-Class Short Story',
    in Blanche H. Gelfant, ed., *The Columbia Companion to the Twentieth-
    Century American Short Story* (New York, 2000), p. 83. Smith observes:
    'of profound influence on twentieth-century working-class stories is
    the fiction of the Russian authors Dostoyevsky, Turgenev, Tolstoy, and
    particularly Anton Chekhov . . . As their stories came into translation,
    American authors were astounded at the deep connections they felt.'

44 'Confessions of a Bad Ass Poet', Part One, *Berkeley Barb*, 26 April–2
    May 1974, p. 13; Vladimir Nabokov, *Lectures on Russian Literature*
    (New York, 1981), pp. 297–8.

45 'Pershing Square, Los Angeles, 1939', in Charles Bukowski, *What
    Matters Most is How Well You Walk Through the Fire* (Santa Rosa, CA,
    1999), p. 43.

46 *Screams*, pp. 55–6; 'Dirty Old Man Confesses', *Portions*, p. 90.

47 *Who's Big in the 'Littles'*, p. 327.

48 Michael Gray Baughan, *Charles Bukowski* (Philadelphia, PA, 2004),
    p. 12.

49 Charles Phoenix, *Southern California in the Fifties* (Santa Monica, CA,
    2001); Lionel Rolfe, *In Search of Literary L.A.* (Los Angeles, 1991).

50 Anthony Heilbut, *Exiled in Paradise: German Refugee Artists in America
    from the 1930s to the Present* (Berkeley, CA, 1997).

51 *Sunlight*, pp. 19, 20. On Bukowski and Los Angeles, see Kevin Starr,
    Coast of Dreams: California on the Edge, 1990–2003 (New York, 2004),
    pp. 477–8, 479, 480.

52 *In/Sert*, 4 (1962); *Mockingbird*, p. 83.

53 *Burning*, p. 127.

54 'Dirty Old Man Confesses', *Portions*, p. 91.

55 Charles Bukowski, *Longshot Pomes for Broke Players* (New York, 1962), n.p.

56 'Dirty Old Man Confesses', *Portions*, p. 91.

57 *Federal Bureau of Investigation File #140-35907, 1957–1970. Henry Charles Bukowski, Jr. (a.k.a. 'Charles Bukowski')*, US Department of Justice, Washington, DC, 20535.

58 *Screams*, p. 56.

59 Letter to William Packard, 23 December 1990, available at www.authenticbukowski.com/manuscripts.

60 *Sun*, 4 (1962).

61 'a note upon starvation', in Charles Bukowski, *Slouching Toward Nirvana* (New York, 2005), p. 254.

62 'Another Portfolio', *Portions*, pp. 234–5; also see Stephen Cooper, 'Madness and Writing in Hamsun, Fante and Bukowski', *Genre*, XIX: *Madness and Literature* (1998), pp. 19–25.

63 Charles Bukowski, *Factotum* (Santa Barbara, CA, 1975), p. 161.

64 *National Underground Review* (15 May 1968), *Portions*, pp. 63–9.

65 'Hard without Music', *Portions*, pp. 15–18.

66 'we the artists', *Burning*, p. 208.

67 Ibid., p. 209.

68 'ww2', *Mockingbird*, p. 91.

69 Ibid., p. 93.

70 *Federal Bureau of Investigation File*.

2 Solitude and Music in Small Rooms: First Stories and Poems, 1944–1959

1 On *Story* magazine, see Frederick J. Hoffman, Charles Allen and Carolyn F. Ulrich, *The Little Magazine: A History and Bibliography* (Princeton, NJ, 1947), pp. 160–61, 303; Margaret Bradham Thornton, ed., *Tennessee Williams's Notebooks* (New Haven, CT, 2006), p. 12; also see Blanche H. Gelfant, ed., *Columbia Companion to the Twentieth-Century American Short Story* (New York, 2000).

2 'Aftermath', p. 2.

3 For Bukowski on Thurber, see *Sunlight*, pp. 110–11, 216, 243, 267, 277. Sigmund Freud, 'Creative Writers and Day-Dreaming', in P. E. Vernon, *Creativity: Selected Readings* (Harmondsworth, 1980), p. 127.

4 'Dirty Old Man Confesses', *Portions*, p. 93.

5 Ibid., p. 94. On this encounter, see also 'the dreamer', *River Rat Review*, 3 (Spring 1988), p. 19.

6 Bukowski submitted stories and corresponded with Burnett from 1945 to 1955. See *Who's Big in the 'Littles'*, p. 118.

7 'Soft and Fat Like Summer Roses', *Matrix*, IX/2 (Summer 1946), p. 10. See *Sifting through the Madness for the Word, the Line, The Way* (New York, 2003), pp. 269–70. On Bukowski's early poetry, see Abel Debritto, 'The Forging of the Ultimate Literary Loner: Charles Bukowski's Early Poetry', in *Das Jahrbuch der Charles-Bukowski-Gesellschaft, 2008* (Riedstadt, 2008), pp. 56–110.

8 See letter to Douglas Goodwin, 15 March 1984: 'You're right on Fante and Celine and James M. Cain, each had something that helped me', *Reach*, p. 56.

9 'The Reason behind Reason', *Absence*, p. 1.

10 Ibid., p. 4.

11 'Hard without Music', *Portions*, p. 16.

12 On Bukowski's preference for instrumental versus vocal music, see his letter to Jon and Louise Webb, 28 March 1963, *Screams*, p.65.

13 'Hard without Music', *Portions*, pp. 17–18.

14 Peter Watson, *The German Genius: Europe's Third Renaissance, the Second Scientific Revolution, and the Twentieth Century* (New York, 2010), p. 163. On music and ecstasy, see also Roald Hoffmann and Iain Boyd Whyte, eds, *Beyond the Finite: The Sublime in Art and Science* (Oxford, 2011), pp. 34–6.

15 Gordon A. Craig defines *Sehnsucht* as 'that irresistible longing for something sensed but not known, that yearning after distant but un-defined gratifications, from which they all [the Romantics] suffered', *The Germans* (New York, 1983), p. 192. Bukowski gives his own inim-itable definition in a letter to William Wantling, 30 October 1965: 'we all have extremities of unfulfilled wanting. We are toys to whatever has created us. We will never get there, and even if we get halfway, the ending will be the same: smashed cat's guts on the boulevard or the last drip of sour blood into the bedpan . . .', *Screams*, p. 222.

16 *Portions*, p. 26.

17 See Andrew Madigan's essay 'Henry Chinaski, Zen Master: *Factotum*, the Holy Fool, and the Critique of Work', *American Studies in Scandinavia*, XLII/2, 2010.

18 See Howard Sounes, *Locked in the Arms of a Crazy Life* (Edinburgh, 2010), pp. 24, 255; also see *Federal Bureau of Investigation File #140–35907, 1957–1970. Henry Charles Bukowski, Jr. (a.k.a. 'Charles Bukowski')*, n.p. The file states under the heading 'Arrested or Received': '7-22-44'; under the heading 'Charge': 'viol. Sel. Serv.' [Violation of Selective Service]; under the heading 'Disposition': '$1000 bond for induction'.

19 'ww2', *Mockingbird*, pp. 91–9; 'Doing Time with Public Enemy No. 1', *Erections*, pp. 248–53.

20 See Michael Basinski, 'Review: 20 Tanks from Kasseldown', *Sure: The Charles Bukowski Newsletter*, 7, p. 29; Caresse Crosby, *The Passionate Years* (New York, 1979); Geoffrey Wolff, *Black Sun: The Brief Transit and Violent Eclipse of Harry Crosby* (New York, 1976).

21 Bukowski letter to Weissner, 28 January 1967, *Screams*, p. 288. There is a fugitive reference to Oswald Spengler in a 16 December 1970 letter to Norm Moser: 'No matter how much the White man may hate himself, he is simply *gifted*, but it may be ending for one reason or another . . . Spengler's *Decline of the West* . . . published in 1918, so long ago . . . although he gave it a 300-year time-table . . . the signs are showing . . . Either Whitey's got to get some *soul* or all his cleverness will be just so much spilled jism . . .'. See Norm Moser, ed., *The Illuminations Reader: Art and Writing from Illuminations, Pulse & Gar 1965–1978* (Berkeley, CA, 1990), n.p. On German Expressionism, see Walter Sokel, *The Writer in Extremis: Expressionism in Twentieth Century German Literature* (Stanford, CA, 1959).

22 'Untitled Essay', in *A Tribute to Jim Lowell*, *Portions*, p. 61.

23 'Confessions of a Bad Ass Poet', *Berkeley Barb* (26 April–2 May 1974), p. 12.

24 Howard Sounes, *Bukowski in Pictures* (Edinburgh, 2000), p. 36

25 See letter to Jim Roman, 26 September 1965, pp. 207–8, *Screams*; also Sounes, *Locked in the Arms of a Crazy Life*, p. 27.

26 Barry Miles, *Charles Bukowski* (London, 2005), p. 83.

27 Neeli Cherkovski, *Hank: The Life of Charles Bukowski* (New York, 1991),

p. 86; Sounes, *Locked in the Arms of a Crazy Life*, pp. 27–8.

28 Charles Bukowski, 'my first affair with that older woman', *You Get So Alone*, pp. 78–9; 'the tragedy of the leaves', *It Catches*, p. 15; *Burning*, p. 15.

29 'Notes of a Dirty Old Man', *Open City* (10–16 August 1967).

30 *Federal Bureau of Investigation File #140–35907.*

31 Unpublished Bukowski letter, 4 November 1953, *Who's Big in the 'Littles'.*

32 *Screams*, p. 115; see 'Life and Death in the Charity Ward', *Erections*, pp. 130–9.

33 *Sunlight*, p. 31.

34 C. G. Jung, *The Red Book*, ed. Sonu Shamdasani (New York, 2009).

35 Edmund Wilson, 'Philoctetes: The Wound and the Bow', in *The Wound and the Bow: Seven Studies in Literature* (Athens, OH, 1997).

36 Friedrich Nietzsche, *Spruche und Pfeile 8*, from *Twilight of the Idols*, *The Portable Nietzsche*, ed. Walter Kaufmann (New York, 1968), p. 467.

37 *Screams*, p. 304.

38 Andrew Robinson, *Sudden Genius?: The Gradual Path to Creative Breakthroughs* (Oxford, 2010).

39 *Hearse*, 8 (1961); *Burning in Water*. Sounes, *Locked in the Arms of a Crazy Life*, pp. 36–41.

40 Charles Bukowski, 'cancer', *Septuagenarian Stew* (Santa Rosa, CA, 1990), p. 49.

41 Gary Snyder, *The Real Work: Interviews & Talks, 1964–1979*, ed. with introduction by W. Scott McLean (New York, 1980), p. 157.

42 Sounes, *Locked in the Arms of a Crazy Life*, p. 39.

43 An example of Bukowski's drawing is featured in *Frank: An International Journal of Contemporary Writing & Art*, 4 (Summer–Autumn 1985), p. 15.

44 'Death Wants More Death', *Harlequin*, 8 (1961).

45 *Charles Darwin's Notebooks, 1836–1844: Geology, Transmutation of Species, Metaphysical Enquiries*, ed. Paul H. Barrett et al. (Cambridge, 2008), p. 429; *The Charles Bukowski Tapes*, 'Nature', dir. Barbet Schroeder (Barrel Entertainment, 2006).

46 Tim Hunt, ed., *The Selected Poetry of Robinson Jeffers* (Stanford, CA, 2001), p. 125.

47 'those sons of bitches', *Mockingbird*, p. 86. On Jeffers, see *Sunlight*, pp. 20, 35, 43, 69, 108, 110, 112, 198, 199, 243. Also see Donald Masterson, 'Jeffers is My God: Charles Bukowski's Commentary on Robinson

Jeffers', *Jeffers Studies*, 5(2) (Spring 2001), pp. 10–20; Ted Olson, 'Two Poets Listening to Life: Bukowski and Jeffers', *Sure*, 4 (1992), pp. 2–8; Lucy Gray, 'Charles Bukowski Remembers John Fante', *Brick: A Literary Journal*, 79 (Summer 2007), pp. 13–28.

48 See 'West Coast School', in Jay Parini, ed., *The Oxford Encyclopedia of American Literature* (Oxford, 2004).

49 'The Rapist's Story', *Harlequin*, II/1; *Absence*, pp. 16–17.

50 '80 Airplanes', *Harlequin*, II/1; *Absence*, pp. 25–31.

51 'Mine', *The Days Run Away*, p. 10.

52 On Wallace Berman, see Stephen Fredman et. al., *Semina Culture: Wallace Berman and His Circle* (Santa Monica, CA, 2005); Bukowski's poem 'mine' is mentioned on p. 54. Also see Hunter Drohojowska-Philp, *Rebels in Paradise; The Los Angeles Art Scene and the 1960's* (New York, 2011), pp. 28–30; Robert Candida Smith, *Utopia and Dissent: Art, Poetry, and Politics in California* (Berkeley, CA, 1995), chapter 8.

53 'The Life of Borodin', *Quicksilver*, XI/3 (1958).

54 'When Hugo Wolf Went Mad', *Odyssey*, II/1 (1959).

55 'The Hunted', *Quicksilver*, XI/2 (1958).

56 Walter Pater, 'Conclusion', in *The Renaissance* in *Essays on Literature and Art*, ed. Jennifer Uglow (London, 1973), p. 45.

57 'Timeline', www.bukowski.net.

58 *Screams*, p. 48.

59 Sounes, *Locked in the Arms of a Crazy Life*, p. 41; 'Confession of A Coward', *Betting on The Muse: Poems & Stories* (Santa Rosa, CA, 1996), pp. 59–65.

60 'The Day I Kicked Away a Bankroll', *Quicksilver*, XII/2 (1959); *Roominghouse*, pp. 73–5.

61 Sounes, *Locked in the Arms of a Crazy Life*, p. 42.

62 *San Francisco Review*, 1 (1958), pp. 66, 67.

63 'The Twins', in *It Catches*, pp. 37, 38. On 'The Twins' and the abuse of Bukowski as a child, see Laura T. Weddle, 'The Healing Power of Art: Bukowski's *The Twins*', *Sure, The Charles Bukowski Newsletter*, 5/6 (1992), pp. 36–9.

64 'The Death of the Father', Parts 1 and 2, *Hot Water Music* (Santa Barbara, CA, 1983) pp. 161–70.

65 'I Taste the Ashes of Your Death', *Nomad*, 1 (1959); *The Days Run Away*, p. 36.

66 Jory Sherman, *Bukowski: Friendship, Fame & Bestial Myth* (Augusta, GA, 1981), p. 15.

67 Ibid.

3 Christ and Dionysus: *Flower, Fist and Bestial Wail* to *Crucifix in a Deathhand*, 1960–1965

1 Arthur Marwick, *The Sixties: Cultural Revolution in Britain, France, Italy, and the United States, c. 1958–c. 1974* (Oxford, 1998); William L. O'Neill, *Coming Apart: An Informal History of America in the 1960's* (Chicago, IL, 2005).

2 Alice W. Flaherty, *The Midnight Disease: The Drive to Write, Writer's Block and the Creative Brain* (New York, 2004); Juvenal, *The Sixteen Satires*, trans. Peter Green (London, 1998), p. 56.

3 Sanford Dorbin, 'Charles Bukowski and the Little Mag/Small Press Movement', *Soundings: Collections of the University Library*, II/1 (May 1970), pp. 17–32.

4 *Sunlight*, p. 215.

5 Ibid., p. 236. In his 'Introduction' to Jory Sherman's *My Face in Wax* (Chicago, IL, 1965), he expanded on this idea: 'When I run my hand across a page of poetry I do not want oil and onionskin, I do not want slick bullshit; I want my hand to come away with blood on it' (n.p.).

6 Lawrence Ferlinghetti, 'Populist Manifesto', *Editor's Choice: Literature & Graphics from the U.S. Small Press, 1965–1977*, ed. Morty Sklar and Jim Mulac (Iowa City, 1980), p. 43.

7 *Notes of a Dirty Old Man* (North Hollywood, CA, 1969), p. 165.

8 *Living on Luck*, p. 180.

9 William Carlos Williams, *Paterson*, ed. Christopher MacGowan (New York, 1995), p. 168.

10 'Looking Back at a Big One', in *Portions*, p. 232.

11 Fredric Jameson, 'Postmodernism and Consumer Society', in E. Ann Kaplan ed., *Postmodernism and Its Discontents* (London, 1988), p. 13.

12 Jack Matthews, 'The Search for Bukowski', in *The Contemporary Literary Scene 1973*, ed. F. Magill (Englewood Cliffs, NJ, 1974), p. 228.

13 *Sunlight*, p. 92. On Aiken, also see p. 198.

14 James Boyer May reviewed the book in *Trace*, 40 (January–March 1961), pp. 53–4. He singled out 'The Twins' as the 'most moving poem' in the collection.

15 Aaron Krumhansl, *A Descriptive Bibliography of the Primary Publications of Charles Bukowski* (Santa Rosa, CA, 1999), pp. 15–16.

16 *Screams*, p. 10.

17 Ibid., p. 25.

18 D. H. Lawrence, letter to Ernest Collings, 17 January 1913, in *The Letters of D. H. Lawrence*, ed. and intro. Aldous Huxley (London, 1934), p. 94. Also see Bukowski's poem, 'Interviewed by a Guggenheim Recipient', *Graffiti*, 2 (1965); *Roominghouse*. Bukowski lists the poets students should read: 'Whitman, T.S. Eliot, D.H. Lawrence's poems about / reptiles and beasts, Auden', p. 110.

19 '10 Lions and the End of the World', *Flower, Fist and Bestial Wail* (Eureka, CA, 1960); *Roominghouse*, p. 96; *San Francisco Review*, 1, 1958; on cummings: 'it was not so much his content as his tricky and lovely and easy way of using and placing his words. That was it', letter to Jon Cone, 14 June 1992, *Reach*, p. 244.

20 'Manifesto: A Call for Our Own Critics', *Absence*, p. 32.

21 On the American underground, see John McMillian, *Smoking Typewriters: The Sixties Underground Press and the Rise of Alternative Media in America* (New York, 2011).

22 Jeff Weddle, *Bohemian New Orleans* (Jackson, MS, 2007), p. 188.

23 *Screams*, p. 21.

24 *Beerspit Night and Cursing: The Correspondence of Charles Bukowski and Sheri Martinelli, 1960–1967*, ed. Steven Moore (Santa Rosa, CA, 2001), pp. 361–71.

25 Ibid., p. 128. Also see Steven Moore, 'Sheri Martinelli: A Modernist Muse', *Gargoyle*, 41 (Summer 1998).

26 *Living on Luck*, p. 17. Bukowski refers to the essay 'The Retreat from the Word', by George Steiner, which originally appeared in the *Kenyon Review*, XIII/2 (Spring 1961), pp. 187–216, reprinted in *Language and Silence: Essays on Language, Literature and the Inhuman* (New York, 1967), pp. 12–35.

27 *Living on Luck*, p. 17.

28 'I Am Visited By an Editor and a Poet', in *Run with the Hunted* (Chicago, IL, 1962), p. 29; *Roominghouse*, p. 217.

29 *Screams*, p. 304: letter to Carl Weissner, 13 May 1967.

30 *Living on Luck*, p. 25.

31 Barry Miles, *Charles Bukowski* (London, 2005), p. 120.

32 'To Jane, When Love Was Not Enough', *The Days Run Away*, p. 42

33 Neeli Cherkovski, *Hank: The Life of Charles Bukowski* (New York, 1991), p. 293. On Los Angeles poetry, see Bukowski, 'A Foreword to These Poems', in *Anthology of l.a. Poets*, ed. Charles Bukowski, Neeli Cherry and Paul Vangelisti (Fairfax, CA, 1972). The 'Foreword' is collected in *Absence*, pp. 126–8.

34 KPFK reading, available at www.bukowski.net and on CD.

35 R. R. Cuscaden, *The Outsider*, 3 (Spring 1963), p. 64; the essay appeared originally in the British magazine *Satis* (Spring–Summer 1962).

36 John William Corrington, 'Charles Bukowski and the Savage Surfaces', *Northwest Review*, VI/4 (Fall 1963), pp. 123–9.

37 *Screams*, p. 48. For Bukowski's tribute to the Webbs, see 'The Outsider', *Absence*, pp. 129–9. On H. L. Mencken, see letter to Stephen Kessler, *Reach*, p. 60; *Living on Luck*, pp. 52, 246.

38 On John Bryan, see McMillian, *Smoking Typewriters*, pp. 92, 127, 239 n. 84.

39 Charles Bukowski, 'Peace, Baby, Is Hard Sell', *Renaissance*, 4 (1962); *Absence*, pp. 34–8.

40 Weddle, *Bohemian New Orleans*, p. 73. On Kaja, also see Barry Miles, *The Beat Hotel: Ginsberg, Burroughs and Corso in Paris, 1958–1963* (New York, 2000), pp. 259–60, 268.

41 Weddle, *Bohemian New Orleans*, p. 97.

42 Gerard Malanga, *Screen Tests, Portraits, Nudes: 1964–1996*, ed. Patrick Remy and Marc Parent (Göttingen, 2000), p. 89.

43 Robinson Jeffers, 'Hellenistics', *The Collected Poetry of Robinson Jeffers, Volume Two, 1928–1938*, ed. Tim Hunt (Stanford, CA, 1989), p. 526.

44 Krumhansl, *A Descriptive Bibliography*, p. 23.

45 Corrington, 'Introduction' to *It Catches*, p. 5.

46 Kenneth Rexroth, 'There's Poetry in a Ragged Hitch–Hiker', *New York Times* (5 July 1964).

47 'Old Man, Dead in a Room', *It Catches*, p. 95; *Roominghouse*, p. 53.

48 Ibid.

49 Walt Whitman, 'Song of Myself', *Leaves of Grass*, intro. Gay Wilson Allen (New York, 1980), p. 96. Bukowski wrote an early, unpublished

essay on Whitman; see *Who's Big in the 'Littles'*, p. 129. On Whitman and the counterculture, see David Stephen Calonne, *Bebop Buddhist Ecstasy: Saroyan's Influence on Kerouac and the Beats with an Introduction by Lawrence Ferlinghetti* (San Francisco, 2010).

50 'the tragedy of the leaves', *It Catches*, p. 15.

51 Ibid.

52 'Conversation in a Cheap Room', p. 31; *Roominghouse*, p. 224.

53 *Living on Luck*, p. 49.

54 Ibid., p. 50.

55 The State of California preserved Bukowski's residence as a historic landmark in 2008.

56 *Bukowski in the Bathtub: Recollections of Charles Bukowski by John Thomas*, ed. Philomene Long (Venice, CA, 1997), p. 15.

57 Ibid., p. 16.

58 *Living on Luck*, p. 138.

59 'Notes of a Dirty Old Man', *Open City* (8–14 December 1967); *Absence*, pp. 59–63. In 'one for old snaggle-tooth', he remembers her more fondly: 'she has hurt fewer people than / anybody I know. / and if you look at it like that, / well, / she has created a better world. / she has won / Frances, this poem is for you.' *Love is a Dog*, p. 66.

60 *The Outsider*, 1/3 (Spring 1963), p. 61.

61 'A Murder', in *Notes from Underground*, 1 (1964), pp. 53–8; reprinted as 'The Blanket' in *Erections*, pp. 231–8.

62 Sigmund Freud, 'The Uncanny', in *The Uncanny*, trans. David McClintock, intro. Hugh Haughton (New York, 2003), pp. 123–62. *Deutsche Erzählungen/German Stories: A Bilingual Anthology*, trans. and ed. Harry Steinhauer (Berkeley, CA, 1984), p. 110.

63 'The Blanket', p. 232.

64 Ibid., p. 238.

65 Charles Rosen, *The Romantic Generation* (Cambridge, MA, 1998), p. 648.

66 'The Blanket', pp. 237–8.

67 See *The Bukowski/Purdy Letters, 1964–1974*, ed. Seamus Cooney (Sutton West & Santa Barbara, CA, 1983).

68 See Steve Richmond, *Spinning Off Bukowski* (Northville, MI, 1996), pp. 20, 32; *Earth Rose 1* (Santa Monica, CA, 1966); on Bukowski and broadsides, see James D. Sullivan, *On the Walls and in the Streets: American Poetry Broadsides from the Sixties* (Champaign, IL, 1997), p. 24.

69 *Screams*, p. 112.

70 *The Days Run Away*, pp. 144–6.

71 Charles Bukowski, *Post Office* (Santa Barbara, CA, 1971), p. 91.

72 *Sciamachy*, 5 (1963).

73 *Living on Luck*, p. 97.

74 *Screams*, p. 113.

75 Ibid., pp. 156, 192–3, 203, 242.

76 *Bukowski in the Bathtub*, ed. Philomene Long (Venice, CA, 1997), p. 12.

77 *Hollywood* (Santa Rosa, CA, 1989), pp. 229, 230. *Betting on the Muse: Poems and Stories* (Santa Rosa, CA, 1996), p.136; first appeared in *Black Ace*, 3 (1991).

78 Bukowski, *More Notes of a Dirty Old Man: The Uncollected Columns*, ed. David Stephen Calonne (San Francisco, 2011), pp. 27–38.

79 'Preface' to *Crucifix in a Deathhand* (New Orleans, 1965), n.p.

80 Bukowski, 'crucifix in a deathhand', in ibid., pp. 23–4; *Burning*, p. 52.

81 'A Report Upon the Consumption of Myself', in 'crucifix', p. 32; *Roominghouse*, p. 105.

82 Ibid., p. 33; *Roominghouse*, p. 106.

83 Ibid.

84 'Foreword', *Roominghouse*, p. 5.

85 'on beer cans and sugar cartons', in *The People Look Like Flowers at Last* (New York, 2007), pp. 249.

86 'A Rambling Essay on Poetics and the Bleeding Life Written While Drinking a Six-Pack (Tall)', *Portions*, pp. 33–40.

87 Unpublished letter, for sale by Addyman Books, ABE, Hereford, UK.

88 *Screams*, p. 190. On Bukowski and Celine, see Ulf Geyersbach, *Louis-Ferdinand Céline* (Hamburg, 2008), pp. 7, 12, 68; *Sunlight*; Bukowski, 'Celine with cane and basket', *Last Night*, p. 242.

89 Martin letter, available at www.authenticbukowski.com/manuscripts. On John Martin and Black Sparrow Press, see *Against the Grain: Interviews with Maverick American Publishers*, ed. Robert Dana (Iowa City, 1986), pp. 113–50.

90 See *Dear Friend: A Letter from Henry Miller to Charles Bukowski on August 22, 1965* (Santa Barbara, CA, 1987). 'I Am Afraid That I Will Continue To Drink Myself To Death . . .', *Kauri*, 11 (Nov–Dec. 1965). Miller had written to the Webbs on 18 December 1963 concerning

the recent publication of *It Catches*: 'I do sincerely like Bukowski's poems. And I don't see why he is not published by a big publisher.' Available at www.authenticbukowski.com/manuscripts.

91 *Confessions of a Man Insane Enough to Live with Beasts*, in *South of No North* (Los Angeles, 1975), pp. 168–89.

92 *Lizard's Eyelid*, Winter Issue, n.d.

93 *Confessions of a Man Insane Enough to Live with Beasts*, p. 168.

94 Ibid., p. 175.

95 Ibid., p. 178.

96 Ibid., p. 185.

4 Age of Aquarius Dawning: A Dirty Old Man among the Beats and Hippies, 1966–1969

1 Arthur Marwick, *The Sixties: Cultural Revolution in Britain, France, Italy, and the United States, c. 1958–c. 1974* (Oxford, 1998).

2 See David Stephen Calonne, 'Introduction' to *Absence*, pp. xv–xvii. Also see Jean-Luc Duval, *Bukowski and the Beats* (Northville, MI, 2002). On Bukowski and the hippies, see 'Dirty Old Man Confesses', *Absence*, pp. 100–102.

3 Bukowski, review of Allen Ginsberg's *Empty Mirror*, *Ole*, 7 (May 1967); *Absence*, pp. 49–53.

4 'A Rambling Essay on Poetics and the Bleeding Life Written While Drinking a Six-Pack (Tall)', *Portions*, p. 38.

5 For Bukowski and Corso, see 'I Just Write Poetry so I Can Go to Bed with Girls', *Absence*, pp. 99–111.

6 'Reading and Breeding for Kenneth', *Portions*, pp. 105–10.

7 'Drawing of A Band Concert on a Matchbox', *Some/Thing*, II/1 (Winter 1966), ed. Jerome Rothenberg and David Antin; *The Days Run Away*, pp. 123–5.

8 On Malanga and Warhol, see Stefana Sabin, *Andy Warhol* (Hamburg, 1992). For Malanga's photograph of Bukowski, see Gerard Malanga, *Screen Tests, Portraits, Nudes: 1964–1996*, ed. Patrick Remy and Marc Parent (Göttingen, 2000), p. 89.

9 See *Intrepid Anthology: A Decade & Then Some Contemporary Literature 1966*, ed. Allen Deloach (Buffalo, NY, 1976).

10 See Bukowski's poem 'The Beats', in *The Best American Poetry 2005*, ed. Paul Muldoon (New York, 2005), pp. 25–6.

11 'the 60's', *The Flash of Lightning Behind the Mountain* (New York, 2004), p. 38.

12 *Reach*, p. 279.

13 Jonathan Cott, 'Reflections of a Cosmic Tourist', *Conversations with Henry Miller*, ed. Frank Kersnowski and Alice Hughes (Jackson, FL, 1994), p. 200.

14 William S. Burroughs, *Nova Express* (New York, 1992), p. 5.

15 On William Wantling, see 'Unpublished Foreword to William Wantling's 7 on Style', *Portions*, pp. 151–5. Wantling's poetry is collected in H. Bruce Franklin, ed., *Prison Writing in 20th-Century America* (New York, 1998), pp. 242–5.

16 Last year one Tamara Swerline wrote to the Bukowski.net website: 'Would you consider donation [sic] Charles Bukowski to our prison library? He's often requested and due to our state budget crisis my funds have been cut.' Accessed 27 January 2011.

17 *Screams*, p. 111. Bukowski on Villon and Genet, see 'Looking for the Giants', *Sunlight*, pp. 44–6.

18 Norman Mailer, 'The White Negro', in *Advertisements for Myself* (New York, 1959), p. 319. According to Al Fogel, Mailer wrote him a letter saying 'Bukowski spit out poetry like nails' (personal communication, 19 July 2010). The two writers met during the filming of *Barfly* at the Château Marmont in Los Angeles.

19 'East Hollywood: The New Paris', *Absence*, p. 200.

20 See Aaron Krumhansl, *A Descriptive Bibliography of the Primary Publications of Charles Bukowski* (Santa Rosa, CA, 1999), pp. 32–5.

21 *Reach*, p. 18.

22 For Bukowski's review of Artaud, see *Portions*, pp. 49–53; *Living on Luck*, p. 68.

23 Marwick, *The Sixties*.

24 *The East Village Other*, 1/23 (1–15 November 1966); *Roominghouse*, p. 31.

25 *The Genius of the Crowd* (Cleveland, OH, 1966); *Roominghouse*, p. 31. On d.a. levy, see Larry Smith and Ingrid Swanberg, eds, *d.a. levy and the mimeograph revolution* (Huron, OH, 2007).

26 Lao Tzu, *Tao Te Ching*, trans. Stephen Mitchell (New York, 2000), verse 57.

27 'Untitled Essay', *A Tribute to Jim Lowell* (Cleveland, OH, 1967), *Portions*, pp. 61–2.

28 On censorship, see Charles Rembar, *The End of Obscenity: The Trials of Lady Chatterley, Tropic of Cancer and Fanny Hill* (New York, 1968); Bill Morgan and Nancy J. Peters, eds, *Howl on Trial* (San Francisco, 2006).

29 'the faces are gnawing at my walls but have not yet come in', *Entrails*, 4 (1967), p. 48.

30 Hart Crane, 'Legend', *White Buildings* (New York, 1972), p. 3.

31 'the faces are gnawing', pp. 48, 49; Michel Foucault, 'A Preface to Transgression', in *Religion and Culture: Michel Foucault*, ed. Jeremy R. Carrette (New York, 1999), p. 58.

32 *Bukowski in the Bathtub: Recollections of Charles Bukowski by John Thomas*, ed. Philomene Long (Venice, CA, 1997), pp. 30, 40, 109.

33 Aldous Huxley, *The Doors of Perception* (New York, 2009). On writers and drugs, see Marcus Boon, *The Road of Excess: A History of Writers on Drugs* (Cambridge, MA, 2005); James Hughes, *Altered States: Creativity Under the Influence* (New York, 1999).

34 'The Marriage of Heaven and Hell', in *William Blake*, ed. Michael Mason (Oxford, 1988), p. 14.

35 *Iconolatre*, 18/19, where Bukowski had published seven poems, edited by Alex Hand and Alan Turner in West Hartlepool, UK. See *Gargoyle*, 35, p. 71. On Weissner, see Jay Dougherty, 'Charles Bukowski and the Outlaw Spirit', and 'Translating Bukowski and the Beats: An Interview with Carl Weissner', *Gargoyle* 35 (1988), pp. 98–103 and pp. 66–87.

36 *Acid: Neue Amerikansche Szene*, ed. R. D. Brinkmann and R. R. Rygulla (Hamburg, 1983): 'Am Fussende die Amsel steht'; 'Lilien in meinem Gehirn', pp. 103, 229.

37 'The Old Pro', *Ole*, 5 (1966); *Absence*, pp. 44–8.

38 *Portions*, pp. 57–60.

39 Barry Miles, *Charles Bukowski* (London, 2005), p. 157.

40 His first appearance was in no. 50 (1967) with the poem 'men's crapper' and in four issues between 1969 and 1970.

41 Bukowski, *More Notes of A Dirty Old Man: The Uncollected Columns*, ed. David Stephen Calonne (San Francisco, 2011), p. 15.

42 *Play the Piano*, p. 52.

43 *Screams*, p. 175.

44 Krumhansl, *A Descriptive Bibliography*, p. 37. See review by Alicia Ostriker, 'Other Times, Other Voices', *Partisan Review*, xxxviii/2 (1971), pp. 220–21.

45 *Simbolica*, 27 (1966).

46 'Author's Introduction', *Burning*; Miles, *Charles Bukowski*, pp. 154–5.

47 Bukowski, *At Terror Street and Agony Way* (Los Angeles, 1968), p. 5; *Burning*, p. 97.

48 Blake, 'Auguries of Innocence, in *William Blake*, ed. Michael Mason, p. 30.

49 *Burning*, p. 108.

50 Ibid., p. 128.

51 Sounes, *Locked in the Arms of a Crazy Life*, pp. 97, 295.

52 Bukowski, *Poems Written Before Jumping Out Of An 8 Story Window* (Glendale, CA, 1968), n.p.

53 *Gedichte die einer schrieb bevor er im 8. Stockwerk aus dem Fenster sprang* (Gersthofen, 1974). On Bukowski's German reception, see Horst Schmidt, *The Germans Love Me for Some Reason* (Augsburg, 2006).

54 *Federal Bureau of Investigation File #140–35907, 1957–1970. Henry Charles Bukowski, Jr. (a.k.a. 'Charles Bukowski')*, n.p.

55 Ibid.

56 Weissner, 'Der Dirty Old Man von Los Angeles', pp. 6–7 in *Gedichte die einer schrieb*. Translation mine.

57 See Terence Diggory, *Encyclopedia of the New York School Poets* (New York, 2009) on the '220-page issue that Gerard Malanga guest-edited for the West Coast magazine Intransit', p. 242.

58 There were three issues of *Laugh Literary*: vol. I, no. 1, 1969; vol. I, no. 2, 1969; vol. I, no. 3, 1971.

59 *Notes of a Dirty Old Man*, p. 87.

60 Krumhansl, *A Descriptive Bibliography*, p. 41.

61 *Notes of a Dirty Old Man*, p. 9.

62 Ibid., p. 65.

63 Ibid., p. 29.

64 Carver met Bukowski in spring 1972 when he invited him to read at UC Santa Cruz. On Carver and Bukowski, see Carol Sklenicka, *Raymond Carver: A Writer's Life* (New York, 2009), pp. 168, 207–9, 210, 448. For Carver's poem inspired by Bukowski, see *Fires: Essays, Poems, Stories* (New York, 1984), 'You Don't Know What Love Is: an evening

with Charles Bukowski', pp. 57–61. On Waits' discovery of Bukowski through the *la Free Press*, see Barney Hoskyns, *Lowside of the Road: A Life of Tom Waits* (New York, 2009), pp. 72–4.

65 Cherkovski, *Hank*, p. 193.

66 *The Days Run Away*, pp. 65, 39, 79; 'remains', p. 65.

67 Ibid., p. 176.

68 Ibid., p. 67.

69 Harold Norse, *Memoirs of a Bastard Angel: A Fifty-Year Literary and Erotic Odyssey* (New York, 1989).

70 'The Day We Talked About James Thurber', *Erections*, p. 140–47.

71 Howard Sounes, *Locked in the Arms of a Crazy Life* (Edinburgh, 2010), p. 102.

72 Poster of Bukowski reading.

73 'The Absence of the Hero', *Absence*, pp. 64–7.

74 Bertolt Brecht, *Baal*, in Walter H. Sokel, ed., *An Anthology of German Expressionist Drama: A Prelude to the Absurd* (New York, 1963), p. 353.

75 'The Absence of the Hero', *Absence*, pp. 64–7.

76 *Federal Bureau of Investigation File*.

77 Sounes, *Locked in the Arms of a Crazy Life*, p. 101.

78 Sounes, based on conversations with Martin, ibid., p. 101.

79 Barry Miles, *In the Sixties* (London, 2002), p. 259.

5 A Professional Writer and the Dogs from Hell, 1970–1978

1 On the genesis of *Post Office*, see *Sunlight*, p. 241; Howard Sounes, *Locked in the Arms of a Crazy Life* (Edinburgh, 2010), pp. 103–6.

2 Louis-Ferdinand Céline, *Voyage au bout de la nuit* (Paris, 1952) p. 15.

3 Andrew Madigan, 'Henry Chinaski, Zen Master: *Factotum*, the Holy Fool, and the Critique of Work', *American Studies in Scandinavia*, xlii/2 (2010).

4 Charles Bukowski, *Post Office* (Santa Barbara, ca, 1971), p. 25.

5 See Mark Ames, *Going Postal: Rage, Murder, and Rebellion* (Brooklyn, ny, 2005), pp. 72–8. Also see Stanley Aronowitz, *False Promises: The Shaping of American Working Class Consciousness* (Durham, nc, and London, 1992), p. 311.

6 Valentine Cunningham, 'Male Order', *Times Literary Supplement*, 4030

(20 June 1980), p. 706.

7 'East Hollywood: The New Paris', *Absence*, p. 188.

8 *Bukowski in the Bathtub: Recollections of Charles Bukowski by John Thomas*, ed. Philomene Long (Venice, CA, 1997), p. 23.

9 'The L.A. Scene', *Portions*, pp. 111–20.

10 'I Just Write Poetry So I Can Go to Bed with Girls', *Rogue*, 29 (April 1971); *Absence*, pp. 99–111. Bukowski also writes about Corso in the poem 'Tarot', *Wormwood Review*, 53 (1974), pp. 22–3.

11 Archilochus, trans. Guy Davenport, *7 Greeks* (New York, 1980), p. 63.

12 For sale of the archive, see Michael Gray Baughan, *Charles Bukowski* (Philadelphia, PA, 2004), p. 67; Sounes, *Locked in the Arms of a Crazy Life*, p. 102.

13 *Living on Luck*, p. 234; Barry Miles, *Charles Bukowski* (London, 2005), p. 185.

14 For Bukowski's comments on writing for mens' magazines, see *Sunlight*, p. 181.

15 His first poem appeared in 1971, issue 7.

16 William Packard, 'Notes on the Bukowski', *Small Press Review*, IV/4 (May 1973), p. 9.

17 Letter to Packard, 17 April 1992, *Reach*, p. 235.

18 *Me and Your Sometime Love Poems*, 4th edn (Phoenix, AZ, 2009), p. 37.

19 Sounes, *Locked in the Arms of a Crazy Life*, p. 112.

20 See Liza Williams, *Up the City of Angels* (New York, 1971).

21 Bill Morgan, *The Beat Generation in San Francisco: A Literary Tour* (San Francisco, 2003), p. 63.

22 For Robert Crumb on Bukowski, see *R. Crumb: Conversations*, ed. D. K. Holm (Jackson, FL, 2004).

23 'consummation of grief', *Mockingbird*, p. 85.

24 Tennessee Williams, *A Streetcar Named Desire* (New York, 2004), p. 147.

25 'the mockingbird, *Mockingbird*, p. 71.

26 'Hurt Hawks', in *The Selected Poetry of Robinson Jeffers*, ed. Tim Page (Stanford, CA, 2001), pp. 165, 166. Also see Donald Masterson, '"Jeffers is my god": Charles Bukowski's Commentary on Robinson Jeffers', *Jeffers Studies*, V/2 (Spring 2001), pp. 10–20.

27 Ibid., p. 161.

28 'style', *Mockingbird*, p. 156.

29 Ibid., p. 114.

30 Bob Dylan, 'Subterranean Homesick Blues' (1965).

31 'style', *Mockingbird*, pp. 115–16.

32 Raymond Carver, 'You Don't Know What Love Is', *Fires: Essays, Poems, Stories* (New York, 1984), pp. 57–61.

33 *Reach*, p. 158.

34 On Carver and Bukowski, see Carol Sklenicka, *Raymond Carver: A Writer's Life* (New York, 2009) pp. 207–9. On Carver, see Martin Scofield, *The Cambridge Introduction to the American Short Story* (Cambridge, 2006), pp. 226–35.

35 *Reach*, p. 158.

36 *Living on Luck*, p. 146.

37 Aaron Krumhansl, *A Descriptive Bibliography of the Primary Publications of Charles Bukowski* (Santa Rosa, CA, 1999), p. 50. David Evanier reviewed *Erections* in *Event*, II/2, 'Would You Suggest Writing as a Career?' Also see Thomas R. Edwards, 'News from Elsewhere', *The New York Review of Books* (5 October 1972), pp. 21–3.

38 'The Birth, Life, and Death of an Underground Newspaper', *Erections*, p. 119.

39 'The Day We Talked About James Thurber', ibid., p. 140.

40 Ibid., p. 141

41 Ibid.

42 'The Fuck Machine', ibid., pp. 35–46.

43 'The Fiend', ibid., pp. 207–12. For Bukowski's response to the controversy generated by the story, see *Sunlight*, p. 116.

44 'The Copulating Mermaid of Venice, Calif.', *Erections*, pp. 156–63.

45 'The Big Pot Game', ibid., p. 468; Lester Bangs, *Creem*, VI/5 (October 1974), p. 59.

46 Sounes, *Locked in the Arms of a Crazy Life*, p. 133. Bukowski composed a two-part column for the *Los Angeles Free Press* about the trip, later revised and included in *Women*.

47 See 'Notes of a Dirty Old Man', *LA Free Press* (28 June 1974); *Absence*, pp. 157–61.

48 Neeli Cherkovksi, *Hank: The Life of Charles Bukowski* (New York, 1991), p. 239.

49 Letter to Weissner, available at www.authenticbukowski.com/manuscripts.

50 'No Way to Paradise', *South of No North* (Los Angeles, 1973), pp. 28–32.

51 'Class', ibid., pp. 65–9. For Bukowski's review of A. E. Hotchner's *Papa Hemingway*, see 'An Old Drunk Who Ran out of Luck', *Portions*, pp. 54–6. 'The Night Nobody Believed I Was Allen Ginsberg', *Portions*, pp. 70–77.

52 'This is What Killed Dylan Thomas', *South of No North*, p. 129.

53 Ibid., p. 130; Jeffers, *Selected Poems*, p. 23.

54 Kenneth Rexroth, 'Thou Shalt Not Kill', *The Collected Shorter Poems of Kenneth Rexroth* (New York, 1967), p. 267.

55 'This is What Killed Dylan Thomas', *South of No North*, p. 131.

56 See 'Notes of a Dirty Old Man', *Los Angeles Free Press* (28 June 1974); *Absence*, pp. 157–61.

57 *Bukowski in the Bathtub*, ed. Long, p. 8.

58 Published in *Oui* in two instalments, February/March 1985; *Absence*, pp. 221–44.

59 Bukowski declared 'there's a great deal of Puritan in me', *Sunlight*, p. 123.

60 Ann Menebroker, *Surviving Bukowski: The Relationship between Ann Menebroker and Charles Bukowski* (Boulder, CO, 1998), p. 17.

61 Ric Reynolds, 'Partying with the Poets', *Sunlight*, pp. 74, 75.

62 Ibid., p. 75.

63 *Sunlight*, p. 85. Also see Ernst Kris, 'Inspiration', *Psychoanalytic Explorations in Art* (New York, 1971), p. 295; Vladimir Nabokov, 'Inspiration', *Strong Opinions* (New York, 1973), pp. 308–14.

64 *The Night Torn Mad with Footsteps* (Santa Rosa, CA, 2001), pp. 292–3.

65 Sounes, *Locked in the Arms of a Crazy Life*, p. 173.

66 Ibid., p. 174.

67 *Burning*, pp. 166, 200; reviewed by Robert Peters, 'Gab Poetry . . .', in *Where the Bee Sucks: Workers, Drones and Queens of Contemporary American Poetry* (Santa Maria, CA, 1994), pp. 56–66.

68 *Sunlight*, p. 117.

69 Ibid.

70 Ibid., p. 102.

71 Charles Bukowski, *Factotum* (Santa Barbara, CA, 1975), p. 11.

72 Ibid., p. 12.

73 Ibid., p. 185.

74 Ibid., p. 67.

75 Galen Strawson, 'Bottoming Out', *Times Literary Supplement*, 4092

(4 September 1981), p. 1,000.

76 Richard Elman, *New York Times Book Review* (8 August 1976).

77 'Workout', *Portions*, p. 169.

78 Sounes, *Locked in the Arms of a Crazy Life*, p. 164. Also see Mike Watts's interview with Linda in *Mean Magazine*, II/7 (March–April 2006), p. 88.

79 Cherkovski, *Hank*, p. 255.

80 Ibid., p. 256. He wrote to Jon and Louise Webb, 6 August 1963: 'I like crab. You can get a big crab down at one of the stores for around 80 cents and it takes you all day to eat him and you don't feel very sorry for the crab. That makes it nice. Although they say they boil them alive? But they boil me every time I walk out the door.' See *Screams*, p. 84.

81 '240 pounds', *New York Quarterly*, 57 (1997).

82 Sounes, *Locked in the Arms of a Crazy Life*, p. 171.

83 Charles Bukowski, *The Cruelty of Loveless Love* (New York, 2001); 'Carson McCullers', *The Pleasures of the Damned*, *Poems*, 1951–1993 (New York, 2007), p. 98.

84 Uncollected letter to Jojo Planteen, at www.authenticbukowski.com/manuscripts.

85 Joan Jobe Smith, *Art, Survival and So Forth*, uncollected letter, 22 April 1976, pp. 85–6. On Bukowski and Waits in Pittsburgh, see Paul Maher, ed., *Tom Waits on Tom Waits: Interviews and Encounters* (Chicago, IL, 2011), p. 50; Barney Hoskyns, *Lowside of the Road: A Life of Tom Waits* (New York, 2009), pp. 146–7; 'The Big Dope Reading', *Absence*, pp. 171–87.

86 She has recently published a memoir: Pamela Wood, *Charles Bukowski's Scarlet* (Northville, MI, 2010).

87 Bukowski inscription in *Scarlet* (Santa Barbara, CA, 1976).

88 Peter Green, trans., *The Poems of Catullus*: *A Bilingual Edition* (Berkeley, CA, 2005), pp. 190–91.

89 *Living on Luck*, p. 211. See Carl Sesar, trans., *Selected Poems of Catullus* (New York, 1974).

90 *Reach*, p. 125.

91 'the crunch', *Love is a Dog*, pp. 162, 163.

92 Richard T. Kelly, *Sean Penn: His Life and Times* (New York, 2004), p. 166; on Schroeder, see Cherkovski, *Hank*, pp. 276–7.

93 Krumhansl, *A Descriptive Bibliography*, p. 73.

94 On Boccaccio, see *Sunlight*, p. 179.

95 *Living on Luck*, p. 249.

96 Ibid., pp. 147, 149.

97 *Bukowski in the Bathtub*, ed. Long, p. 8.

98 Walter Burkert, *Structure and History in Greek Mythology and Ritual* (Berkeley, CA, 1979), p. 35.

99 Walter Burkert, *Greek Religion* (Cambridge, MA, 1985). On Bukowski and Dionysus, see Alexander Thiltges' superb *Bukowski ou les contes de la violence ordinaire* (Paris, 2006), pp. 24–7. The classic discussion remains E. R. Dodds, *The Greeks and the Irrational* (Berkeley, CA, 1964).

100 Charles Bukowski, *Women* (Santa Barbara, CA, 1978), p. 291. The novel was positively reviewed by Lucy Ferris, *San Francisco Review of Books*, IV/8 (1979), p. 14.

101 On Derschau's invitation, see Jay Dougherty, 'Translating Bukowski and the Beats: An Interview with Carl Weissner', *Gargoyle*, 35 (1988), pp. 80–81; *Living on Luck*, p. 241.

102 On Günter Grass, see Dougherty, 'Translating Bukowski', p. 81.

103 Miles, *Charles Bukowski*, p. 231; On *Apostrophes*, see Jean-François Duval, *Bukowski and the Beats* (Northville, MI, 2002), pp. 151–4. Also see Pierre Chalmin, *Dictionnaire des Injures littéraires*, (Paris, 2010).

104 *Living on Luck*, p. 274.

105 Ibid.

106 *Reach*, p. 236. In his 1991 interview with Donald McRae, Bukowski returned to Sartre: 'You know he really wanted to meet me but I said 'no way baby!' I wasn't into Sartre one little bit, I just had my bottle to take care of. But I've been reading some of his better writing lately and it's damn fine. I regret turning him down but then I think 'what the hell we'd probably just've ended up boring each other' and I remember my bowing Paris [sic: Nice] waiters instead . . .', from *Sunlight*, p. 273.

107 Sounes, *Locked in the Arms of a Crazy Life*, p. 138.

108 'A Conversation between Mike Watt and Linda Lee Bukowski about Charles Bukowski', *The Rise and Fall of the Harbor Area*, 4 (May–August 2005), p. 14.

6 Turning Sixty in San Pedro: 1979–1986

1 'Céline with cane and basket', *Last Night*, p. 242; on *beedies*, see Roger Ebert review of *Bukowski: Born Into This* (16 July 2004), at rogerebert.suntimes.com.

2 Charles Bukowski, *Hollywood* (Santa Rosa, CA, 1989), p. 63.

3 Howard Sounes, *Locked in the Arms of a Crazy Life* (Edinburgh, 2010), pp. 190–91.

4 *Reach*, pp. 10, 13, 16; 'slow night', *Dangling in the Tournefortia* (Santa Barbara, CA, 1981), p. 268.

5 'the recess bells of school', *The Continual Condition* (New York, 2009), p. 16.

6 *Bukowski in the Bathtub: Recollections of Charles Bukowski by John Thomas*, ed. Philomene Long (Venice, CA, 1997), p. 70.

7 'Notes of a Dirty Old Man', *Los Angeles Free Press* (9–15 May 1975), *Portions*, p. 162; 'Interview with Linda Bukowski', *Freethought*, II/1 (2000), p. 7.

8 Bukowski's daily life is chronicled in Michael Montfort, *Bukowski Photographs 1977–1987, with an Introduction and Poem by Charles Bukowski* (Santa Barbara, CA, 1987).

9 Charles Bukowski, *Shakespeare Never Did This* (Santa Rosa, CA, 1998), Sec. 21, n.p.

10 Sounes, *Locked in the Arms of a Crazy Life*, p. 192.

11 *Living on Luck*, p. 274.

12 Stephen Cooper, *Full of Life: A Biography of John Fante* (New York, 2000), p. 309. For Bukowski and Fante, also see pp. 9, 169, 307–10, 311, 314, 317–18, 322–3, 326, 327.

13 Bertolt Brecht, *Baal*, in *An Anthology of German Expressionist Drama: A Prelude in the Absurd*, ed. Walter H. Sokel (New York, 1963).

14 '40,000 flies', *Play the Piano*, p. 27.

15 Pablo Neruda, 'Walking Around', *The Essential Neruda: Selected Poems*, ed. Mark Eisner (San Francisco, 2004), pp. 42–5.

16 Cherkovski, *Whitman's Wild Children* (Venice, CA, 1988), p. 13.

17 Ben Pleasant's 1975 interview with Bukowski, *Sunlight*, pp. 111–12

18 See Vladimir Nabokov, *Strong Opinions* (New York, 1973), pp. 54, 57, 102, 118.

19 *Play the Piano*, p. 98.
20 Ibid., p. 112.
21 *Living on Luck*, p. 275.
22 'My Friend the Gambler', *High Times* (October 1984), pp. 40–45, 71–5, 88; Bukowski, *More Notes of a Dirty Old Man: The Uncollected Columns*, ed. David Stephen Calonne (San Francisco, 2011).
23 Sounes, *Locked in the Arms of a Crazy Life*, p. 193.
24 For Bukowski's meeting with Godard, see Colin McCabe, *Godard: A Portrait of the Artist at Seventy* (London, 2005), p. 329.
25 Sounes, *Locked in the Arms of a Crazy Life*, p. 196. 'Mad Enough', *Septuagenarian Stew* (Santa Rosa, CA, 1990), pp. 362–71. Also see Jack Sargent, *Naked Lens: An Illustrated History of Beat Cinema* (London, 1997), pp. 227–28.
26 'the lady in red', *Dangling in the Tournefortia*, p. 13. Reviewed by Gerald Locklin, *American Book Review*, IV/5 (July–August 1982), p. 6.
27 'fear and madness', *Dangling in the Tournefortia*, pp. 194–5.
28 'the secret of my endurance', ibid., p. 270.
29 'guava tree', ibid., p. 232.
30 'bad fix', ibid., pp. 106, 107.
31 Uncollected letter, available at www.authenticbukowski.com/manuscripts.
32 Bukowski on Salinger, see *Sunlight*, pp. 57, 94, 114, 130; Jean-François Duval, *Bukowski and the Beats* (Northville, MI, 2002), p. 178.
33 *Ham on Rye*, p. 70.
34 Ibid., p. 167.
35 Arthur Schopenhauer, *The World as Will and Representation* (New York, 1969), p. 354. Also see Roni, 'Bukowski-Nietzsche-Schopenhauer', *Jahrbuch der Charles Bukowski Gesellschaft 2004*, pp. 40–55; the poem 'a funny guy', *You Get so Alone*, p. 124, which refers to volume II of *Parerga*, chapter 30, 'Über Lerm und Gerausch', 'On loudness and sound'; *Sunlight*, p. 134; *Reach*, p. 135; *Screams*, pp. 79, 186; *Living on Luck*, p. 271; *Beerspit Night and Cursing: The Correspondence of Charles Bukowski and Sheri Martinelli, 1960–1967*, ed. Steven Moore (Santa Rosa, CA, 2001), pp. 92, 149.
36 *Ham on Rye*, p. 168.
37 Ibid., p. 91.

38 Paul Ricoeur, 'Life: A Story in Search of a Narrative', in Mario J. Valdes, ed., *A Ricoeur Reader: Reflection and Imagination* (Toronto, 1991), p. 432.

39 *Ham on Rye*, pp. 217, 219.

40 Ibid., pp. 258, 272, 267.

41 Ibid., p. 274.

42 Ibid., p. 281.

43 Ibid., p. 283.

44 Barry Miles, *Charles Bukowski* (London, 2005), pp. 245–6.

45 Ibid., p. 247.

46 Russell Harrison, *Against the American Dream: Essays on Charles Bukowski* (Santa Rosa, CA, 1994),p. 253.

47 Gay Brewer, *Charles Bukowski* (New York, 1997), p. 65. See *Who's Big in the 'Littles'*, pp. 301–2.

48 *NOLA*, 91 (1971). The version in *Hot Water Music* (Santa Barbara, CA, 1983), differs from the original, pp. 17–18.

49 Ibid.

50 'I Meet the Master', *Oui* (December 1984 and January 1985); *Portions*, pp. 205–29. Also see Miles, *Charles Bukowski*, pp. 237, 239; Cooper, *Full of Life*, p. 326.

51 *Betting on the Muse: Poems and Stories* (Santa Rosa, CA, 1996), pp. 366–70; Cooper, *Full of Life*, p. 327.

52 Charles Bukowski, 'Preface' to John Fante, *Ask the Dust* (Santa Rosa, CA, 1991).

53 Bukowski, *More Notes of a Dirty Old Man*, pp. 169–74.

54 'overhead mirrors', *War All The Time: Poems, 1981–1984* (Santa Barbara, CA, 1984), p. 237.

55 Ibid., p. 238, 239.

56 Miles, *Charles Bukowski*, p. 242.

57 *Reach*, p. 65.

58 Charles Bukowski, *The Wedding* (San Pedro, CA, 1986); Neeli Cherkovski, *Hank: The Life of Charles Bukowski* (New York, 1991), p. 283; Sounes, *Locked in the Arms of a Crazy Life*, pp. 206–7.

59 Gundolf S. Freyermuth, *That's It: A Final Visit with Charles Bukowski* (n.p., 2000), p. 20.

60 'quiet', *You Get So Alone*, p. 308.

61 Ibid., p. 309.

62 Ibid., pp. 309–10.

63 Ibid., pp. 310–11.

64 'no help for that', *You Get So Alone*, p. 26.

65 Ibid., p. 26.

66 'sunny slice down', *You Get So Alone*, p. 57.

67 'The Invader', *Absence*, pp. 255–70.

68 'Looking Back at a Big One', *Portions*, pp. 232.

69 Cherkovski, *Hank*, p. 282.

70 Faye Dunaway, *Looking for Gatsby: My Life* (London, 1995), p. 358.

7 Journey to the End of the Night: Late Style, 1987–1994

1 On filming, see Neeli Cherkovski, *Hank: The Life of Charles Bukowski*
   (New York, 1991), p. 285; Howard Sounes, *Locked in the Arms of a Crazy
   Life* (Edinburgh, 2010), p. 214.

2 See Chris Hodenfield, 'Gin-Soaked Boy', *Film Comment*, XXIII/4
   (July/August 1987), p. 58. On Bukowski's admiration for *Eraserhead*,
   see *Sunlight*, p. 230. For his birthday in August 1979, Carl Weissner
   sent Bukowski *Ecce Homo* by George Grosz and Bukowski thanked
   him: 'Ecce homo by George Grosz was an astonishing birthday gift.
   You certainly know my taste, Some of this man's work reminds me
   of my own short stories,' *Living on Luck*, p. 273. On *Barfly*, see Jack
   Sargent, *Naked Lens: An Illustrated History of Beat Cinema* (London,
   1997), pp. 229–31.

3 Sargent, *Naked Lens*, p. 230; Margot Dougherty and Todd Gold,
   People, 17 November 1987, in *Sunlight*, p. 224.

4 Jules Smith, *Art, Survival and So Forth: The Poetry of Charles Bukowski*
   (Hull, 2000), p. 213; Barry Miles, *Charles Bukowski* (London, 2005),
   p. 252.

5 Vincent Canby reviewed the film enthusiastically. See '*Barfly*, Doing
   the Best with the Worst of Life', *New York Times* (30 September 1987).
   Roger Ebert called it 'a truly original American movie, a film like
   no other . . . *Barfly* was one of 1987's best films.' See *Roger Ebert's
   Four-Star Reviews, 1967–2007* (Kansas City, MO, 2007), p. 63.

6 Charles Bukowski, *The Movie 'Barfly'* (Santa Rosa, CA, 1987), p. 47.
   On the bar in American history and literature, see Christine Sismondo,

America Walks Into A Bar: A Spirited History of Taverns and Saloons, Speakeasies and Grog Shops (Oxford, 2011); on O'Neill, p. 199; Saroyan, p. 238; Bukowski, p. 267.

7 William Saroyan, *The Time of Your Life* (New York, 1939), p. 72.

8 Walter Goodman, in *New York Times* (18 March 1988). Also see Sargent, *Naked Lens*, pp. 228–9.

9 Howard Sounes, *Locked in the Arms of a Crazy Life* (Edinburgh, 2010), p. 218.

10 Bukowski, 'Foreword', *Roominghouse*, p. 5.

11 Sounes, *Locked in the Arms of a Crazy Life*, p. 218.

12 *Sunlight*, p. 230.

13 Tom Dardis, *Some Time in the Sun: The Hollywood Years of F. Scott Fitzgerald, William Faulkner, Nathanael West, Aldous Huxley and James Agee* (New York, 1976).

14 Pamela Cytrynbaum, 'Rhythm, Dance, Quickness', *New York Times Book Review* (11 June 1989); *Sunlight*, p. 246.

15 Charles Bukowski, *Hollywood* (Santa Rosa, CA, 1989), p. 9.

16 Ibid., p. 10.

17 Ibid., p. 63.

18 Ibid., p. 10.

19 Ibid., p. 34.

20 Ibid., p. 38.

21 Ibid., p. 30.

22 Ibid.,p. 33.

23 Ibid., pp. 222–3.

24 Ibid., p. 239.

25 Uncollected letter, available at www.authenticbukowski.com/manuscripts.

26 Sounes, *Locked in the Arms of a Crazy Life,* p. 218.

27 Ibid., p. 219.

28 Ibid.

29 Cherkovski, *Hank*, p. 290.

30 'The Other', *Portions*, pp. 236–48.The doppelgänger is another theme beloved by the German Romantics. See Andrew J. Webber, *The Doppelgänger: Double Visions in German Literature* (Oxford, 1996).

31 Letter to Steve Richmond in *Charles Bukowski and Alpha Beat Press, 1988–1994* (New Hope, PA, 1994), ed. Ana & Dave Christy, n.p.

32 'Action', *Septuagenarian Stew* (Santa Rosa, CA, 1990), pp. 119–32. For review, see Doren Robbins, 'Drinking Wine in the Slaughterhouse with Septuagenarian Stew'. *OntheBus*, 8/9, pp. 282–5.

33 'the burning of the dream', *Septuagenarian Stew*, pp. 42–8.

34 'nowhere', *Septuagenarian Stew*, pp. 160–61.

35 'birthday party', *Septuagenarian Stew*, p. 270.

36 Miles, *Charles Bukowski*, p. 258.

37 'computer class', *What Matters Most is How You Walk Through the Fire* (Santa Rosa, CA, 1999), p. 307.

38 Miles, *Charles Bukowski*, p. 259; 'animal poem', *The Night Torn Mad with Footsteps* (Santa Rosa, CA, 1999), pp. 327, 328.

39 *Sunlight*, p. 213; 'exactly right', *The Night Torn Mad with Footsteps*, p. 164.

40 Sounes, *Locked in the Arms of a Crazy Life*, p. 227.

41 *Sunlight*, p. 275.

42 Miles, *Charles Bukowski*, p. 262.

43 *Reach*, p. 277.

44 'no leaders, please', *Come On In!* (New York, 2006), p. 270.

45 'nobody but you', *Sifting Through the Madness for the Word, the Line, the Way: New Poems* (New York, 2003), pp. 393–4; 'the laughing heart', *Prairie Schooner* (Fall 1993) and *Betting on the Muse: Poems and Stories* (Santa Rosa, CA, 1996), p. 400; 'roll the dice', *What Matters Most is How You Walk Through the Fire*, pp. 408–9.

46 Neeli Cherkovski, *Hank: The Life of Charles Bukowski* (New York, 1991); Howard Sounes, *Locked in the Arms of a Crazy Life* (Edinburgh, 2010); Barry Miles, *Charles Bukowski* (London, 2005); Aubrey Malone, *The Hunchback of East Hollywood* (Manchester, 2003); Michael Baughan, *Charles Bukowski* (Philadelphia, PA, 2004).

47 Marcus Grapes, *OntheBus*, 17/18 (2002), p. 26.

48 *The Captain is Out to Lunch and the Sailors Have Taken Over the Ship*, illustrated by Robert Crumb (Santa Rosa, CA, 1998), p. 10.

49 'Timeline', www.bukowski.net.

50 'the beggars', *Last Night*, p. 254; Michael Basinski, 'Life and Death in Charles Bukowski's *The Last Night of the Earth Poems*', in *Last Call: The Legacy of Charles Bukowski*, ed. R. D. Armstrong (San Pedro, CA, 2004), pp. 103–7.

51 'Dinosauria, we', *Last Night*, pp. 320, 321. Masterson detects the influence of Jeffers's 'The Beautiful Captive', which envisions the end

of humanity: 'Now, if we die like the dinosaurs, the beautiful / Planet will be the happier'. *The Collected Poetry of Robinson Jeffers, Volume Three: 1939–1962*, ed. Tim Hunt (Stanford, CA, 1991), pp. 428. Donald Masterson, '"Jeffers is my god": Charles Bukowski's Commentary on Robinson Jeffers', *Jeffers Studies*, V/2 (Spring 2001), p. 17. The poem's repeated chant 'born into this' supplied the title for John Dullaghan's documentary on Bukowski, *Born Into This* (2003).

52 'confession', *Last Night*, p. 139.

53 'the bluebird', ibid., p. 120.

54 Ibid., pp. 120, 121.

55 'sitting with the IBM', ibid., p. 223.

56 Ibid., p. 225.

57 See 'Charles Bukowski's Los Angeles for Li Po', *Portions*, p. 230; 'immortal wino' ('Li Po, I keep thinking of you as I / empty these bottles of / wine / you knew how to pass the days and / nights'), *Septuagenarian Stew*, p. 336.

58 'the riots', in *The Verdict Is In*, ed. Kathi Georges and Jennifer Joseph (San Francisco, 1992), p. 74; altered in posthumous version: 'riots', *Sifting Through the Madness*, p. 165; 'the con job', *Sifting Through the Madness*, p. 167.

59 'Basic Training', *Portions*, p. 250.

60 'Playing and Being the Poet', *Absence*, p. 272.

61 Aaron Krumhansl, *A Descriptive Bibliography of the Primary Publications of Charles Bukowski* (Santa Rosa, CA, 1999), p. 157.

62 Smith, *Art, Poetry, Survival and So Forth*, p. 202; Gerald Locklin, *The Case of the Missing Blue Volkswagen* (Long Beach, CA, 1984). The in-joke of the title is that Bukowski himself owned a much-driven-and-loved 1967 blue Volkswagen. On Bukowski's influence on Locklin, see Norman Friedman, 'Locklin, the Beats, and Bukowski', *Spring: The Journal of the E.E. Cummings Society*, n.s. 10 (October 2001), pp. 128–37.

63 31 March 1989, *Reach*, pp. 120–21.

64 Charles Bukowski, *Pulp* (Santa Rosa, CA, 1994), p. 14.

65 Ibid, pp. 15, 19, 119.

66 Ibid., p. 30.

67 Ibid., p. 108. On Woody Allen, see *Sunlight*, pp. 178, 200; Jean-François Duval, *Bukowski and the Beats* (Northville, MI, 2002), pp. 181–2.

68 Bukowski, *Pulp*, pp. 152–3.

69 Ibid., p. 174.

70 Ibid., p. 148.

71 Ibid., pp. 150–51.

72 Miles, *Charles Bukowski*, p. 264.

73 *Reach*, p. 269.

74 'fingernails; nostrils; shoelaces', ' a not so good night in the San Pedro of the World', *Poetry*, CLXII/6 (September 1993); 'cold summer', *Poetry*, CLXIV/4 (July 1994). *Poetry*, CLXIV/2 (May 1994), has an epigraph from 'to kiss the worms goodnight' (*At Terror Street and Agony Way*) on the inside front cover *in memoriam* to 'Charles Bukowski 1920–1994 when my heart stops / the whole world will get quicker / better / warmer / summer will follow summer / the air will be lake clear / and the meaning / too'.

75 *Prairie Schooner*, LXVII/3 (Fall 1993); *What Matters Most*, p. 407. Following his death, *Prairie Schooner* devoted the cover of the LXVIII/2 Summer 1994 issue to the text of 'the laughing heart', illustrated by Bukowski drawings.

76 Sounes, *Locked in the Arms of a Crazy Life*, p. 234.

77 *Reach*, p. 287.

78 Ibid., p. 290.

79 Ibid., pp. 294, 299; on *Run with the Hunted*, see Krumhansl, *A Descriptive Bibliography*, p. 151.

80 *Reach*, p. 297.

81 Ibid., p. 300.

82 *Mean*, II/7 (March/April 2006), p. 89.

83 Richard T. Kelly, *Sean Penn: His Life and Times* (New York, 2004), p. 286.

84 Sounes, *Locked in the Arms of a Crazy Life*, p. 241.

85 Ibid., p. 243–4.

86 *Bukowski in the Bathtub: Recollections of Charles Bukowski by John Thomas*, ed. Philomene Long (Venice, CA, 1997), p. 112.

87 Ibid., p. 112.

88 Willi Winkler, 'Ein deutscher Dichter: Zum Tod von Charles Bukowski', *Die Zeit*, 12 (18 March 1994), p. 61. The American press was less intelligent. See William Grimes, 'Charles Bukowski is Dead at 73: Poet Whose Subject Was Excess', *New York Times* (11 March 1994).

89 Marco Mannone, 'Charles Bukowski Is Rolling In His Grave', *Forth magazine.com*, 5 September 2009.

90 'A Freethought Interview with Linda Bukowski', *Freethought*, II/1 (Summer 2000), p. 7.

91 Geneviève Duboscq, 'A Flashing Heaven of Luck: Black Sparrow Press leaves a mighty legacy', *North Bay Guardian* (4–10 July 2002).

92 See review by Stephen Holden, 'A Poet Weaned on Pain and Reared by Adversity', *New York Times* (4 June 2004).

93 Camille Paglia, *Vamps and Tramps: New Essays* (New York, 1994), p. 327.

94 Jim Harrison, review of *The Pleasures of the Damned: Poems, 1951–1993* (New York, 2007), *New York Times Book Review* (25 November 2007).

95 David Lehman, ed., *The Oxford Book of American Poetry* (New York, 2006), 'my old man', 'freaky time', 'comments upon my last book of poesy', 'me against the world', 'so you want to be a writer?', pp. 651–8. Garrison Keillor, *Good Poems* (New York, 2002); *Good Poems for Hard Times* (New York, 2006); *Good Poems, American Places* (New York, 2011); *The Best American Poetry*, 1993, 1994, 2005.

96 See *The Rough Guide to Cult Fiction* (London, 2005), pp. 38–9; Andrew Calcutt and Richard Shephard, *Cult Fiction: A Reader's Guide* (Chicago, IL, 1999), pp. 34–6; Martin Seymour-Smith, *Who's Who in Twentieth Century Literature* (New York, 1976), p. 85; Julian Patrick, ed., *501 Great Writers* (London, 2008), p. 456; Bill Morgan, *The Beat Generation in San Francisco: A Literary Tour* (San Francisco, 2003), pp. 40, 46, 63, 68.

Select Bibliography

Works by Charles Bukowski

Flower, Fist and Bestial Wail (Eureka, CA, 1960)

Longshot Pomes for Broke Players (New York, 1962)

Poems and Drawings (Crescent City, FL, 1962)

Run with the Hunted (Chicago, IL, 1962)

It Catches My Heart in Its Hands (New Orleans, 1963)

Cold Dogs in the Courtyard (Chicago, IL, 1965)

Confessions of a Man Insane Enough to Live with Beasts (Bensenville, IL, 1965)

The Genius of the Crowd (Cleveland, OH, 1966)

All the Assholes in the World and Mine (Bensenville, IL, 1966)

At Terror Street and Agony Way (Los Angeles, 1968)

Poems Written Before Jumping Out Of An 8 Story Window (Glendale, CA, 1968)

Notes of a Dirty Old Man (North Hollywood, CA, 1969)

A Bukowski Sampler (Madison, WI, 1969)

The Days Run Away Like Wild Horses Over the Hills (Los Angeles, 1969)

Post Office (Los Angeles, 1971)

Erections, Ejaculations, Exhibitions and General Tales of Ordinary Madness (San Francisco, 1972)

Mockingbird Wish Me Luck (Los Angeles, 1972)

Me and Your Sometimes Love Poems (Los Angeles, 1972)

South of No North (Los Angeles, 1973)

Burning in Water, Drowning in Flame (Los Angeles, 1974)

Factotum (Santa Barbara, CA, 1975)

Scarlet (Santa Barbara, CA, 1976)

Love is a Dog from Hell (Santa Barbara, CA, 1977)

Women (Santa Barbara, CA, 1978)

Play the Piano Drunk Like a Percussion Instrument until the Fingers Begin to Bleed a Bit (Santa Barbara, CA, 1979)

Shakespeare Never Did This (San Francisco, 1979)

Dangling in the Tournefortia (Santa Barbara, CA, 1981)

Ham on Rye (Santa Barbara, CA, 1982)

Horsemeat (Santa Barbara, CA, 1982)

Bring Me Your Love (Santa Barbara, CA, 1983)

Hot Water Music (Santa Barbara, CA, 1983)

The Bukowski/Purdy Letters (Santa Barbara, CA, 1983)

The Most Beautiful Woman in Town and Other Stories (San Francisco, 1983)

Tales of Ordinary Madness (San Francisco, 1983)

There's No Business (Santa Barbara, CA, 1984)

War All The Time (Santa Barbara, CA, 1984)

Barfly: The Continuing Saga of Henry Chinaski (Santa Barbara, CA, 1984)

The Wedding (San Pedro, CA, 1986)

You Get so Alone at Times that it Just Makes Sense (Santa Rosa, CA, 1986)

The Movie: Barfly (Santa Rosa, CA, 1987)

The Roominghouse Madrigals (Santa Barbara, CA, 1988)

Hollywood (Santa Rosa, CA, 1989)

Septuagenarian Stew: Stories & Poems (Santa Rosa, CA, 1990)

The Last Night of the Earth Poems (Santa Rosa, CA, 1992)

Run with the Hunted (New York, 1993)

Screams from the Balcony: Selected Letters, 1960–1970 (Santa Rosa, CA, 1993)

Pulp (Santa Rosa, CA, 1994)

Living on Luck: Selected Letters, 1960s–1970s: Volume 2 (Santa Rosa, CA, 1995)

Betting on the Muse: Poems and Stories (Santa Rosa, CA, 1996)

Bone Palace Ballet (Santa Rosa, CA, 1997)

The Captain is Out to Lunch and the Sailors Have Taken Over the Ship (Santa Rosa, CA, 1998)

What Matters Most is How Well You Walk Through the Fire (Santa Rosa, CA, 1999)

Reach for the Sun: Selected Letters, 1978–1994: Volume 3 (Santa Rosa, CA, 1999)

Open All Night (Santa Rosa, CA, 2000)

The Night Torn Mad with Footsteps (Santa Rosa, CA, 2001)

Beerspit Night and Cursing: The Correspondence of Charles Bukowski and Sheri Martinelli, 1960–1967 (Santa Rosa, CA, 2001)

Sifting Through the Madness for the Word, the Line, the Way (New York, 2003)

The Flash of Lightning Behind the Mountain (New York, 2004)

Slouching Toward Nirvana (New York, 2005)

Come on In! (New York, 2006)

The Pleasures of the Damned (New York, 2007)

The People Look Like Flowers at Last (New York, 2007)

Portions from a Wine-Stained Notebook: Uncollected Stories and Essays, 1944–1990 (San Francisco, 2008)

The Continual Condition (New York, 2009)

Absence of the Hero: Uncollected Stories and Essays, Volume 2: 1946–1992 (San Francisco, 2010)

More Notes of A Dirty Old Man: The Uncollected Columns (San Francisco, 2011)

Critical Literature

Armstrong, R. D., ed., *Last Call: The Legacy of Charles Bukowski* (San Pedro, CA, 2004)

Basinski, Michael, 'Charles Bukowski', in *Dictionary of Literary Biography, Volume 130: American Short Stories since wwii*, ed. Patrick Meanor (Detroit, MI, 1993)

Berlin, Isaiah, *The Roots of Romanticism* (Princeton, NJ, 1999)

Blanning, Tim, *The Romantic Revolution* (London, 2010)

Brewer, Gay, *Charles Bukowski* (New York, 1997)

Calonne, David Stephen, 'Two on the Trapeze: Charles Bukowski and William Saroyan', *Sure: The Charles Bukowski Newsletter*, 5/6 (1992)

——, *Bebop Buddhist Ecstasy: Saroyan's Influence on Kerouac and the Beats*, with an Introduction by Lawrence Ferlinghetti (San Francisco, 2010)

——, ed., *Charles Bukowski, Sunlight Here I Am, Interviews and Encounters 1993–2003* (Northville, MI, 2003)

——, *William Saroyan: My Real Work Is Being* (Chapel Hill, NJ, and London, 1983)

Carruth, Hayden, 'Images', *Harper's Magazine* (orig. pub. in *Bookletter*, 31 March 1975)

Cherkovski, Neeli, *Hank: The Life of Charles Bukowski* (New York, 1991)
——, *Whitman's Wild Children* (Venice, CA, 1988)
Christy, Jim, and Claude Powell, *The Buk Book: Musings on Charles Bukowski* (Toronto, 1997)
Crumb, Robert, and Peter Poplaski, *The New Crumb Handbook* (London, 2005)
Dardis, Tom, *The Thirty Muse: Alcohol and the American Writer* (New York, 1989)
Debritto, Abel, *Who's Big in the 'Littles': A Critical Study of the Impact of the Little Magazines and Small Press Publications on the Career of Charles Bukowski from 1940 to 1969*, PhD thesis (Universitat Autonoma de Barcelona, May 2009)
Dorbin, Sanford A., *A Bibliography of Charles Bukowski* (Los Angeles, 1969)
Duval, Jean-François, *Bukowski and the Beats: A Commentary on the Beat Generation* (Northville, MI, 2002)
Fogel, Al, *Charles Bukowski: A Comprehensive Checklist* (Miami, FL, 1982)
Fox, Hugh, *Charles Bukowski: A Critical and Bibliographical Study* (Somerville, MA, 1971)
Freyermuth, Gundolf S. and Michael Montfort, *Das War's: Letze Worte mit Charles Bukowski* (Hamburg, 1996); English translation, *That's It: A Final Visit with Charles Bukowski* (n.p., 2000)
Gair, Christopher, *The American Counterculture* (Edinburgh, 2007)
Gelfant, Blanche H., ed., *The Columbia Companion to the Twentieth-Century American Short Story* (New York, 2000)
Glazier, Loss Pequeno, *Small Press: An Annotated Guide* (Westport, CT, 1992)
——, *All's Normal Here: A Charles Bukowski Primer* (Fremont, CA, 1985)
Harrison, Russell, *Against the American Dream: Essays on Charles Bukowski* (Santa Rosa, CA, 1994)
Heilbut, Anthony, *Exiled in Paradise: German Refugee Artists and Intellectuals in America from the 1930s to the Present* (Berkeley, CA, 1997)
Holm, D. K., ed., *R. Crumb Conversations* (Jackson, MS, 2004)
Krumhansl, Aaron, *A Descriptive Bibliography of the Primary Publications of Charles Bukowski* (Santa Rosa, CA, 1999)
Locklin, Gerald, 'Charles Bukowski', in *Updating the Literary West*, ed. Thomas J. Lyon (Fort Worth, TX, 1997)
Long, Philomene, ed., *Bukowski in the Bathtub: Recollections of Charles Bukowski by John Thomas* (Venice, CA, 1997)

Marwick, Arthur, *The Sixties: Cultural Revolution in Britain, France, Italy, and the United States, c. 1958–c. 1974* (Oxford, 1998)

McMillian, John, *Smoking Typewriters: The Sixties Underground Press and the Rise of Alternative Media in America* (New York, 2011)

Miles, Barry, *Charles Bukowski* (London, 2005)

Montfort, Michael, *Bukowski Photographs 1977–1987* (Hollywood, CA, 1987)

O'Brien, John, ed., *The Review of Contemporary Fiction: Charles Bukowski/Michel Butor*, v/3 (Fall 1985)

O'Neill, William L., *Coming Apart: An Informal History of America in the 1960's* (Chicago, IL, 2005)

Paglia, Camille, 'Love Poetry', in *Vamps & Tramps: New Essays* (New York, 1994)

Packard, William, *The Art of Poetry Writing: A Guide for Poets, Students, and Readers*, foreword by Karl Shapiro (New York, 1992)

——, 'Notes on the Bukowski', *Small Press Review* (May 1973)

Parini, Jay, ed., *The Oxford Encyclopedia of American Literature* (Oxford, 2004)

Pells, Richard H., *Radical Visions and American Dreams: Culture and Social Thought in the Depression Years* (New York, 1973)

Phoenix, Charles, *Southern California in the 50s* (Santa Monica, CA, 2001)

Pivano, Fernanda, *Charles Bukowski: Laughing with the Gods* (Northville, MI, 2000)

Sherman, Jory, *Bukowski: Friendship, Fame and Bestial Myth* (Augusta, GA, 1981)

Sklenicka, Carol, *Raymond Carver: A Writer's Life* (New York, 2009)

Smith, Jules, *Art, Survival and So Forth: The Poetry of Charles Bukowski* (Hull, 2000)

——, 'Charles Bukowski and the Avant-Garde', *Review of Contemporary Fiction*, v/3 (Fall 1985'

Sollers, Philippe, 'Bukowski et la folie ordinaire', *Éloge de l'infini* (Paris, 2001)

Sounes, Howard, *Charles Bukowski: Locked in the Arms of a Crazy Life* (Edinburgh, 2010)

——, *Bukowski in Pictures* (Edinburgh, 2000)

Starr, Kevin, *Coast of Dreams: California on the Edge, 1990–2003* (New York, 2004)

Sullivan, James D., *On the Walls and in the Streets: American Poetry Broadsides from the 1960s* (Champaign, IL, 1997).

Thiltges, Alexandre, *Bukowski ou Les Contes de la Violence Ordinaire* (Paris, 2006)

Wakoski, Diane, 'Charles Bukowski', in *Contemporary Poets*, ed. James Vinson and D. L. Kirkpatrick, 4th edn (New York, 1985)

Watson, Peter, *The German Genius: Europe's Third Renaissance, the Second Scientific Revolution, and the Twentieth Century* (New York, 2010)

Weddle, Jeff, *Bohemian New Orleans: The Story of the Outsider and Loujon Press* (Jackson, MS, 2007)

Websites

The Academy of American Poets
www.poets.org

Charles Bukowski, American Author
www.bukowski.net

Charles Bukowski Gesellschaft
www.bukowski-gesellschaft.de

Poetry Foundation
www.poetryfoundation.org/bio/charles-bukowski

Journal devoted to Charles Bukowski

Das Jahrbuch der Charles-Bukowski Gesellschaft

Acknowledgements

Thanks as always *für alles* to Maria. Many thanks to Roni, head of the Bukowski Gesellschaft in Germany, who helped me immensely with the preparation of the illustrations. Thanks as well to Daisy Montfort and David Barker. Sue Hodson, curator of literary manuscripts at the Huntington Library and Natalie Russell kindly supplied the photograph of Bukowski's typewriter. I am also grateful to Bukowski.net to which I repeatedly turned for the resolution of thorny chronological and bibliographical issues. I thank Linda Lee Bukowski for her help and encouragement. And my deep gratitude to J. S. Bach, who accompanied me daily as I wrote this book.

Photo Acknowledgements

The author and publishers wish to express their thanks to the following sources of illustrative material and/or permission to reproduce it.

From *Ein Ablehnungsbescheid und die Folgen* (Frankfurt: Edition Büchergilde, 2007): p. 30; reproduced courtesy Agence Litteraire Lora Fountain & Associates: p. 168; reproduced courtesy of Ulf Andersen: p. 132; reproduced courtesy David Barker: p. 67; reproduced courtesy of Edwin Blair and Gypsy Lou Webb: pp. 57, 58; from Charles Bukowski, *The Captain Is Out to Lunch and the Sailors Have Taken Over the Ship* (Santa Rosa, Calif.: Black Sparow Press, 1998): p. 168; reproduced courtesy of The Estate of Charles Bukowski: pp. 41, 71, 95, 100, 117, 123, 150, 165; reproduced courtesy the Charles-Bukowski-Gesellschaft: p. 138; photo Linda Bukowski: p. 138; photo by Sam Cherry, courtesy of Neeli Cherkovski: p. 78; reproduced courtesy Heinrich Fett: p. 11; reproduced courtesy Handelskammer Bremen (www.passagierlisten.de): p. 9; reproduced courtesy the Huntington Library, San Marino, Calif.: p. 119; reproduced courtesy of Melodie Marnell, Roswell High School, New Mexico: p. 37; photos Michael Montfort (reproduced courtesy Daisy Montfort and the estate of Michael Montfort): pp. 12, 77, 88, 115, 124, 126, 136, 153, 175, 178; reproduced courtesy of the artist (Thomas Müller): p. 30; reproduced courtesy Jean-Régis Roustan/Roger-Viollet/The Image Works: p. 6; photo Smalltown Boy: p. 8.